The Corsete

"*The Corseted Skeleton: A Bioarchaeology c* and entanglement with, the practices of wonderfully engaging act of scholarship that synthesizes osteological, archaeological, anthropological, gendered and historical perspectives, weaving them into a robust narrative about bodies, agency, materials, and society."
—Agustín Fuentes, *Professor of Anthropology, Princeton University, USA*

"In this important contribution, Gibson shows how bioarchaeology can be historical, theoretical, and relevant to modern discourse. Alongside stunning skeletal images and osteobiographies, she details a history of corseting, fashion, and women's agency usually overlooked in both historical and modern times. Her integration of social theory, archival history, and bodies pushes us to consider our own modern assumptions about how skeletons are 'made.'"
—Meredith A. B. Ellis, *Assistant Professor of Anthropology, Florida Atlantic University, USA, and author of* The Children of Spring Street: The Bioarchaeology of Childhood in a 19th Century Abolitionist Congregation *(2019)*

"Dr. Gibson puts corset wearing into context within the lifestyle, class, and socio-economic landscape of the time. She uses data collected from extant garments, skeletal remains, and contemporary written sources to establish whether or not corsets were harmful, and if women wore them out of choice or societal pressure. Was it about body image or did corseting have a practical purpose? This is a fascinating look at women's agency in a time when modern perception often tells us they had none."
—Virginia Crawford, *Historical Costumier, Bath, England, UK*

Rebecca Gibson

The Corseted Skeleton

A Bioarchaeology of Binding

Rebecca Gibson
Department of Anthropology
University of Notre Dame
Notre Dame, IN, USA

ISBN 978-3-030-50391-8   ISBN 978-3-030-50392-5   (eBook)
https://doi.org/10.1007/978-3-030-50392-5

Cover illustration: "Merydolla" and "SciePro"/Shutterstock

This Palgrave Macmillan imprint is published by the registered company Springer Nature Switzerland AG
The registered company address is: Gewerbestrasse 11, 6330 Cham, Switzerland

This book is dedicated to those who worked to ensure that I would fly, when others desired to see me fall.

To those others: this is not for you.

Acknowledgments

For their help and support throughout this project, I would like to thank: my parents, John and Judy Horwitz, who always welcomed my love of bones and weird dark things, for being the best parents ever; Ellen Schattschneider at Brandeis University in Waltham Massachusetts, who believed in me enough to step in when I needed her, for her love and kindness, which are limitless; Jay VanderVeen at Indiana University South Bend, my occasional writing partner and indispensable dear friend, who has heard me talk about this more than any other person in the world, for his patient acceptance of my chaos field; Wendy Birch of University College London, for experimental use of her lab and her amazing kindness at a particularly low point in my career; and Agustín Fuentes at Princeton University, who has been steadily supportive, for the inspiration and friendship he provides on a daily basis. I would also like to recognize Aurelie Fort and Veronique Laborde of the Muséum Nationale d'Histoire Naturelle in Paris; Virginie Varenne of le Maison des Canuts in Lyon, France; Rebecca Redfern and Jelena Bekvalac of the Centre for Human Bioarchaeology at the Museum of London; Hanne Faurby and Sarah Westbury at the Victoria and Albert Museum's Blythe House fashion and textiles collection in London; Fleur Johnson at the

Fashion Museum in Bath, England; Elen Phillips at St. Fagans Museum in Cardiff, Wales; Emily Taylor at the National Museum of Scotland in Edinburgh; Bill Edwards at the Gordon Museum in London; Martyn Cooke and Laura Sintado at the Hunterian Museum in London; and Lowell Flanders at the Mütter Museum in Philadelphia for providing access and assistance at their various museums. It was an honor to walk their distinguished halls and learn from their scholars. My thanks as well to the many semesters-worth of brilliant and dedicated undergraduate students that I have had the privilege to teach, and who have listened to me lecture on bones and corsets, as their questions helped strengthen my arguments. Finally, I would like to send my unending gratitude to my editorial team, Mary Al-Sayed and Madison Allums, as it has been a delight to work with them a second time, and I am still in awe of their promptness, thoroughness, and kindness to me throughout this process.

Contents

List of Figures

List of Tables

1

Introduction: Shaping the Garment, Shaping the Woman

If I asked you to imagine a corset, you might see one of several things in your mind's eye. Costumes from period dramas, usually seen on PBS or the BBC. Lingerie from specialty shops. Renaissance faire garb. The cultural imprint of the corset lies deep in our psyche—we can all identify it, link it to memories of favorite movies, or recite the myths of women who were harmed by their corset. However, this cultural consciousness is very much based on just that: myths.

Referring to that mental picture, modern-day garments of the same shape and function would overlay any pure conceptualization of the object. You would most likely be picturing fabrics that are more diverse than the options on offer in the time period, or colors that had not yet been invented. This is because our current understanding of the world is the default in our minds, and the first thing that occurs to us may be significantly colored by our modern perceptions.

Were I then to ask you why a woman would wear a corset, similar overlaying would take place. Modern corsets are marketed as sexy, exotic, and erotic, and in many cases are quite uncomfortable—meant to only be worn for minutes at a time, and then taken off; a prelude to the main act. But that is not what women wore them for, for the

© The Author(s) 2020
R. Gibson, *The Corseted Skeleton*,
https://doi.org/10.1007/978-3-030-50392-5_1

majority of time while the fashion persisted. This book will examine what we think we know, and why, and deconstruct our preconceived notions that are all bound up in lives we currently live, using the lens of bioarchaeology. To do this, I will examine skeletons from St. Bride's church in London, and compare them to examples from the Musée de l'Homme in Paris. I will also look at four collections of corsets, dozens of reports from doctors and women of the time, and historical and contemporary takes on the idea of the corseted woman.

The corset, as seen by examples from the Victoria and Albert Museum, the Fashion Museum in Bath, St. Fagans Museum in Wales, and the National Museum of Scotland, is a garment that supports and shapes the female body in various distinct ways. Always covering the waist, but variably covering the breasts and/or hips, the corset can be used as an undergarment, used as a structural overgarment, or built into tops or dresses as the underlying structure. It began as a simple way to stiffen and shape the front of the garment with a busk—a long, straight, stiff length of material—and went through many changes in form such as the additions of sets of stays (side stiffeners, often called bones, that radiate from the busk around the sides of the body), the overbust (from above the nipples down past the waist), the underbust (beginning under the breasts and stopping either just below the waist or at the hips), and included specialty corsets such as ones designed to accommodate pregnancy and nursing.

While the practice of wearing such garments began in the late 1500s, I will be looking only at the years between 1700 and 1900 CE. This is the time for which there is physical evidence—existing corsets and skeletal remains—and so this book will focus on that short time period, resisting the temptation to focus solely on the Victorian and Edwardian periods. While these were decidedly the heyday of corsetry, and the periods where much of our corset iconography comes from, focusing so narrowly would force the data I have gathered into very tight spaces, squeezing it down to fit a narrative that we have built, rather than allowing it to tell its own story. That narrative needs to be pulled apart as well: out of 150 unique articles written about corsetry and health that were condensed to a bibliography by a writer in the early twentieth century (O'Brien 1929) and which were published between 1750 and

1930 (24 in German, 52 in French, 74 in English), 74 were identifiable as written by doctors. 16 were in support of corseting (or at least not in total condemnation of the practice). Only two were identifiably written by women. The people who create the narrative control it. And the data should tell that story, instead of the accepted narrative, for the corset is much, much more than we believe it to be. A garment which persisted for centuries, the corset reveals much more than it conceals, and this book will explore those revelations—what women wore, how they wore their corsets, and what those corsets did to their bodies. But before we begin, a lexicon:

Glossary

Agency/Agentive: The concept of agency refers to a person's ability or perceived ability to make choices regarding their own behaviors. When a person is faced with a choice between multiple actions, and they can or feel that they can make that choice, they are behaving agentively. Agency and agentive behavior are tempered or mitigated by several things: physical limitations (i.e., the choice is not physically possible); cultural limitations (the person feels that their choice would be too sanctioned or controversial, and therefore it is not considered as possible); and actual or perceived powerlessness (the person feels, correctly or not, that they do not have the ability to choose for themselves).

Anatomical normal: In this context, anatomical normal refers to the standard presentation of a skeleton or skeletal element (a bone, which makes up part of the skeleton). This is what you see if you open up a textbook on skeletal biology. The anatomically normal bone has no anomalies, deformations, or pathologies—no disease, damage, or congenital malformations. It is your average bone, looking like a typical or standard representation of that particular bone.

Binding: To constrict something by artificial means. In this context, we will discuss binding done with fashion, or for aesthetic purposes—corseting will be the main topic, but this book will also selectively discuss foot-binding and orthodontic braces, among other types.

Bioarchaeology: A term coined in the late 1960s to refer to the intersection of biological anthropology, that is the examination of the human condition by way of human biology, with archaeology, which is the study of material culture. This book will give a bioarchaeological look at the practice of corseting; integrating the corset's effect on the skeleton with what the corsets themselves can tell us about the women who wore them.

Boning: The material used to stiffen a corset. Various materials were used, depending on origin, plentitude, availability, cost, and fashion. Historically, wood, leather, whalebone, and steel were prevalent, with plastic not appearing until after our time period, and whalebone eventually falling out of popularity as steel became cheaper and easier.

Busk: The stiff material that created the front line of the corset. Depending on the shape of the garment, busks were either single (if the garment did not lace or hook in the front), or double (if it did). Busks were initially removable and changeable, but then became fully integrated into the garment, to the point that one was no longer able to purchase them for personal use, instead being available only for dressmakers, corset makers, or the repairing of both.

Corset: An undergarment or overgarment usually, though not exclusively, worn by women. The purpose of the corset was to provide shape to the wearer's garments, creating a distinct bust, waist, and hips. Eventually the corset was replaced by the brassiere and girdle, as fashions and textile manufacture changed. The terms corset and stays are often used interchangeably in texts from the time period, and modern corset theorists and enthusiasts are not in agreement over any meaningful distinction between the two. Thus, both terms are used in this book.

Critical Discourse Analysis (CDA): Developed by Norman Fairclough (2003), the practice of Critical Discourse Analysis allows a writer to examine texts for deeper meanings than what one would get from a surface reading. Such things as a text fitting into a certain genre (letters to the editor) or collocation (what words are grouped near other, significant, words) give depth and nuance to the evaluation of the written word.

Damage/deformation: In this context, this refers to deviation away from the anatomical normal, particularly changes in the shape and structure of skeletal elements such as ribs and vertebrae due to the long-term pressure of the corset. This usage does not imply trauma, or even necessarily excessive pain, merely that the bone was altered or deformed by corset use.

Hegemonic Patriarchy: The idea that a male-oriented social order is currently the dominant (or hegemonic) social order, and has been for a considerable amount of recent history. This concept is generally understood to be referring to the geographic and cultural "west" (Europe and North America), and reflects the social realities of women being seen as culturally less than their male counterparts. These social realities contain multitudes of exemplars, but can be shown by women being expected to compromise their careers if they want to bear and raise children, women being paid less than men for similar jobs, women's pain levels being taken less seriously than men's, and women's clothing and personal presentation emphasizing beauty standards over comfort. How much these social realities effect individual women varies within time periods, locations, and from woman to woman, but the concept of hegemonic patriarchy provides the overarching structure under which we experience them.

Rib: The human skeleton contains 24 ribs, 12 pairs, which are attached in the back of the body to the thoracic vertebrae, and in the front of the body to the sternum by way of cartilage. Both male and female bodies contain ribs in the same number and configuration, and apart from variations in size, there is no real way to tell male from female just by examination of these skeletal elements.

Sexual dimorphism: The natural phenomenon of different biological sexes having different body shapes or sizes. This is not present in all animal species, but is present in various ways in our species. Male Homo sapiens are generally larger and more robust than females, and various markers on the skeleton (landmarks on the skull, pelvis, and femur, primarily) indicate the sex of the individual to a trained eye. This is not to ignore nonbinary or intersex individuals, or trans individuals. Those categories are marked by the biological anthropologist as well, and we proceed with a recognition that biological sexing is not exact, and that a skeleton cannot ever completely give us the lived experience of the individual, and so says very little about gender identity or presentation unless other things are known about that person.

Skeletal remains or skeleton: Skeletal remains, or the skeleton, are what is left when a body has naturally decayed or artificially been defleshed. Generally consisting of 206 bones (if an adult, as were most I will discuss here), the skeleton forms the substructure of the human body, and is comprised of a collagenated matrix onto which a calcium-based cell structure is deposited. Skeletal remains can reveal age, sex, ancestry, stature, what a person ate and drank, and within reason what stresses (repetitive motions, pressure and constriction, breaks, diseases, and malnourishments) the body has undergone.

Spinous process: The bony protrusion on the back of the vertebra. It points downward at an approximately 45-degree angle on an anatomically normal vertebra. This is what you feel if your run your fingers down your own back.

Stays: The word stay or stays is occasionally used interchangeably with corset, and refers to a bound undergarment that contains boning, but which may or may not contain a busk.

Vertebra/vertebrae: The elements of the spinal column—humans have seven vertebrae in the cervical or neck region, 12 in the thoracic region, and 5 in the lumbar, or lower back region. Those referred to in this book are the thoracic vertebrae unless otherwise indicated.

*   *   *

As a practice in urban areas, like London, where the main skeletal evidence originates, corseting crossed socioeconomic lines, spanning the gamut of female stations from the very wealthy to the impoverished. London, among other centers of trade and fashion, had a thriving second-hand market of clothing of all types. Corsets were not a once-in-a-lifetime purchase for upper-class London women, but a fashionable, yearly changing garment that would be updated as the styles changed. As such, older, out of fashion corsets would either be passed to the servants as gifts, or sold to garment merchants. Clothing stalls would resell old garments for pence on the pound, making the styles of the previous years affordable to all but the poorest of women. Additionally, much as women of the twenty-first century would think twice about going out to dine without wearing a bra, likewise did city women of the 1700–1900 period consider their corset an integral part of polite dress for civilized interactions in public.

Why, you may be asking yourself, have I chosen to concentrate on the rather neatly squared off time period of AD 1700–1900? Why not look at the Victorian period, or the Early Modern period, or other use-ful shorthanded designations? The short answer is the availability of archaeological data. Because I will be approaching this topic from the standpoint of a bioarchaeologist, I need to be able to examine physical things—remains and garments from the time period. I ran into issues of artifact scarcity when I considered moving backward in my timeline, with corsets being rarities in the archaeological record before the 1700s, and with skeletal material too friable and fragile to examine for data collection.

Furthermore, such designations as "Victorian" are limiting and in some cases confuse the ability for analysis. If you say "Victorian" then you are de facto talking and thinking about England during the years 1837–1901. This eliminates the possibility of bringing in data from outside the British Empire, apart from doing a cross-cultural compari-son. Or data from before 1837. So, for ease and nuance of analysis, and to make the best use of the data I collected, I chose the easily encapsu-lated two-century period between 1700 and 1900.

And in fact, these were indeed the heyday of corseting, and of European fashion in general, which was occasionally competitive between England and France. Despite being at war with each other at various irregular intervals in this time period, and despite the American and French revolutions, fashions flitted back and forth across both the English Channel and the Atlantic Ocean with regularity. An arms race (bodice race?) of innovation in fashion swept the known world, and cultural fashion norms, such as the use of stays and busks, diffused throughout all "civilization."

"Civilization" and the Corseted "Savage"

To do an historical study, one must accept that ideas of what is right and proper and respectful shift over time, and that the ideas and lan-guage used to express proper concepts in one era will not always be seen as respectful in subsequent eras. Thus, I need to address the fact of scientific and anthropological racism. Anthropology has always had a problem with hierarchies in general, and the "racial hierarchy" specifically. The science of anthropology began with experiments on cranial capacity, which were not at all accurate, nor that scientific, and which "found" that nonwhite, non-European peoples (as well as white European women) had smaller cranial capacities than white European males. In the spirit of being selfless and magnanimous, the earliest anthropologists wanted to try to lift up the rest of the world to their level by "civilizing" the "savage." You can no doubt see from my excessive use of scare quotes that this idea is both wrong-headed and patronizing—as is currently widely acknowledged, no so-called racial group living on the planet is inherently better, smarter, or more fit than any other. We are all one race: Homo sapiens, human, all the same.

Yet, the racial and racist (and sexist) implications of this work survive in various ways. One of these ways is the idea that certain types of dress, certain fashions, are more proper than others. Specifically, that civilization is imparted to a person by the clothing that they wear—we see it daily, from an overall denigration of fashion worn by young Black people, to the glorification of the business suit and tie. Thus, in the period between 1700 and 1900, the corset was seen as the height of civilized clothing—it bound and constrained women, delineating them from men, and showing their adult status, while also emphasizing femininity in a way that was both sexual and nonsexual. Sexual, in that it outlined and showed the body, but nonsexual because it created a barrier between the woman and the outside world. This, of course, contrasted sharply with the "savage" dress of non-Europeans, who often went unclothed or barely covered, a discussion that will occur in much more detail in regard to the comparative collection for this book, the skeletons from the Musée de l'Homme.

The Corseted Skeletons: FAO90—St. Bride's Lower Churchyard

At the end of this section, I will give you a short overview of each of the following chapters, and how they build on themselves to recreate the narrative of the corset in history. However, I first want to introduce you to the women of FAO90—St. Bride's Lower Churchyard. We will be spending the entire book in their company, and they are an interesting group of women.

Currently held at the Museum of London's Centre for Human Bioarchaeology, the postmedieval skeletal collection with the accession designation FAO90 comprises some 606 individual skeletons. Of these, a significant portion are female and were above the age of 18 years at the time of death. How they came to be in the Museum of London is a bit of a longer story.

St. Bride's parish church, at Fleet Street, is centuries old; almost as old as London itself (St. Bride's 2019). With confirmed history spanning from AD 43 to the present, the foundations, tribute to Brigid (the eponymous "Bride" herself), have outlasted the growth of the city, the rise and fall of the Roman empire, and the rise and fall of the British empire. The church has stayed through times of war and peace, famine and flood, plagues and industrialization. And in 1940, on what would have been an average day for the church itself, but what was the middle of the war for London, St. Bride's was bombed and the church and churchyard damaged (ibid.). A decade later, the Museum of London's Archaeology division excavated the lower churchyard, which was heavily damaged, and retrieved the 606 skeletons which would become FAO90, 125 of them determined to be female (Museum of London 2019).

So, who were these women? Fleet Street, also known as Printer's Row, was home to the magazines, newspapers, circulars, and bookbinders of the postmedieval city of London. While women in the industry were few at the time, wives and daughters of men of industry abounded. Being a parish, St. Bride's served a relatively delineated area of London, which I will discuss in detail later on. It also served a poorhouse or workhouse, and a prison. The lower churchyard, based on the burial records of the time, was at first an overflow of the main burial ground, and then a place to bury low-socioeconomic-status individuals (St. Bride's Register 1770–1849). Regrettably, the bombing of the cemetery removed what information there was about which skeletons went with which exact graves, and that data was scarce to begin with, as burials were often stacked on top of each other, sometimes as much as six deep, to save space.

We can make certain observations about these women based on what we know of St. Bride's: they were at least nominally Christian, or Christian enough to be buried in a parish church; they ranged in socioeconomic status from impoverished to upper-middle class; they lived in a relatively small area of the city, most of them for their entire lives; they were exposed to London water, food, pollution, and pathogens; and based on their socioeconomic status, they wore London fashions—whether as primary purchasers of the clothing or as wearers of second-hand garments from London's vast resale market. These were not the rich and famous, though they too have their place in this reshaping of the corseting narrative. These were, by and large, "regular" women—women who grew up and married and had children and went to church and had opinions and did various types of labor, some of it hard and physical, day after day until they died. Keep this in mind, this idea of the everyday woman, as we move forward through this book. The very act of not glamorizing their existence is revolutionary when compared to what we are ordinarily told about the corset.

Corseting "Myths" and How We Can Bust Them

Misogyny sits at the heart of the myths surrounding corseting. Every idea about corseting that the data demonstrate as being factually incorrect stems from one thing: the conceptualization of women as inferior to men. What are those myths? Let's look at a few. (1) Women who corseted died early. (2) If a woman did not die early from her corset, she was at least incommoded to the point of being unable to work, making her dependent on support from her family, if she had a family. (3) The corset was physically harmful, impeding liver function, causing miscarriages, influencing tuberculosis, and literally cutting women in half. (4) The corset was exotic/erotic and scandalous, and the corseted woman was an inherently sexual being. (5) Women did not want the corset and/or were being forced into it.

Some of these appear to be based in fact, but only if we do not interrogate them further. We are oft told that the projected lifespan of a woman during this time period was approximately 35 years old, and we feel we know intuitively that if you compress the body then weird things are going to happen to the person's insides. It also stands to reason that if you cannot bend in the middle, a lot of work, particularly physical work, is going to be off the table. And if all this were true, why would a woman want to do that to themselves?

However, intuitions, reasonable assumptions, and hyperbolic questions are not data-driven and tested facts. While **overall** the life expectancy of a woman was indeed around 35 years old at death, that number changes significantly if you remove childhood deaths from your dataset. This allows the researcher to understand how adult women lived and died, having eliminated the noise of the most death-heavy portion of life. The fact is that most women were not dying at or younger than 35, but rather that many female children died from accidents or disease before their 18th birthday, thus bringing the average sharply downward. The actual average lifespan of a woman who had reached adulthood will be discussed in detail in a later chapter.

Now, how about women and work? The idea that a corseted woman was a woman who did not produce or did not labor in the sense of working for money or barter is one that assumes that all corsets are the same, and that all women wore them in the same way—tight-laced and worn to below the hips. This is very much our cultural perception of the corset at play, seen in costume dramas from various historical periods. These movies and TV shows focus mostly on the upper class, and if they show the lower classes at all, they usually show them uncorseted, which is not historically accurate. Women exercised a great deal of agency over how they wore their fashions, which will similarly be deconstructed in the body of this book.

To refute the next point, we must go back to who is creating this narrative of the woman harmed by the corset, and what they have to gain from it. In subsequent chapters, I will bring in reports from physicians of the time period, beginning with the source of much of their own information, Ambroise Paré, and moving into the 1700s and 1800s. Medical knowledge during much of this time was passed down by rote, rather than by experimentation and observation, and it was not uncommon for patients and doctors to never even meet, holding consultations by letter (Fitzharris 2017). Additionally, much of what was known of female anatomy came from inaccurate medical illustrations, which occasionally showed the uterus as bilobed like a pig or a dog uterus, and looked at women as merely men with the capacity to bear children. What knowledge was gleaned from actual human subjects was taken from operating theaters and dissection chambers. Operations were generally done as a last-ditch effort to save the patient's life, when it was deemed that nonintervention would kill them quicker, though often the surgical patient ended up on the dissection table themselves, due to lack of cleanliness causing infection, and eventual death (ibid.).

So, doctors with little practical knowledge of living surgical patients were creating the narrative of the woman harmed by her corset, but why? On one hand, people genuinely did go into medicine for altruistic purposes. They were scientifically curious, and wanted to help their patients by finding reasons for what was, at that time, mysterious. They wanted to be able to treat, and hopefully cure, that which ailed their patients, no matter their sex. However, they were also in a profession, and a profession's purpose is to make money for those who choose it. There will most likely always be a necessity for doctoring. There's no shortage of people getting sick or becoming hurt or being born or developing anomalous physical characteristics.

There is, however, an additional way in which doctors earned money during this time: by becoming famous for and the sole provider of something innovative. Whether a new patent medicine or a new patent corset, doctors often had a side business in various cures or treatments for the disorders in which they specialized. Of the many articles, book chapters, and books on corseting, many found in that previously mentioned bibliography (O'Brien 1929) had subtitles or descriptions that indicated that the doctor's new patented corset was the one true medically acceptable corset, and that readers who wanted to be seen as both at the cutting edge of fashion and as medically good subjects should buy and wear Dr. So-And-So's patented corset.

It is important here to distinguish between change to the body and harm or trauma or violence to the body. The fact that the corset **changed** the body is indisputable. It decidedly did, and I will show those changes with skeletal evidence. But change is not necessarily harmful, or traumatic, or violent. Change over time can be neutral, and does not always cause pain, lasting trauma to the body or psyche, or imply violence to the person. To put it differently, while women's bodies were changed by the corset, this was not de facto an issue that needed to be fixed. There are several modern industries devoted to changing the body into a more culturally or visually "pleasing" shape, and all but the very extreme are accepted into the mainstream behaviors of most cultures of the European-derived world. We use orthodontic braces, elective cosmetic surgery, nutritional control programs, exercise programs, and tattoo and piercing to express our inner selves outwardly, and we do not blink at that. Corseting is not so very different.

The next two ideas went hand in hand—that the woman who wore a corset was inherently sexual, and that she was being forced to wear the corset (presumably by men or the overarching patriarchical structure, but forced in general). The idea of the sexuality of the corset as separate from the sexuality of undergarments in general is a distinctly modern one. This is because we see the corset as an outlier in clothing, rather than an example of a standard undergarment. This view of the corset is incorrect. For the amount of time that it was in fashion, the corset was used by women to shape their garments a certain way, to create a silhouette, and as a support structure for the breasts and trunk of the body. This does not preclude it being inadvertently or purposefully sexy, but being sexy was not the main purpose. Bras can be sexy; their purpose is to shape and support the breasts.

If we remove the idea that the purpose was to be sexy, in effect, to appeal to heterosexual men (during this time period, there is a heavy emphasis on default heterosexuality, though I will address that in further chapters as well), then the idea that women were forced into corsets to pander to the male gaze falls apart as well. In fact, an examination of the available data will show that women were the perpetuators of corseting, as they made or bought most of the clothing, filed most of the patents on corsets, and participated in a counter-discourse refuting the idea that wearing a corset was any sort of burden. They could, of course, have been participating due to internalized sexism—we often latch onto ideas of the hegemonic discourse and use them as our own, in negation of a feeling of powerlessness. However, that idea leaves no room for agency, no room for intentionality, no room for women being aware of their own societal status and rebelling against it. It strips women of their voices and implies that they are all dupes of the patriarchy. I am not comfortable with such an unnuanced approach to women during any time period, and particularly not during one in which their narrative has been repressed.

Why This Matters

You may be saying to yourself, why does this matter? What can a bioar-chaeological look at the practice of corseting tell us that is of any import to the world we currently live in? The way we talk about women, and the way women think about themselves, is deeply rooted in the physi-cality of our bodies. Current views on these issues stem from our cul-tural understanding of women's bodies. If we take these myths, outlined above, at face value, we can easily fall into the trap of looking at women as weaker, more frail, less able, and less civilized than men. We are only as knowledgeable as our best data, and as of yet, our narrative relies on outmoded data riddled with assumptions and mythologies built up over the past few centuries. We can do better. The data I have collected here support an entirely different narrative, one that shows that women were and are strong, capable, long-lived, and agentive, similar to men. This is the narrative that you will read in the upcoming chapters.

*   *   *

This primary chapter has given an overview of the main themes of the book, explained terminology, and introduced you to the idea of the corset and its impact on the female body/the discourses around women who corseted. It has outlined some of the myths that we believe about corseting and given a brief refutation of those myths. Perhaps most importantly, it has introduced you to the women of St. Bride's lower churchyard, London, and explained the significance of the "ordinary" woman. Each following chapter will have an opening vignette that will introduce you to a specific person or object associated with this updated take on the bioarchaeology of the corseted woman.

The next chapter will look at clothing as a multiple signifier, with a garment never simply representing itself but also representing the culture within which it exists and the intentions of the woman wearing it. This multiple signification is determined by an interplay between what is shown, what is meant, and what is perceived—so the form of the garment interacts with the wearer and the viewer to create sociocultural meanings, and these meanings are often both intentional and incidental.

It begins with a look at what fashion historians say about uses of the corset. The current conversation highlights a certain subset of letters to magazines or journals, which are a combination of reader-titillation and writer-exhibitionism, but also can be read as the way in which women, who were supposed to be nonpublic, participated in the public sphere. The intended readership was male, though both men and women would have read the letters.

Among these women, several felt compelled to respond to societal outcry against the corset, detailing a thoroughly unerotic use of the corset. In this subgenre of the letters, the women wrote about everyday wear, and about the support and comfort of a well-fitted corset. They were intent on setting the record straight, and a few of the letters were so detailed as to be downright boring. The intended audience was, again, male—in this case, in order to counteract the imprecations of "bad" corset use, to remove the focus from sexuality and refocus the attention on how normal corseting actually was.

Next, I will provide a nuanced view as to who wore a corset, what an "average" corset might look like, and data on the specific dimensions and materials from the corsets in the Victoria and Albert Museum in London, the Fashion Museum in Bath, St. Fagans Museum in Cardiff, and the National Museum of Scotland in Edinburgh's collections.

The bulk of Chapter 3 will detail those collections, looking at trends in fabric and other material use over time, whether or not there was a change in size dependent on the fineness of the garment, and showing the abovementioned peculiarities. This will be done with data in aggregate, divided by decades. I will also discuss the finances of affording a corset—how much they might cost, what materials were available, who had access to them, and whether or not there were socioeconomic barriers to corseting.

The narrative then returns to theoretical arguments that corseting can be a barrier between a woman and the outside world, analyzing such ideas as thoughts about civilization and corset wearing, and what was considered by women when they wore their garments.

The discussion surrounding women's place in the home vs. their public personas is one that must be approached with nuance. In Chapter 4, I will draw from multiple sources to tease out the various strands of that discussion as it intersects with corsets, tight clothing, and the dress reform movement of the 1890s and 1900s. As seen previously, women's relationship with their corsets and other clothing as arbiters of social standing and defense against the world was deeply ingrained, yet also contested from both men and women from this time. Health and morality were deeply linked, with ill-health and/or the poverty that occasionally caused such ill-health being seen as moral failings rather than failings of the flesh. Through this time, we see a change and a conflict in this narrative, one from the men railing against the tight stays of earlier times, to the women creating their own dress reform movement to remove tight/hot clothing and release the burden on women's waists.

This is a narrative that incorporates various ideas from earlier chapters—that women were more active in society than measured merely by their participation in the home; that they were responsible for corseting patents much of the time; that they were more agentive than how they were viewed by society and more nuanced than their salacious contributions to magazines. The practice of corseting lasted 400 years, and although it is often seen as a patriarchal imposition of men onto women, women were instrumental both in its perpetuation and in ultimately ending that practice through dress reform.

Continuing the analysis in a different vein, another conversation around corseting is that of men of medicine. The study of the body is respected, and the knowledge of one's own body discounted, until what remains of the narrative of women's health and corseting is that pushed by physicians of the time. Women are seen as the object of medical discourse, rather than the subjects of their own lives. In Chapter 5, I will examine what doctors say about the corset, and what motivated their assessments, and look at whether those assessments were accurate when compared to what we now know about female physiognomy. This presses back against prejudices that are found among doctor's statements about the corset, and determines what the corset could have realistically done to the female body, based on lifespan and skeletal data. This chapter will examine several doctors, but will primarily discuss Ludovic O'Followell, whose 1908 book on corseting is the most cited among cultural historians today.

The next chapter will introduce the history of St. Bride's as well as data from the St. Bride's parish archive and discuss the longevity of the women buried there, as well as their causes and locations of death. Who were these women? How long did they live? Where, and how, did they die? These questions have direct bearing on one of the central questions of this book—was the corset responsible for maiming and killing women? If it is, then a deep look into the demographic data of St. Bride's Parish will give us an idea of that.

The penultimate chapter will look at the skeletal data, keeping in mind all the previously introduced information about the lives of these women and the discourses surrounding them. I will also briefly discuss the comparison between St. Bride's and the French skeletal collection at the Musée de l'Homme. Having previously looked at the corsets themselves, here I will examine what an uncorseted skeleton looks like in relation to a corseted one, how the location of death can determine whether or not the person would have corseted, and I will detail precisely what changes have occurred to the St. Bride's skeletons that indicated deformation from corseting. I will look at three different skeletal markers—the angles of the spinous processes, and the shape and relative size of the ribs/thoracic cage.

The final chapter will address modern corseting and why the subject matters so much to a twenty-first-century understanding of women and the various discourses in which we participate. In it, I take the reader from the reform movement to 2019, looking at such things as the move from the corset to the bra/girdle combination and back to modern corseting. Corseting has recently undergone a resurgence in popularity, and I examine this in the lens of body modification, as well as fashion and reenactment styles. I look at the language we continue to use regarding women, and how that language ties back to the historical practice of corseting. Finally, I revisit the myths about corseting, and look at the impact those myths have on what women do now within the current instantiation of the hegemonic patriarchy. Before we begin, however, I must say a bit about two topics: the male/female dichotomy which is used throughout this book and the use of skeletal remains and photos in this research.

The Gender Binary: Why I Use "Women" and "Female"

As an anthropologist, specifically as a biological anthropologist, I am very clear on the fact that what we call biological sex[1] does not determine a person's gender,[2] that there are more than two sexes and more than two genders, and that clothing is not deterministic, so we cannot guarantee that people who corseted were "women." There will be a discussion later in this book about how sex is determined in skeletal remains. However, it bears emphasizing here that many of our current understandings about sex and gender post-date the time period in which the people I will discuss lived. The modern acceptance of multiple sexes and multiple genders is not retroactively applicable to the eighteenth and nineteenth centuries when people did not discuss themselves in such terms.

This is not to say that intersex individuals, trans individuals, and nonbinary individuals did not exist; certainly, they did. Human biological variation is as old as humans ourselves, and the tendency for self-expression that represented that variation is just as old. However, due to social stigmatization and censure, people who did not at least visibly and behaviorally conform to the sex and gender binaries were variably ostracized or held up as examples of "how not to be." This led

---

[1]Biological sex in this reference can be understood as a selection of biological characteristics—sex chromosomes, primary and secondary sex characteristics, and skeletal traits—that, when grouped together, are referred to as male, female, or intersex.

[2]Gender in this reference can be understood as a selection of behavior and cultural traits—too many to mention, but often inclusive of clothing, hairstyles, levels of aggression, and social "strength"—that, when grouped together, are referred to as male/masculine, female/feminine, or nonbinary, agender, bigender, gender fluid, or other currently evolving self-referential terms.

to a minimization of their presence in the historical record. When I have encountered such individuals, I have made note of it. In all other circumstances, I have used either the self-identification of the person (using female pronouns for people who sign their written contributions as "A Lady" for example), or based my identifications on commonly used skeletal markers, as will be discussed in detail.

Ethical Use of Remains in Skeletal Collections

The discussion about the storage and use of human remains has long been a contested one, with more participants than just religious organizations and various governmental agencies. Native/aboriginal groups, surviving relations, and anti-dissectionists all bring varied ideas to the table in regard to where, how, and whether human remains should be held and displayed (Jenkins 2011; Lohman and Goodnow 2006). In regard to the St. Bride's cemetery collection, neither native groups nor anti-dissectionists have had issues with the idea of continued storage of the remains and their scientific access within the Museum of London's laboratories, as the collection does not likely include remains that were the product of hospital use, nor any remains from native or aboriginal contexts. However, there was at one point slight pushback from at least one distant descendant of one woman buried at St. Brides (Fuller 2015).

Due to the nature of the St. Bride's excavation, and indeed of the majority of the excavated materials currently held at the Centre for Human Bioarchaeology through the Wellcome project, the linking of individual skeletal material to their identifying historical records of births, deaths, and burials is not possible (Lohman and Goodnow 2006, p. 108). Yet ethical concerns do arise when a family member asks for reinterment and cannot be accommodated. These concerns are dealt with one at a time as they occur, and in the case of Jodi Fuller, the descendant of Hannah Rapson (neé Fulford), late of London and buried in St. Bride's, I was able to assist in rendering assurance that all skeletal remains are handled with respect, and that the scientific knowledge derived from them is beneficial in many ways. That particular issue has been mitigated in this instance, in part because I am writing this book with her knowledge and cooperation (Fuller 2020). We owe it to the descendants of the people whose remains we use to consult and gain their consent, in a timely manner as possible.

One reason this continues to be so highly contested is the long history of body snatching in England or "resurrection" for the purpose of scientific and/or medical research. Eighteenth-century experiments with electrical restimulation of the human body (Ghosh 2015; Montillo 2013) and the desperate need for a better understanding of anatomy in order to properly treat disease and dysfunction (Aptowicz 2014; Dwight 1896; Ghosh 2015; Hutton 2006; Jones 2011; Montillo 2013) clashed with the concept of complete and final Christian burials (Lohman and Goodnow 2006, pgs. 86-90). While the legal ability to claim corpses from executions and the illegal trade of body snatching both supplied the anatomists with intellectual fodder, they were inconvenient, time consuming, and in some cases dangerous (Montillo 2013). These practices were augmented by the 1832 Anatomy Act, which made it legally permissible to obtain bodies from deaths that occurred at workhouses (Dwight 1896; Hutton 2006). The facts that not all people buried as Christians stayed buried, and not all professed Christians received proper burial (were they to die in a workhouse) has certainly colored the way recent anatomically based scandals, such as Alder Hey in 1999 and the Marchioness disaster in 1989, were seen by the British public (Jenkins 2011, p. 30; Lohman and Goodnow 2006, p. 111).

Regardless of the debate surrounding the practice of collecting and displaying human remains, be they wet specimens or skeletal remains, the fact is that current museum practice is to do so. It becomes, therefore, a question of what is the best practice, and what can be done to mitigate any potential harms done to the living. Historically, in both England and France, there were three main ways to acquire anatomical cadavers for use by hospitals and medical schools: donation; deaths of those who had in some way forfeited their claim on burial, be that via dying intestate with no relatives or being sentenced to death by the state (Dwight 1896); or grave robbing. In only one of these was permission directly granted—if a person willed their body to an anatomist, as was done in the case of Jeremy Bentham (Jenkins 2011, p. 107), then such was done without coercion and with informed consent. However, for the unfortunate circumstances of dying poor, or of going to the rope, or having the worst fortune of all, being buried in a cemetery besought by grave robbers, one could find oneself on display without notice or permission, in ways that the English public saw as distinctly grotesque (Bates 2008).

Many works have been written about consent and the display of human remains, not the least of which by historian Stephen Jay Gould, explicitly critiquing the naturalist Georges Cuvier's mistreatment of Sartje Baartman (Gould 1982).[3] Perhaps the most egregious of harms that can be done to a dead human, Baartman's genitals and buttocks were on display, along with her skeleton, in the Musée de l'Homme under the title "The Hottentot Venus." Collected by Cuvier after her death, and paraded around as a sideshow exhibit in life, she stands as a reminder that the history of anthropology is one riddled with racism. Hottentot is the name given by European explorers to the Khoisan People of southern Africa. The term Venus was used to connect Baartman to the Roman goddess of love, and to hyper-sexualize her representation to the European viewing public. While Baartman's skeleton was returned to her home country of South Africa in 2002, the wet mounts of her body parts were lost during one of the museum's moves, and have not yet been found or returned to her homeland. With this type of display, during life and death, to contend with, one can clearly see how care and tending of existing human remains must be at the forefront of their use.

Furthermore, there needs to be a distinction made between museum collections that contain relatively modern and non-contiguous collections, such as the Musée de l'Homme, and ones that contain the results of archaeological excavation, like the Museum of London. Archaeological excavations generally occur under circumstances which ensure that the dead have no remaining family members—generally speaking, older cemeteries or other types of interments are those most

---

[3]Various spellings/Anglicizations of her name exist—I am using the one present in Gould's text.

likely to be threatened by development projects or disasters like the WWII bombing that disturbed St. Bride's Lower Churchyard. An argument can be made that the fate of such collections would be worse if nothing were done to preserve them, and that repatriation, with no one to claim the remains, would be well-nigh impossible. It is then up to the museums and scientists to ensure that such remains are curated well and treated fairly. Yet what of the question of consent?

One recent article highlights how all methods of obtaining remains, other than by donation, are ethically unsound. One researcher (Jones 2011) emphasizes how New Zealand's current system—that of an informed consent based bequest system (ibid., p. 20) came to pass due to a scandal, the 2002 revelation that in many hospitals in the country doctors had been removing the hearts of dead children and using them for cardiac surgery experimentation (ibid.). This came after the similar scandal, often called the Alder Hey scandal, in the United Kingdom (ibid.; Jenkins 2011, pp. 25–26, 28–32, 41, 46–47, 51, 86, 105, 120, 123; Lohman and Goodnow 2006, p. 111). The contention of the physicians was that consent to autopsy was de facto consent to the removal of tissue; the families of the deceased children did not agree (Jenkins 2011, pp. 28–32). In regard to their disagreement, one article states that the issue of consent and/or proper use of remains lies in how they are seen by the nonscientific public.

While Floris Tomasini, archaeologist and philosopher, discusses organ and tissue donation, in his paper on the treatment of the dead, indeed the very question which was at the center of Alder Hey, the three categories he proposes for relevant nonscientific viewpoints regarding that treatment are applicable to osteological collections as well. He states that how we relate to human remains is based on seeing them as "… [C]adavers…[A]nte-mortem persons…[or as if] [B]y significant others…" (Tomasini 2008, p. 7). Each category comes with its own set of value judgments, according to Tomasini. A cadaver has no (or reduced) humanity, and can be used, displayed, with less ethical quandaries (ibid.). An ante-mortem person, however, has rights, possesses full humanity, and can exercise their rights via wills or bequests (ibid.). This ability to negotiate the treatment and disposal of one's remains prior to death negates the next viewpoint, that of the loved ones left behind. Yet if we allow the third to supersede the first or second, that could lead to the loss of pre-death autonomy from donations and bequests.[4]

Additionally, one must ask the question of benefits vs. risks. The above literature has concentrated on the risks, primarily to living humans, but not explored how much benefit comes from having collections available to a multitude of types of researchers. Knowledge production for the sake of production alone is no longer the norm of the archaeological sciences, and collections no longer are simply assembled and left to gather dust.[5] Both the Musée de l'Homme skeletons and the postmedieval St. Bride's remains are working collections, attracting droves of scientists asking myriad questions and using diverse techniques. The curators of the Museum of London's Centre for Human Bioarchaeology aver that to reinter or repatriate all osteological collections would be a great loss to the fields of anthropology, archaeology, forensics, and medicine, among others (Lohman and Goodnow 2006, pp. 110–116). Through the use of trauma and taphonomic analysis, DNA studies, isotopic analysis, and geometric morphometrics, we access the information that ancient and historical bones can give us. Several curators from the British Museum's Department of Ancient Egypt and Sudan call it "holding [information] for the future" (Fletcher et al. 2014, p. 20). New techniques have been developed very recently, and one does not know what shape future developments will take—it can be seen as irresponsible by scientists who wish to use this untapped knowledge, to unmake the opportunity and potential that waits in the skeletons already available.

---

[4]This, it should be noted, applies only to a specific subset of death ideas and rituals—other cultural burial beliefs and rituals would either have no problem with organ removal and/or display, or would have an even bigger problem, based on beliefs that the body should remain intact after death. As this research is based on a Protestant Christian church population (St. Bride's) and a population created by the purposeful disregard of native burial practices (Musée de l'Homme), the Western perspective is what I have chosen to highlight.

[5]In the case of the Musée de l'Homme collection, this is quite literal—the skeletons were left uncovered for much of their tenure in the museum, and as such are coated in a thick layer of dust and soft tissue remnants. The museum is undertaking a cleaning and preservation project, and has instituted a system of plastic bags to ensure the coating does not grow thicker in the meantime.

Finally, we must address two things: the use of photographs of skeletal material in this book, and the potential for scientific hypocrisy in the work-arounds that are proposed as alternatives for using said photographs. Certainly, if I have not already done so, then by the end of this book I will have convinced you that we can learn numerous interesting, scientifically important, and socially relevant things from the study of the human skeleton, past and present. Those things are only possible to unearth and comprehend by the direct measurement and observation of those skeletons—there is a point where theoretical observations and discussions must be left off and concrete examination must occur. It is at that point where, through the scientific method, our understanding of the human condition, the very thing that *is* anthropology, is produced. There are no substitutes for having one's hands on one's subject material, for looking at, touching, measuring, and recording the normalities and anomalies of the human skeleton.

This is recognized throughout bioanthropological science—it is how we teach our students, it is how we conduct our research, it is how we produce our knowledge. The second-best method, if one cannot access the physical remains, is to use high-quality photos to illustrate points. This book does just that. In several places, you will see photographs of skeletal remains from the Museum of London's Centre for Human Bioarchaeology, and from the Musée de l'Homme. Both museums have explicitly given their permission to use those photographs in this work, with the understanding that the purpose of doing so is to broaden the scientific understanding of this under-explored topic. Throughout the course of my research, over the past eight years, I have worked with both museums to create images that would give you, my readers, the experience of how I created these datasets which are discussed here. However, just as scholars debate whether or not to store human remains, so to do we debate whether to use such photos in our work.

As is no doubt obvious, I come down on the side of "yes." But why? How is this justified after the last several pages about consent, and respect for the human body, etc.? There are three reasons I feel that scientists are justified in their use of actual photographs of human remains, rather than in using work-arounds such as line-drawings, diagrams, or intensely descriptive prose: the first lies in that above-discussed value of photographs as illustrations for those who cannot physically access the remains—there's no need to reiterate this; the second is that to refuse to share information to which I have access, after having gathered that information to begin with, would be intensely hypocritical of me; and the third lies in the restoring of a story, a personal narrative, to each woman I examined in my research. I will expand on the second and third reasons.

It is becoming more and more common, during gatherings of scholars—particularly gatherings of anthropologists—to acknowledge the use of spaces and land that was taken from Indigenous American groups by the United States government. Generally, the formula goes like this: "…before we begin, we would like to acknowledge that we are standing on the ancestral homelands of [insert your local group's name here] and that these groups were forcibly removed from this land." There are variations, but you get the gist. However, only very rarely does the acknowledgment go further—that we acknowledge the removal of Indigenous Americans from their ancestral homelands, that this was wrong and regrettable, and requires that we make mention of it…and yet we are still using the land, still building the structures on it, still participating in this institution which has been used to oppress and marginalize these people.

In much the same way, then, do scholars who work with human remains treat the data they create—marking a divide between the use of that data among themselves, and the use of that data to "outsiders." We create photographs of skeletal remains to show our colleagues at conferences, to publish in scientific journals, and to illustrate ideas to our students, but draw an invisible line when it comes to sharing these photographs to the world. We have accepted that we will use the remains to create data, and through that, that we will produce the images in the first place for our own use or for use by our colleagues. But then we stop when it comes to sharing that information, that only-one-step-removed-from-bones information, with you, the reader of a pop-sci book. I do not agree with that line being drawn. We must not stifle access to valid and valuable information and datasets because the people reading it lack our own formal training. If we did so, how would we interest the next generation of scientists in their own future work?

How can we, many of whom grew up on popular science works in such magazines as National Geographic and Smithsonian Magazine, refuse to share what we know?

And what I know, in this particular case, are some of the stories of the women of St. Bride's Parish, and of the Musée de l'Homme collection. Not every story. I am not that lucky, nor is there enough time in one life for me to track down and collate the records for each person, named and unnamed, in both collections. But some of them. I have been able to attach stories to a few skeletons—whether those stories are completely accurate or not is something I cannot verify, but they are, at the very least, completely plausible. Through this book, among others, you will meet Jodi Fuller's ancestor Hannah Rapson. You will meet a young English woman who presents a quandary to researchers, and follow me as I explore how she ended up in the Musée de l'Homme. You will meet women who did not corset, and those who did, and learn about their lives—as illustrated by the skeletons they left behind. You will see the science that I used to discover these stories through the photos, the next best thing to being able to examine the bones yourself. Thank you for joining me on this exploration of these corseted skeletons and what they can tell us about the bioarchaeology of binding. Please consider becoming an organ donor, or donating your body to forensic research—your story is important as well, in our effort to create a better, more just scientific landscape for the future of biological anthropology—and enjoy the rest of the book!

Bibliography

Aptowicz, C. (2014). *Dr. Mütter's Marvels*. New York, NY: Penguin.

Bates, A. (2008). "Indecent and Demoralizing Representations": Public Anatomy Museums in mid-Victorian England. *Medical History, 52*(1), 1–22.

Dwight, T. (1896). Anatomy Laws Versus Body-Snatching. *Forum* (p. 493).

Fairclough, N. (2003). *Analyzing Discourse: Textual Analysis for Social Research*. New York, NY: Routledge.

Fletcher, A., Hill, J. D., & Antoine, D. (2014). *Regarding the Dead: Human Remains in the British Museum*. London, UK: The British Museum Press.

Fitzharris, L. (2017). *The Butchering Art: Joseph Lister's Quest to Transform the Grisly World of Victorian Medicine*. New York, NY: Macmillan.

Fuller, J. (2012). http://www.wiltshire-opc.org.uk/Items/Salisbury/Salisbury%20 -%20Hannah%20Fulford%20(St.%20Edmund)%201762-1838.pdf.

Fuller, J. (2015). Pers. Corrs.

Fuller, J. (2020). Pers. Corrs.

Ghosh, S. (2015). Human Cadaveric Dissection: A Historical Account From Ancient Greece to the Modern Era. *Anatomy and Cell Biology, 48,* 153–169.

Gould, S. (1982). The Hottentot Venus. *Natural History, 91,* 20–27.

Hutton, F. (2006). The Working of the 1832 Anatomy Act in Oxford and Manchester. *Family and Community History, 9*(2), 125–139.

Jenkins, T. (2011). *Contesting Human Remains in Museum Collections: The Crisis of Cultural Authority*. New York, NY: Routledge.

Jones, D. (2011). The Centrality of the Dead Human Body for Teaching and Research—Social, Cultural, and Ethical Issues. *South African Journal of Bioethics and Law, 4*(1), 18–23.

Lohman, J., & Goodnow, K. (2006). *Human Remains and Museum Practice*. Paris, France and London, UK: UNESCO and The Museum of London.

Montillo, R. (2013). *The Lady and Her Monsters: A Tale of Dissections, Real-Life Dr. Frankensteins, and the Creation of Mary Shelley's Masterpiece*. New York, NY: HarperCollins.

Museum of London. (2019). https://www.museumoflondon.org.uk/collections/ other-collection-databases-and-libraries/centre-human-bioarchaeology/ osteological-database/post-medieval-cemeteries/st-brides-lower-post-medieval.

O'Brien, R. (1929). *Bibliography on the Relation of Clothing to Health* (Miscellaneous Publication No. 62). Washington, DC: United States Department of Agriculture.

St. Bride's. (2019). http://www.stbrides.com/history/index.html.

St. Bride's Register. (1770–1849). ancestry.co.uk.

Tomasini, F. (2008). Research on the Recently Dead: An Historical and Ethical Examination. *British Medical Bulletin, 85,* 7–16.

2

The Corset in Our Collective Consciousness: Exotic, Erotic, or Other?

For your consideration of the erotic/exotic vs. everyday undergarment narrative, I would like to bring to your attention three corsets at extremes of the spectrum: T.90-1928 from the Victoria and Albert fashion annex, I.27.107 from the Fashion Museum in Bath, and F83.173.4 from St. Fagans in Cardiff, Wales. These corsets could not be less alike. From size to utility, they share nothing in common apart from the fact that they are corsets and serve the same general purpose; to shape the female body.

T.90-1928, from the year 1905, is elaborate, highly decorated, with bows and ribbons and fleurettes made of silk. It is delicate, almost fragile because of the material. While it can be laced completely closed, I would hazard a well-educated guess that it never was—the materials simply would not be able to withstand the strain of being tugged on. It is lightly boned, and obviously meant to be lingerie. Its dimensions are 68.0 cm at the bust, 46.0 cm at the waist, and 61.0 cm at the hips, which corresponds to 26.8in × 18.1in × 24.0in or a ratio of 1:.67:.89. This is an erotic corset, and it is in the minority in all the collections I examined. It is pretty, flashy, and delicate, but not "normal."

© The Author(s) 2020
R. Gibson, *The Corseted Skeleton*,
https://doi.org/10.1007/978-3-030-50392-5_2

I.27.107, dated to between 1870 and 1880, is one of the largest corsets I examined in all four museum collections, with measurements of 110.5 cm at the bust, 80.5 cm at the waist, and 122.0 cm at the hips. This corresponds to 43.5in × 31.7in × 48.0in, and a ratio of .91:.66:1 showing a definite corseted effect at the waist. The material is utilitarian—made of cotton canvas, heavily boned, with very minimal decoration. It can be laced fully closed, or worn more open, as it has laces in the back and hooks in the front. This is an everyday corset. It is also fairly typical of the corsets I examined, in that it is unexceptional, plain, has a few decorations, but is meant to be worn and indeed shows wear patterns.

F83.173.4 from St. Fagans in Cardiff, Wales, is a "Wedding Corset" specifically created to go underneath a wedding dress. It was made in 1883 and measures 86 cm × 51.5 cm × 93.5 cm. This corresponds to 33.8in × 20.3in × 36.8in, in a ratio of .92:.55:1. It is both fronted and lined with silk and has embroidered details. The accompanying dress, 65.81/21, can be seen in Photos 2.1, 2.2, 2.3, and 2.4, as worn by the bride, a Miss G. Morgan, of Tynycymmer Close, Porth, Glamorgan, Wales, approximately 18 miles northwest of Cardiff. In it, she married Phillip Dunn. It is a lovely shimmery gold color and radiates wealth and sophistication.

What can be said about these garments, so representative of differing types? These show that the practice of corseting was not simplistic or predictable. There were gradations of fineness, in the type of fabric and how the corset was constructed. The corsets were as individual as the women who wore them, with different styles creating different looks and moods. We cannot see corseting as monolithic, being only for one purpose or representing only one type of narrative discourse, because the options were multiple.

These are also representative of only one small snapshot of corseting, as they are from the latter part of the era under discussion. Earlier corsets emphasized different ideas of femininity and were not very comparable in shape to later ones. For example, corsets 38.262 and 53.119 from St. Fagans Museum in Cardiff, Wales, are both representative of the styles of the late 1700s, which focused on creating a cone-shaped torso that ended in a point near the pubic bone of the woman (Photos 2.5, 2.6, and 2.7).

Photo 2.1   F83.173.4—The Wedding Corset (Photo by author and used with permission from St. Fagans Museum, Cardiff, Wales)

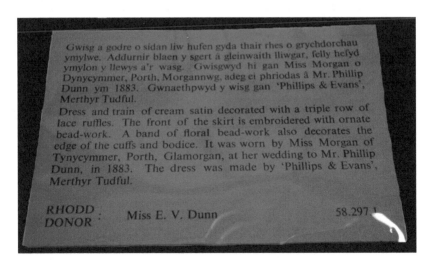

Photo 2.2   Description tag for The Wedding Corset (Photo by author and used with permission from St. Fagans Museum, Cardiff, Wales)

Photo 2.3   Photo of the bride, Miss G. Morgan of Tynycymmer Close, Porth, Glamorgan, Wales (Photo by author and used with permission from St. Fagans Museum, Cardiff, Wales)

We can see that tapering effect in the above photo, of 53.119, a corset from the late eighteenth century, which has waist and hips measurements that are remarkably similar—the corset measures 87.5 cm x 68 cm x 66 cm or 34.4in × 26.8in × 26.0in. Our perception of corsets more closely resembles the later examples, however, so I have created a

Photo 2.4 Photo of the bride, Miss G. Morgan of Tynycymmer Close, Porth, Glamorgan, Wales (Photo by author and used with permission from St. Fagans Museum, Cardiff, Wales)

diagram using the abovementioned Wedding Corset, to show what the various parts of corsets look like in situ (Photo 2.8).

* * *

This chapter will look at clothing as a multiple signifier, with a garment never simply representing itself but also representing the culture within which it exists and the intentions of the woman wearing it. This multiple signification is determined by an interplay between what is shown, what is meant, and what is perceived—so the form of

53.119

Photo 2.5 Corset 53.119, 1770–1780, exterior view, closed, from the front (Photo by St. Fagans Museum, Cardiff)

the garment, in this case, the corset, interacts with the wearer and the viewer to create sociocultural meanings, and these meanings are often both intentional and incidental. As mentioned in the introduction to this book, modern perceptions of corseting view it as an exotic/erotic practice, due to the current literature, which pushes that narrative discourse. We can see that in lingerie advertising, in the glorification of the Kardashian sisters, and in the popularity of corseting as a shorthand for femininity that occurs in movies adaptations of books set during the time period—particularly ones like the 1994 version of "Little Women"

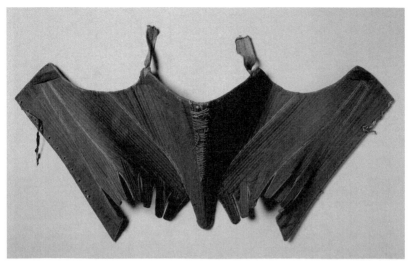

53.119

Photo 2.6   Corset 53.119, 1770–1780, exterior view, open (Photo by St. Fagans Museum, Cardiff)

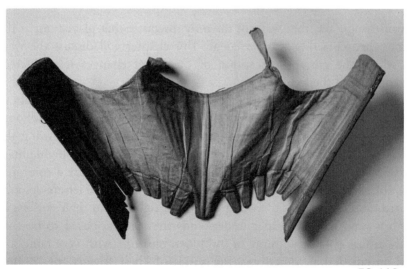

53.119

Photo 2.7   Corset 53.119, 1770–1780, interior view, open (Photo by St. Fagans Museum, Cardiff)

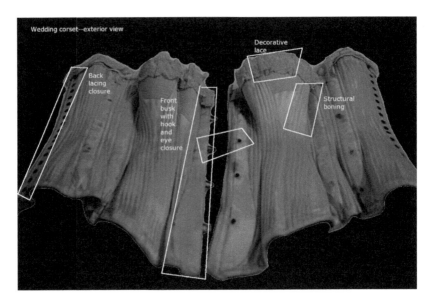

Wedding corset--exterior view

Decorative lace

Back lacing closure

Front busk with hook and eye closure

Structural boning

Photo 2.8 The Wedding Corset, a diagram (Photo by author and used with permission from St. Fagans Museum, Cardiff)

(Armstrong). Yet, that was not the only discourse that played out at the time when corseting was prevalent. This chapter will discuss the ways in which the current perception of the corset changes if a different discourse is at the forefront.

This narrative begins with a look at what fashion historians say about uses of the corset—looking at such issues of the creation of childhood, the creation of the middle class, and the ideals of fashion during the time. The current conversation among cultural historians highlights a certain subset of letters to magazines or journals, which are a combination of reader-titillation and writer-exhibitionism. These letters describe boarding school antics of young girls laced tightly into their corsets, in such a way that the reader understands they are supposed to be covertly arousing—the epitome of forbidden pleasure, with very tame/soft girl-on-girl action, describing the antics of "best friends" or "dearest companions." The intended readership was male, though both men and women would have read the letters.

Indeed, women felt compelled to respond to those possibly fabricated and decidedly hyperbolic letters with ones of their own, detailing a thoroughly unerotic use of the corset. In this second subgenre, the women wrote about everyday wear, and about the support and comfort of a well-fitted corset. They were intent on setting the record straight, and a few of the letters were so detailed as to be downright boring. The intended audience was, again, male—in this case, in order to counteract the imprecations of "bad" corset use, to remove the focus from sexuality and refocus the attention on how normal corseting actually was. This forms the backbone of a discourse that passed back and forth between the writers and their audience.

Fashioning the Narrative: What Cultural Historians Say About the Corset

To begin, I need to make clear the distinction between the disciplines of cultural historian and historical bioanthropologist. While the two are quite similar, and use much of the same language, theory, and sources, the cultural historian generally has not been trained to evaluate artifacts or evaluate the human body in relation to their work. Their interpretations, therefore, are lacking in dimensionality—they look at documentation and apply anthropological and historical theory to that documentation, but do not examine the material culture left behind by the people. In the next few chapters, I will also examine the documentation, and then I will connect it to the artifacts and skeletal remains that have as yet been unexamined in this way.

This is not to deride the contributions of the cultural historians, which are many and valuable. For example, the examination of documents of theft gives us a better look at what women of all classes wore, and busts one of the minor myths about corseting—that only rich women corseted. In "The Dress of the People" John Styles writes, regarding theft records: "The fact that so few stolen stays appear in the indictments may result from many poorer women owning only one pair, which they were wearing when the thefts took place. Alternatively,

cheaper stays may have been less attractive to thieves than other garments, or when not being worn they may have been stored in ways that
made them less vulnerable to theft" (Styles 2007, p. 43). In reference
to the types of stays worn, he also states "Stays, which women wore
over their shifts, could be expensive items. Although they are conspic-
uous by their rarity in the criminal indictments, they were crucial to
achieving the correct posture and silhouette. Poorer women who could
not afford the more expensive boned stays wore cheaper versions in
leather….It seems likely that all but a few of the many women whose
stolen clothes appear in the indictments would have worn some kind of
stays, although it was not unknown for women to go without" (ibid.,
pp. 42–43).

Here he is discussing the town of Brandon, about 90 miles to the
northeast of London—decidedly not a bustling urban area like London,
yet still conscious of fashion and figure. However, Styles' mentions of
stays are rather incidental in his larger work—on the subject of what
constituted everyday fashion. And like the heavily boned fancy clothing of the "ton," which was rare in Brandon, discussions of the everyday
are rare among cultural historians of the corset itself. Styles' book is also
nontypical of the corseting narrative in another way—it is a distinctly
scholarly work, as opposed to pop-science or coffee table, which most
works on corseting personify. There is nothing wrong with either of
those genres, of course. This book that you are holding now can be clas-
sified as pop-sci, and I do hope you might keep it on your coffee table.

However, the overall "point" or "type" of Styles' work is not to be
popular or flashy or necessarily catch your eye as you walk through the
bookstore. The title is not meant to titillate. The cover is not a scantily
clad woman, or an abstract corset. In fact, the cover is a painting of a
beer-maid handing a young man a stein, and the subtitle is "Everyday
Fashion in Eighteenth-Century England." This book is meant for people interested in historic fashion, not in the flashy, showy, exotic corset.

Contrast Styles book, then, with the most known cultural history of corsets, Valerie Steele's book "The Corset: A Cultural History"
(2001/2011). Steele's book is **gorgeous**. And it is meant to be.
Appealing to the eye, and to the hand, it is an oversized book with a

photograph of a corseted woman on the front. The woman is not wearing a shift underneath her corset, so her shoulders and arms are bare. She is looking down the length of her right arm, in a posture that suggests that if she heard you call her name, she would turn to look back at you. The whole feel of the scene is seductive and sexy, enticing and exotic.

The interior is no different, with heavy emphasis put on the narrative that the corset is meant to be erotic. Primarily concerned with tight-lacing, the practice of reducing one's waist by more than a few inches at any given time, Steele makes heavy use of advertisements and the common magazine-based discourse. This is not unreasonable at all, and it makes for a very interesting and attractive book. However, it also subsumes any other potential narrative, and puts this version of history at the forefront of our cultural consciousness.

Steele is not alone in this. The prevailing pattern in corset scholarship often relies on salacious puns and wordplay to draw in readers, with such titles as "Fashion and Fetishism" (Kunzle 1982); "Whalebone to See-Through" (Colmer 1980); "Bound and Determined" (Seleshanko 2012); "Bound to Please" (Summers 2001); "Support and Seduction" (Fontanel 1992); and "An Intimate Affair" (Fields 2007). All of these also have photos or drawings of semi-nude women on the covers or dust jackets. Sex sells, and forbidden, seductive, erotic sex sells harder.

Yet as I mentioned earlier, women, people in general, are multifaceted, and sex is not the main focus of most people's daily lives. As much as it is of cultural importance, it is had or done in relatively minor proportions to the rest of daily activities. Although Summers points out that much of the advertising of corsets during the 1800s was focused on the nude female form (2001, p. 83), she also concurs that these were for the male gaze, not the female consumer. We spend far more time sleeping, eating, reading, working, being athletic, or simply just **being** than we do having sex. And during those times, we generally give very little thought to the various states of our undergarments, unless they happen to be uncomfortable. So where is **that** in the discourse? Where is the ordinary, the everyday, the mundane? To find it, we have to go back to the idea that clothing is a multiple signifier.

Moving Beyond Exotic/Erotic: A Deeper Look at Gender and Its Intersection with Fashion Theory

We understand corseting as many things. A clothing, a way to barricade the body from the outside world, an undergarment that lasted centuries, and as a body modification (Stone 2012). All of these are also seen to as ways to create identity (Geller 2009). While much of the literature surrounding this type of identity deals with futuristic cyber-enhancements, (Campbell 2010; Downey et al. 1995; Haraway 1991; Hartsock 2006), the same principles can be applied backward in time if we extend the idea of technology to include clothing, which is often recognized as such (Barthes 1967; Entwistle 2000). Seen thusly, corseting becomes an outer shell, formed in the image of the bodyscape of the day (Geller 2009), used by the woman to enhance or minimize her own image. She could choose to identify with the current style, emphasizing breasts, bottom, or waist as the fashions changed, or she could choose to go without a corset, becoming a bad subject, a bad and uncivilized woman (Pêcheux 1975).

Two modern theories of identity—disidentification (Pêcheux 1975); and bodyscape theory (Geller 2009) give us the underpinning of a discourse that does not focus on sex, sexuality, or exoticism. These two schools of thought incorporate the concepts of agency—the ability to choose otherwise—and habitus—the cultural conditioning that lets us understand what is appropriate in various social situations—but that also allow for the self-creation of subjectivity. Basically, self-identity is created by an interaction between what we are expected to do in our culture (habitus) and the ability to understand that cultural conditioning and react in ways that accept, subvert, or deny it (agency).

The women of St. Bride's and the wearers of the various corsets I examined were subjects in many ways—all to their countries of origin, some to the people who enslaved them, some to husbands or fathers, yet to reduce them to merely their unautonomous subjectivities is a logical fallacy. Within every overarching social structure, there is a means of resistance. Within every cultural system, there are fringe members, who are, to various degrees, recognized, ignored, punished, or reincorporated by the system. Moreover, the human psyche is complex and nuanced, allowing for the possibility of multiple subjectivities, multiple reasons for performing agentive actions, such as choosing how, or whether, to wear a corset.

The repetition of a certain bodyscape one day at a time becomes a practice that creates identity (de Certeau 1984; Perry et al. 1992). We have established that the corset is a choice women make, so what does that choice say about their identification with or disidentification from the prevailing ideology of the time? This ability—to assent, modify, or refuse to use the corset—shows us that there are three subjectivities, the good subject, the bad subject, and disidentification.

We can see how women who corseted had the ability to perform any or all of these at various points in her life. A good subject would be a woman who corseted from an acceptably early age; wore the garment without complaint, and with restraint in its use, neither tight-lacing nor "allowing" herself to become too large for one (though this is a misnomer—as shown by the examples at the beginning of this chapter, the garment expanded to fit the woman, not vice versa); and did not use it in improper ways, for example, to induce miscarriages. A bad subject would be a woman who refused the corset or was unable to wear one. Reasons for this abound, but in the time period being analyzed the most common reasons would be madness, illness, or wantonness. Women who were diagnosed with mental or physical illnesses, and women who practiced prostitution, were somewhat seen as outside of society's purview, and therefore the social rules of corseting did not generally apply to them (Flanders 2012). The disidentified subject, therefore, would be any woman who used the societal expectation of corseting against itself, for her own desires and purposes.

This use could take many forms, but they all have one thing in common: the self-creation of the woman, in relation to, but not exclusively for, society's ideals. Examples include women who used corsets to self-abort; those who practiced extreme tight-lacing; those whose laces were always a bit loose; those who followed fashion slavishly, and those who did not; and those who, fed up with heavy skirts and the confines of the corset, fought for dress reform. In each of these examples, the women are creating a bodyscape, taking from many versions of the ideal to form their own pastiche. It is this bodyscape—influenced by society but not dictated by it—that the corset can so usefully reify and/or create new ways for women to control what they symbolize and how they are seen. You will also note: none of the above examples are focused on sexuality.

Yet that narrative persists. Why? Theorist and symbological scholar Barthes (1967) tells us that clothing can contain many meanings within a single garment. He also tells us that what is signified by the wearer is not always what is perceived by the viewer (ibid.). This opens up room for the possibility that the internal subjectivities of the women who corseted were left out of history because their own ideas about their existence were often silenced or misinterpreted. The use of magazine correspondence was one way they pressed back on this negation. We have to bring the nuance back to the discussion, as the data shows a diversity of corset fashions and a multiplicity of voices from women who wore the corset.

However, even when women were able to move more into the public sphere, their words were discounted, ridiculed, or decried as satire. Some saw noted nineteenth-century historian William Berry Lord's (1868/1870) long book on corseting and tight-lacing through history, in which he reproduced positive letters about the experience, as "shamelessly biased" (Kunzle 1982, p. 225). Let us now take a look at some of those letters and see what they can tell us about the women who wore corsets.

Talking About Talking About Things: Critical Discourse Analysis and Its Uses

The practice of Critical Discourse Analysis (CDA), made prevalent by twenty-first-century linguistic theorist Norman Fairclough (2003), is a useful tool for assessing the way we talk about things and what that shows us about the things themselves. I use "things" as a purposely very broad category because CDA can be used to analyze everything from hashtags to horror movies to the corset. As mentioned in Chapter 1, women's voices surrounding the wearing of the corset are incredibly sparse in the historical record. This was due to the cultural context—as women were "supposed" to not participate in public spaces, and were "supposed" to be modest and private during the good majority of the time under discussion, the publication of written works under one's own name and gender was frowned upon. What, then, was left? Anonymity, the magazine genre, the use of one's family's power and influence, or, very rarely, daring forays into science and medicine—though those were considerably more visible toward the end of the nineteenth century than at any other time in these 200 years.

The Magazine Genre: On Being Anonymous in the Public Sphere

To discuss women's role in shaping the discourse surrounding corsets, we must return to the word in quotation marks above, "supposed." European thought during this time emphasized the notion of separate spheres, the public where men rightfully met and mingled, and the private, where women did the same (de Tocqueville 1840). Supposedly. Reality, as is usually the case, was considerably messier. Separate spheres worked well enough under a very cultivated set of circumstances—if the male was employed or independently wealthy enough to support a wife that only worked inside the home; if the wife was not what was euphemistically called "high spirited" and was content to remain in the private sphere; if the family was "comfortable" and could live within their means, requiring only one income[1]; if the man's trade did not require the wife to work at a public-facing support role, for example, that of an innkeeper or a smith. If all these and other unnamed requirements were met, then the woman of the house could remain in the private sphere, tending to hearth, home, babies, and domesticity.

---

[1]"Annual income twenty pounds, annual expenditure nineteen nineteen and six, result happiness. Annual income twenty pounds, annual expenditure twenty pounds ought and six, result misery," (Dickens 1850, pp. 125–126).

However, this was very rarely the case. Women were, as they are at all points in history, dynamic in their roles, both public and private facing, with public interactions running the gamut from having their own land and business to being in charge of the domestic arena yet still interacting with tradespeople, servants, and the like. Here again, we see a discrepancy between reality and the perception of women's roles. However, much was invested, culturally, in maintaining that perception—while women did participate fully, they were cautious about being **seen** to participate fully. Anonymity in the form of letters to various magazines and circulars of the day was one way to do both, to maintain their appearance of circulating solely in the domestic or private sphere, while also participating in the public discourse on topics of import, such as the corset. For this reason, among others, such letters are much of what is left of the female corseting discourse. Many of our examples of this genre come from William Berry Lord's excellent book "Freaks of Fashion: The Corset and the Crinoline" (1868/1870) which was largely a defense of the practice and an expiation of the women involved.

In one letter to the Guardian, dated Thursday, June 18, 1713, a young lady laments that other ladies of the time, and some of the gentlemen, thought her figure (given by nature, and only slightly augmented with a corset) to be outrageous. I shall reproduce portions of her letter here, and then unpack it:

...one of the gentlemen, who had been very facetious to several of the ladies, at last turned to me. 'And as for you, madam, Prior has already given us your character:—

"That air and harmony of shape express,
Fine by degrees and beautifully less,"'

...[the ladies asked] the gentleman...what Congreve said about Aurelia...[he] instantly repeated the verses—

'The Mulcibers who in the Minories sweat,
And massive bars on stubborn anvils beat,
Deformed themselves, yet forge those stays of steel,
Which arm Aurelia with a shape to kill.'

...What is beauty worth that makes the possessed this unhappy? Why was Nature so lavish of her gifts to me as to make her kindness prove a cruelty? They tell me my shape is delicate...but I wish...these limbs only not deformed, and then perhaps I might live easie [sic] and unmolested, and neither raise love and admiration in the men, nor scandal and hatred in the women. (Lord 1868/1870, pp. 121–122)

Although not explicitly stated, the girl writing the letter was certainly wearing stays, and defending herself only against the charge of tight-lacing. We can see that in the shape that is "fine by degrees and beautifully less," where one is made less beautiful when made smaller. Her figure, slender of waist already, needed little extra help, however, the ladies and gentlemen of her acquaintance believed her to be pulled together tightly with "stays of steel." This account is of a young woman who wants to corset to a moderate degree, neither being seen as a slattern for wearing her stays too loose, nor as unsubstantial for tighten them too finely. She is choosing her own bodyscape, while still making sure to be seen as being not overly concerned with doing just that.

Lord goes on to say that a mantua-maker (one who crafted the garment that went over the stays and pannier/bustle/crinoline) must "know how to hide all the defects in the proportions of the body, and must be able to mould [sic] the shape by the stays so as to preserve the intestines, that while she corrects the body she may not interfere with the pleasures of the palate" (ibid., p. 123). The stays, or the corset, was a garment worn everyday, all day long, often to bed—there was no point in making it as uncomfortable as possible, and every point in making it fit well. Here she is writing against genre norms—she is not praising the corset per se, nor is she expressing an erotic satisfaction from wearing it. She is writing as herself.

A century and a half later, in 1867, another woman writes a letter signed "Mignonette" to the Englishwoman's Domestic Magazine:

Owing to the absence of my parents in India, I was allowed to attain the age of fourteen before any care was bestowed upon my figure; but their return home fortunately saved me from growing into a clumsy, inelegant girl; for my mamma was so shocked at my appearance that she took the unusual plan of making me sleep in my corset. For the first few weeks I occasionally felt considerable discomfort, owing, in a great measure, to not having worn stays before, and also to their extreme tightness and stiffness. Yet, though I was never allowed to slacken them before retiring to rest, they did not in the least interfere with my sleep, nor produce any ill effects whatever. …fearing that, at so late an age, I should have great difficulty in securing a presentable figure, [my mamma] considered ordinary means insufficient, and consequently had my corsets filled with whalebone and furnished with shoulder-straps, to cure the habit of stooping… The busk, which was nearly inflexible, was not front-fastening…effectually prevented any attempt on my part to unloose my stays…the testimony of one who has undergone [the rigorous regimen] without the least injury to health cannot fail to be of value in proving that the much less severe system…be even less likely to do harm….What is most required, however, are the personal experiences of the ladies themselves, and not mere treatises on tight-lacing by those who, like your correspondent Brisbane, have never tried it. (ibid., pp. 149–150)

Several things stand out about this letter—primarily, that it is not in the least sensational, exotic, erotic, or indicative of a sadomasochistic desire to be punished, nor even a fantasy of that notion, as twentieth-century historians Kunzle and Steele allege women who tight-laced evinced (Kunzle 1982, pp. 37 and 237; Steele 2001, pp. 90–92, 109).

I am more inclined to take it at face value than I would be were it about erotics or the pleasure/pain of the corset, due to the letter's very ordinariness—as in, I cannot imagine a situation where confessing to something so unexceptional would be gratifying or self-sensational. Yet it does indeed emphasize the concept of the good/moral corset, a concept which is shown quite clearly later in this book to be related to the judgmental practices of male doctors of the day. Conversely, however, the signature of "Mignonette" or a diminutive of the word mignon, which means lovely cute thing, indicates that she is aware of the genre which she is subverting, and that she wishes to be perceived a certain way—small, delicate, domestic, appropriately female despite lending her voice to the public discourse. Yet on the whole, with its emphasis on personal experience, good health, and reference to the appropriate shape of the day, this rather supports the notion that women wanted to be in control of their own bodies, and did not wholly repudiate the practice of corseting, but used it to make their own agentive choices, which were decidedly unsexual in nature.

Refuting the Exotic/Erotic—A Focus on Health

While Steele does make the distinction between the minority fetishistic practice of BDSM (bondage/domination/sadism/masochism) tight-lacing and the everyday practice of fashionable tight-lacing, Kunzle does not. The difficulty with making this distinction at a historical distance, however, is that by all accounts the general view of tight-lacing (though not the view of tight-lacers) at the time period did not make that distinction, as shown by the need of letters like the above. Lord goes on to quote a Madame La Sante, who discusses the practice of sleeping in a tight-laced corset, stating, "...those girls who have been subjected to this discipline...say that for the first few months the uneasiness by the continued compression was very considerable, but that after a time they became so accustomed to it that they felt reluctant to discontinue the practice" (Lord 1868/1870, p. 153). Although he does not specify, most of these letters are written pseudonymously, and Madame La Sante is probably French or wants to be seen as French, given that sante is the French word for health.

He also firmly states that "A great number of ladies who, by the systematic use of the corset, have had their waists reduced to the fashionable standard are to be constantly met in society. The great majority declare that they have in no way suffered in health..." (ibid., p. 155). Health, wellness, and quality of life are subjective, meaning that what is unbearable for one person may not bother another at all. It also means that although the changes in the skeleton that women experienced due to long corset wear were significant, women were able to become accustomed to it, feel no injury to health, and no ill effects or disruption of sleep. This directly refutes the idea that the corset was a violent and harmful, and sexualizing, tool of the hegemonic patriarchy, as is the contention of certain modern theorists (Stone 2012), since we can see clearly that some women from the time said, with no equivocation, that it was not. To deny their viewpoint or to give it any less validity than the physical evidence of their longevity, undeterred by corseting, is to deny their agency and multiple subjectivities.

One of those subjectivities is very clearly shown in a letter from 1866, published in the periodical "A Flag of our Union," which I am very tempted to reproduce in its entirety as it is a masterwork of pointed writing. However, I shall refrain, and quote only the most salient parts. The author, listed only as "a lady correspondent" (p. 110) writes:

> …I am the envied possessor of a waist of sixteen inches….as to the dreadful effects of tight-lacing. When stays were made of buckram and iron, the doctors might have had some cause to write against them; but look at the beautiful French corsets now universally worn [ed. note: I am not certain from which location she is writing, but England and America both produced multiple brands of corsets during this decade, so no, not **universally** worn.] They are quite a different article of dress. Besides, even in the last century, when stays were made so stiff and cut so straight, ladies enjoyed good health, and were even more robust than those of the present day. Again, there are actually more women in the kingdom than men, which would not be the case if, during so many years (I may say centuries), tight-lacing had *really* been the 'suicide' it has been called. I have often thought it very hard that, if a young lady faints or dies suddenly, she should immediately be accused of having brought it on by tight-lacing. Do men never faint or die suddenly? and [sic.] are *they* not subject to consumption, spinal deformities, and those other diseases which have been ascribed to the corset. For my own part, I have never suffered any inconvenience from this fashion, and my waist is smaller than the majority. (ibid.)

Yet, as part and parcel to the nuance of such concepts, not all women agreed with the above writers. "A Lady" writing in the 1883 edition of the journal Knowledge begins using the new-fangled "divided skirt" (p. 162) without the use of stays or tight-lacing. She expresses her delight at the freedom afforded to her, and states that her waist, far from growing larger, has in fact shrunk by 2 inches since leaving off stays. However, even with her appreciation for the "lightness and freedom" (ibid.) experienced afterward, she goes on to say this:

> I do not suppose that ladies who are so unfortunate as to have no waist would care to leave off stays, for the general prejudice has been, and is, in favour of some slight diminution of the circumference at the waist. But that need not prevent them from trying the divided skirt; indeed, I should imagine that it would be possible, though I do not say it would be wise, to lace tighter when wearing the divided skirt than when, in addition to the bad effects of undue compression, the weight of several heavy petticoats is dragging the body down. (ibid.)[2]

In particular, the women of the Rational Dress movement, as demonstrated by D. O. Teasley, believed that corseting was unhealthful in numerous ways (1904). There are several ways one can view dress reform, an idea that began in the 1850s, gained steam in the latter part of the century and became mostly accepted by the war years, but the fact that corseting lasted so long was a fashion oddity, and during this time the tide was turning. New ideas about women's health were gaining ground, and rational dress was a reaction to the notion that women's requirements were being seen as more equal to men's. Moreover, the woman's right to speak in public as a concept was being born, spurring rational dress, temperance, and suffrage as female-driven causes.

Teasely goes on to state that "[I]t is possible for a woman to dress perfectly neat and still have every garment supported from the shoulders. The skirt bands may have buttonholes. A waist made of light material, with buttons on, will serve to fasten the skirts to, which will throw the weight upon the shoulders; or if preferred, instead of buttons, the skirts may be sewed on to a waist" (1904). This emphasis on the shoulders was influenced by the thought that the body had various temperature zones, and that the temperatures should be equalized, and in balance, rather than one cold zone (shoulders) and one hot zone (the

---

[2]I feel compelled to note that later in the volume from which this quote was taken is a short letter about the practice of "wart charming" which is a method of making warts fall off by simply telling them to do so. That such a practice does not actually work need not detract from the legitimacy of the other scientific contributions to this periodical (Knowledge 1883, p. 630).

waist and what lay below) (Steele 2001/2011, p. 62). Yet, despite being progressive, neither Teasley, nor the idea of dress reform, was at all feminist. She purported to be speaking for women, with their voices, using her position of a wife and mother to add the idea of authenticity.

She was also not alone, however—she was backed up by the overall discourse of the day, and that discourse was resolutely controlled by men. As we can see, however, the discourse was not dominated by the erotic/exotic concepts highlighted by twentieth- and twenty-first-century cultural historians—that was very much in the background. Whether the men controlling the eighteenth- and nineteenth-century discourse were the editors which published the letters, or laypersons weighing in with their own opinions, the discourse was mostly about how the corset harmed the woman. So, how can one get at what women really felt and/ or meant about their own corseting experiences?

Biocultural Analysis or Looking at Behavior to Explain Everyday Choice

To understand what women at the time meant to say about their corset wearing, we have to look not only at the discourse but also their patterns of behavior. We have to integrate the biological into the cultural, to look at the artifacts and skeletal remains, as well as the historical documentation, which I will do in subsequent chapters. What we can see from the above Discourse Analysis is that much of the dialogue of the time should be taken with a grain of salt. Women were happy in their corsets, or they were not. Women were harmed by their corsets, or they were not. Women thought of the corsets as male-oriented and sexual, or they did not. Women, as should be very obvious, are individuals, not a monolith of a group with one opinion or set of reasons for their behaviors. But what women actually did, as a group, was create, patent (Swanson 2011), purchase, use, and mend corsets for hundreds of years.

Chapter 3 will cover their physical behavior in much more detail, and will also look at the corsets as artifacts. However, there is still much to be learned from the above letters and other sources, from their verbal behavior, if you will, that replaces the idea of the corset as exotic/erotic.

Three aspects shown by the discourse strike me as incredibly important to our continued discussion of the corseted woman: that socioeconomic class was no barrier to the desire to be fashionable or the access to style; that women entered the narrative surrounding corseting in ways that were socially acceptable for the time; and that women knew they were working within the patriarchal worldview that pervaded their lives, and used that to their advantage. I will summarize these individually, with a nod toward turning the narrative toward women's agentive choice to use this everyday garment.

While the differences between the various classes will also be explored later, this current discussion does allow us to explore several ways in which the lower classes could have kept their wardrobe current. As mentioned by the historian Styles (2007), women had several options when it came to creating their own garments, indeed as most women did before industrialization and commercialization. They could make stays out of cheaper materials, such as leather or wood or stiffened fabric. They could make over old garments into newer, fresher styles. They could create their own patterns, relying on a knowledge of the craft of textile work, rather than needing to purchase patterns. They could purchase things second hand, or receive new or finer clothing as gifts, or barter for materials. They could, as Styles also pointed out, steal stays. A poor woman was not necessarily an uncorseted woman, because she had these options open to her.

And knowing this, the women did enter the discourse around corsets to express their choices and opinions. This, of course, **was** determined at least in part by socioeconomic class. Women who were able to join the discourse were, necessarily, ones who could write well enough to be published. They had some education, and some knowledge that there was even a discourse to be had. Perhaps they read the very journals they wrote into, like the women who penned "A Plea for Tight-Lacing" (1866) and "The New Skirt" (1883). Some of them were able to understand other languages, such as those who signed themselves "Mignonette" and "Madame La Sante" (Lord 1868/1870). Yet what all the letters have in common, despite their discrepancies in content, is the desire to take control of the subject of corseting, knowing that in order to do so they were constrained by what was considered "proper."

The proper way to be a woman in public was to be dainty, polite, not too tight-laced, and modest, like the unnamed woman in the first excerpt from Lord (1868/1870, pp. 121–122). Or to be uncomplaining, grateful, and a dutiful daughter, like Mignonette. Or to be visibly, verbally, and demonstrably "A Lady," like in "The New Skirt" (1883). One needed to demonstrate the civilizing aspects of the corset, to be molded into a proper female form, yet not show too much enthusiasm for a tiny waist, seeing it as incidental, something for which one might long, but not strive. And, as mentioned, Summers (2001) concurs that depictions of the corseted woman as purely sexual, such as in advertisements, were aimed toward the male gaze, not toward the actions or the desires of the women themselves. All of the examples, even those firmly against corseting such as Teasley's plea from a mother to daughters (1904), are demonstrations of the third point—that women were aware of the patriarchal mores by which they were expected to live, and that they used and occasionally subverted them, living their own authentic agentive lives despite expectations of propriety.

So, what about that patriarchy? How do the dominating expectations of the world we live in effect our behaviors? As shown by the above, the answer is dual: both very much, and very little. Very much in that certain legal and/or cultural proscriptions kept women from fully participating in society. One such way was the legal inability to sign contracts or hold property until the end of coverture laws in the 1880s. Additionally, there was the cultural expectation of at least a nod in the direction of separate spheres, which was enforced in various institutional contexts such as schools and intellect-based workplaces. Yet, individually, each woman could use the abovementioned means to work around some of those restrictions. Women would occasionally dress in "drag," passing as male to achieve their goals (Adams 2010). Women would make social, financial, and legal moves through agreeable or biddable husbands. Women would make contributions to the discourse either using their own status as demonstrably proper women, or by again using anonymity or posing as male (famously, Mary Wollstonecraft Shelley originally published Frankenstein anonymously with a ton of edits made or suggested by her husband, Percy Bysshe Shelley, and everyone thought that **he** was the author; she was certainly not the only author to use such a ruse). And finally, women at both ends of the socioeconomic spectrum, the very wealthy and the extremely impoverished, were somewhat exempt from many social rules, for opposite reasons.

This last point bears more thought. The artifact and skeletal data show this dichotomy, particularly as many of the women of St. Bride's Lower Churchyard were there as a result of dying at the work-house/poorhouse, and many of the corsets from the various museums are from wealthy donors and/or of fine make and material. Therefore, with both sides of the spectrum (and everything in between) repre-sented, we can draw better conclusions about how women could choose to identify, or not, with the cultural norm of corseting. The ability to go without a corset in polite society was restricted to those perceived as wealthy enough to make a scandalous decision and live with it, or those poor enough to be seen as pitiably unable to follow or out of touch with current fashion, until very late indeed in our time period. All of this will be unpacked further, as we move to examining the corsets and learning what they can tell us about the women inside them, in Chapter 3.

Bibliography

Adams, A. (2010). *Ladies of the Field*. Vancouver, BC, Canada: Greystone Books.

Anonymous. (1866, February 17). A Plea for Tight-Lacing. *Flag of Our Union, 21*(7), 110.

Anonymous. (1883, March 16). The New Skirt. *Knowledge, 3*.

Aptowicz, C. (2014). *Dr. Mütter's Marvels*. New York, NY: Penguin.

Armstrong, L. (1994). *Little Women*. Columbia Pictures, British Columbia, Canada.

Barthes, R. (1967). *The Fashion System* (M. Ward & R. Howard, Trans.). Berkeley: The University of California Press.

Campbell, N. (2010). Future Sex: Cyborg Bodies and the Politics of Meaning. *Advertising and Society Review, 11*(1), 50–101.

Colmer, M. (1980). *Whalebone to See-Through: A History of Body Packaging*. Cranbury, NJ: A. S. Barnes.

de Certeau, M. (1984). *The Practice of Everyday Life*. Berkeley: The University of California Press.

de Tocqueville, A. (1840). *Democracy in America*. New York, NY: Penguin.

Dickens, C. (1850). *The Personal History, Adventures, Experience and Observation of David Copperfield the Younger of Blunderstone Rookery*. London, UK: Bradbury and Evans.

Downey, G. L., Dumit, J., & Williams, S. (1995). Cyborg Anthropology. *Cultural Anthropology, 10*(2), 264–269.

Entwistle, J. (2000). *The Fashioned Body*. Malden, MA: Blackwell.

Fairclough, N. (2003). *Analyzing Discourse: Textual Analysis for Social Research*. New York, NY: Routledge.

Fields, J. (2007). *An Intimate Affair: Women, Lingerie, and Sexuality*. Berkeley: University of California Press.

Fitzharris, L. (2017). *The Butchering Art: Joseph Lister's Quest to Transform the Grisly World of Victorian Medicine*. New York, NY: Macmillan.

Flanders, J. (2012). *The Victorian City: Everyday Life in Dickens' London*. New York, NY: Macmillan.

Fontanel, B. (1992). *Support and Seduction: A History of Corsets and Bras*. New York, NY: Harry N. Abrams.

Geller, P. (2009). Bodyscapes, Biology, and Heteronormativity in American. *Anthropologist, 111*(4), 504–516.

Haraway, D. (1991). A Cyborg Manifesto. In *Simians, Cyborgs and Women: The Reinvention of Nature* (pp. 149–181). New York: Routledge.

Hartsock, N. (2006). Experience, Embodiment, and Epistemologies. *Hypatia, 21*(2), 178–183.

Knowledge. (1883). *Killed by Stays*, p. 283. London, UK.

Kunzle, D. (1982). *Fashion and Fetishism: A Social History of the Corset, Tight-Lacing, and Other Forms of Body-Sculpture in the West*. Totowa, NJ: Rowman and Littlefield.

Lord, W. B. (1868/1870). *Freaks of Fashion: The Corset and the Crinoline*. London: Ward, Lock, and Tyler.

Montillo, R. (2013). *The Lady and Her Monsters: A Tale of Dissections, Real-Life Dr. Frankensteins, and the Creation of Mary Shelley's Masterpiece*. New York, NY: HarperCollins.

Pêcheux M. (1975). The Subject Form of Discourse in the Subjective Appropriation of Scientific Knowledges and Political Practice. In H. Nagpal (Trans.), *Language, Semantics, and Ideology* (pp. 155–170). New York: St. Martins Press.

Perry, L. A., Turner, L. H., & Sterk, H. M. (1992). *Constructing and Reconstructing Gender: The Links Among Communication, Language, and Gender.* Albany, NY: The State University of New York Press.

Seleshanko, K. (2012). *Bound and Determined: A Visual History of Corsets 1850–1960.* Mineola, NY: Dover.

Summers, L. (2001). *Bound to Please: A History of the Victorian Corset.* Oxford: Berg.

Steele, V. (2001/2011). *The Corset: A Cultural History.* New Haven, CT: Yale University Press.

Stone, P. (2012). Binding women: Ethnology, Skeletal Deformations, and Violence Against Women. *International Journal of Paleopathology, 2–3,* (2), 53–60.

Styles, J. (2007). *The Dress of the People: Everyday Fashion in Eighteenth-Century England.* New Haven, CT: Yale University Press.

Swanson, K. (2011). Getting a Grip on the Corset: Gender, Sexuality, and Patent Law. *Yale Journal of Law and Feminism, 23*(1), 57–115.

Teasley, D. (1904). *Private Lectures to Mothers and Daughters on Sexual Purity: Including Love, Courtship, Marriage, Sexual Physiology, and the Evil Effects of Tight Lacing.* Moundsville, WV: Gospel Trumpet Company.

3

The Corset as a Garment: Is It a Representative of Who Wore It?

Here I would like to draw your attention to an exception: a woman who assuredly did not corset. The import of this particular case study is twofold—first, as we have seen from Styles (2007) and will continue to discuss, socioeconomic status was no barrier to corseting—women from impoverished classes did so. Thus, it is difficult to find female-presenting skeletal material from this time period which we can concretely say should not bear the marks of long-term corseting. Second, I must digress for a moment into a discussion of the paucity of skeletal material from contemporary non-corseted women.

While drawing from older skeletal collections—those from before 1700—leaves one with fragmented bones and degradation of the small skeletal elements which I use for this study, drawing from more modern ones—post-1900—exposes one of the flaws of bioanthropology: the privilege of staying buried is an unequal one, leading to bias in the makeup of the collected materials. Privilege is a factor in most things in this world, whether we are talking about socioeconomic class, race, being of the religious majority, or any of the many ways in which one group may have privilege over another. For the purpose of this discussion, we may grant that staying interred and not having one's bones

© The Author(s) 2020
R. Gibson, *The Corseted Skeleton*,
https://doi.org/10.1007/978-3-030-50392-5_3

in a museum has two factors. Luck, which is something the St. Bride's deceased did not have, as their burial ground was bombed, and the privilege of being a majority race, class, and religion. Skeletal collections from the early 1900s are, by and large, made up of individuals from racial minorities, and the poor. Were I to try to find a group that would be comparable directly to the St. Bride's collection from post-1900, I would run into a few problems: middle-class white Christian women tend to stay buried, and anyone recent enough to have been 100% guaranteed to not corset would be buried in the last 50 years or so, and likely would still have relatives who would object. Therefore, we must press along with comparisons I can make—those between the St. Bride's skeletons and the Musée de l'Homme skeletons, and between those among the later who did not corset and the other individuals that did. This skeleton is unique in a few ways: she is young, taller than average, English, and by all agreed upon skeletal markers, did not corset.[1]

From the Musée de l'Homme collection, MNHN-HA-765 is a young woman between 18 and 26 years of age at death. Her intake data only gives her nationality and year of death—English, 1843. She has mild porotic hyperostosis—a porous and pitted skull from iron deficiency anemia. Her skull sutures are open and differentiated, which merely shows that she is not middle aged or older, and her iliac crests are not completely fused, which indicates that she is not over thirty. She has lost some teeth (perhaps organically, perhaps during reassembly), but has all of her wisdom teeth (the third molars).

The rib cage of MNHN-HA-765 is anatomically normal, showing no rounding of the ribs or distortion toward an overall circular shape. Her vertebrae show minimal changes, which cannot be accounted for by long-term corset wearing. This, at first glance is not surprising. Not all English women corseted. However, what is surprising is what we can learn from her body, and from why and how she ended up in a French museum. While Georges Cuvier, the anatomist who originated the

---

[1]I have tried, where possible, to show skulls, faces, and full-body photos of the skeletons. This is deliberately done to counteract the fragmentation of these bodies, which further contributes to their anonymous and voiceless status.

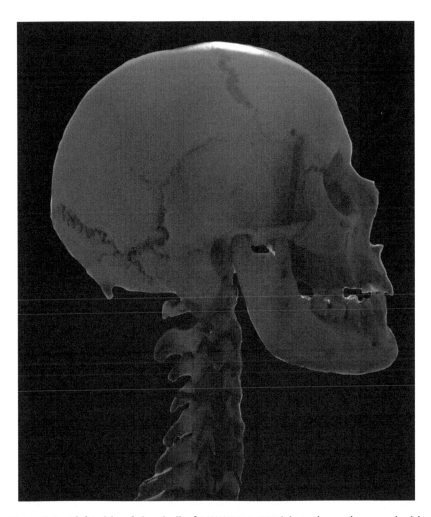

Photo 3.1   Right side of the skull of MNHN-HA-765 (Photo by author, used with the permission of the Muséum National d'Histoire Naturelle)

Musée de l'Homme, died in 1832, before this woman died, his practices for the collection and cataloging of human remains carried on into the continuation of the museum as a whole. He was, after all, considered the father of French anatomy, and so the museum used his methods and means until it was revamped in the 1900s (Photos 3.1, 3.2, and 3.3).

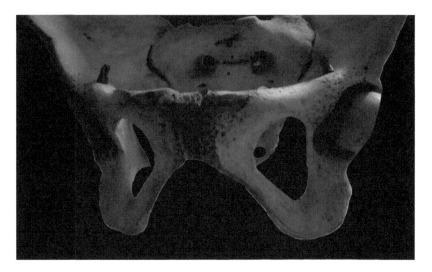

Photo 3.2 Anterior view of the pelvis of MNHN-HA-765 (Showing subpubic angle photo by author, used with the permission of the Muséum National d'Histoire Naturelle)

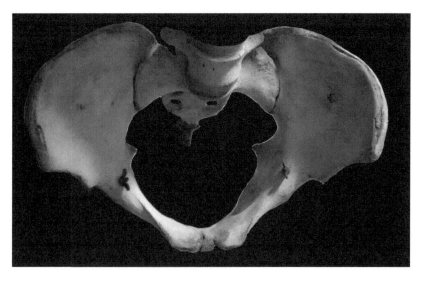

Photo 3.3 Superior view of the pelvis of MNHN-HA-765 (Showing pelvic opening photo by author, used with the permission of the Muséum National d'Histoire Naturelle)

Therefore, we must ask: how **did** an Englishwoman end up in a French museum, an anonymous skeleton among hundreds, with a number instead of a name? Much of the answer to that question lies in the skeleton itself. When I first examined her in 2012, I called over the museum curator, Phillippe Mencier, for a second opinion. MNHN-HA-765 is listed in the record as female, but her skeleton does not completely bear that out. Her pelvis is very, very female— wide iliac crests, wide, obtuse subpubic angle, round pelvic opening through which children could easily have passed.[2] Her skull, however, is distinctly male. With a massive mandible, an ascending ramus closer to 90 degrees than not, a robust and rugged mastoid process, and an immense external occipital protuberance that is pointy, her entire facial presentation is male. The rest of her skeleton is also male-presenting, with huge rugged bones, tall stature, and robust muscle attachment points.

Because the differences are so distinct, it is entirely possible, even likely, that MNHN-HA-765 presented as nonbinary or intersex during her life. As the difference noted exists specifically in the pelvic region, she may also have had anomalous presentation in external and internal genitalia as well. One mechanism is a particular type of genetic chimerism, which codes for gynandromorphy—the presence of both male and female traits—of very specific organ systems (De Marchi et al. 1976; Fitzgerald et al. 1979; Niu et al. 2002). In the mid- to late 1800s, people with such anomalies were often shunned, ridiculed, and cast out from their families. Yet they still needed to make their way in the world, and to make a living, many turned to "freakshows." Depending on the way in which her condition manifested, MNHN-HA-765 could have presented with abnormal facial hair growth (and thus billed herself as a bearded lady), or as a true hermaphrodite (for display in the less-constrained shows, where people were not shy of exposed genitalia). In such a way, she would both travel outside of England, and have

---

[2]There is also a distinct bilateral preauricular sulcus. The utility of using this skeletal marker as a notation of sex and/or childbirth is under debate, but I feel that it is useful in pre- or early-industrial society (Cox and Scott 1992; Gülekon and Turgut 2001; Inskip et al. 2018; Karsten 2017).

been without family to claim her when she died, thus ending up in a museum (Bates 2008). Regardless of the rest of her history, which is lost, she shows no evidence of corseting, unlike the women of St. Bride's which will be discussed in subsequent chapters.

* * *

Who Wore Corsets and Why, an Overview of Corseting

At its most basic form, the corset is a stylistic element of a garment, meant to create a certain shape. Formed of various other elements— busk, stays, fabric, boning, laces—each individual corset can have all or almost no features similar to that of other corsets. The stays, which are a set of stiff strips of material at the front of the garment on either side of the front opening, or a busk, which is one flat strip of material that replaces a front opening, may be the only indication that a garment contains a corset element. Early dresses and blouses were formed with pockets at the front to hold either stays or a busk, which were secured with ribbons at the ends (Bendall 2014). These were called "bodies" (or "corsets," which means "little bodies" in French from the root word corps (body) and the diminutive suffix -et), and were considered the height of fashion in the sixteenth century, in the majority of Western Europe (ibid.). However, the height of fashion, if appealing enough, often becomes the norm of fashion, which is precisely what happened with the corset. Busks and stays are relatively easy to create, requiring only a bit of wood or leather, and the mechanism for creating the garments to hold them was easily copied (ibid.; Salen 2008). Thus began a 400-year trend of infinite variation and endless contention.

Corset trends changed by the decade across Europe, and fashion in the urban centers of Europe moved even more quickly. Both England and France were trendsetters in the European fashion scene (Bruna 2015), and the trends wafted back and forth across the English Channel every few months or so, at least during the periods when the two countries were not at war with each other (Lord 1868). For the purpose of this discussion, there is one main change in fashion that bears a small digression—that of the neoclassical look of the late eighteenth and early nineteenth centuries. Fluctuations in trends led to various fashionable silhouettes, with one decade favoring exaggerated breasts, while another wished the breasts to remain hidden and minimized and the buttocks to be accentuated with bustles, while another created an s-curve with a puffed pigeon breast and a bustled behind. All but one period had one thing in common—the creation of a smaller, rounder, less natural waist. The lone variant that eschewed all such profiles was the neoclassical or Empire period.

This period was characterized by high waists, with bands directly under the breasts, and long skirts that fell from that band straight down to the floor. To the untrained eye, it appears to be unsupported by corseting, prompting a nineteenth-century corset historian to quote the rude couplet from the time "Now a shape in neat stays, Now a slattern in jumps" (Lord 1868/1870, p. 130) quoted in the previous chapter, where jumps are a shortened and not tight-laced corset. However, several factors abound in the continuation of the practice of corseting, including the fact that it was thought, whether medically accurate or not, that wearing a corset created a dependency—once the body was used to it, going without could be incredibly uncomfortable, some said even dangerous (Dickinson 1887). The period of neoclassical fashion did not last long, and afterward corsets went directly back to creating the small waist of their "normal" form, and in fact, the corsets from this era in the collections I examined did not change significantly, perhaps being slightly shorter/not covering the area of the abdomen below the waist or over the hips. Another factor is that not all women could afford to change clothing with the newest fashion, and certainly others merely did not want to.

However, despite being a ubiquitous part of fashion over the years of this study, corset use was differentiated within women of the time. Not by socioeconomic class, as is often surmised, but by location and vocation. For example, one specific set of working women—the Wigan Pit Girls, about whom much is written (Hiley 1979)—wore skirts, pants, and occasionally corsets, though occasionally not. Wigan, approximately 200 miles from London, was a major center of coal production, and many people, both male and female, worked the mines. Men worked below ground, while women worked in the above-ground "pits," shoveling coal into wheelbarrows, separating it from rock, and doing work that involved lifting, carrying, stretching, and bending. We might intuit that such work would have been impeded by the use of a corset, however, photographs from the time (ibid.) show women wearing them, and show women without. It is surmised that garments that may have been considered "special" or "fine" would have been saved for Sundays or important wooing opportunities. This demonstrates the difference in attitude between the country and the town—in photographs from London of the same time period, women are not seen without their corsets unless they are among the poorest of the poor (ibid.). This was also demonstrated by the archival research done by Styles (2007), that I highlighted in Chapter 2.

From this we can also see that some women had considerable autonomy over when, how, and where to use their corsets. We cannot treat women as monolithic in their corset use—as all tight-lacers, or as all following the societal norm, or as all concerned with the standards of beauty of the day. Many factors went into the personal decision of what to wear and how tight to lace one's garments, though given the evidence of the Wigan Pit Girls, and of Styles' work (ibid.), it appears safe to assume that the majority of women, country or city, had at least one corset and used it when appropriate. Furthermore, that appropriate situations would be more prevalent in the city than in the countryside, corsets being de facto required for polite, civilized, public interactions (Bruna 2015; Colmer 1980; Fontanel 1992; Fowler 1870; Kunzle 1982; Lord 1868; O'Followell 1908; Seleshanko 2012; Steele 2001; Summers 2001). This ability to decide for themselves what they wanted and what was appropriate edged into creating their own versions of the garment, in more official ways than merely stitching a new variant at home, as women eventually became the leading patent holders of corsets and corset making materials, which will be discussed below (Swanson 2011).

Variations on a Theme: Practical Corseting and What Women Wore

With the above understanding of what a corset is, I will now explore the variations available to women—not in form, or the way they looked, but in actual construction which would affect the function of the garment. The two major distinctions are underbust and overbust, with overbust beginning anywhere above the woman's nipples, and underbust beginning anywhere below the breasts. Within the two categories, several types exist.

In overbust corsets, whether built into a dress or as a stand-alone garment, the purpose was to support and define both the bust and the waist. Thus, by varying the cut of the corset and the structure of the boning, many styles could be created. A straight front, with little breast definition was popular in the late seventeenth and early eighteenth centuries, whereas a heart-shaped front, which emphasized the bosom, was popular in the mid- to late nineteenth century (Salen 2008).[3] Such corsets could go underneath a larger dress, or overtop of a chemise and skirt combination to form an outer garment. Overbust corsets could also be modified into pregnancy and nursing garments, by creating gussets over the breasts that would lace, snap, or expand to give access for nursing mothers, and other gussets over the hips and abdomen for the purpose of expansion during pregnancy.

These gussets could also be laced tighter, to allow women to control their fertility through forced miscarriages (Fowler 1870; Kunzle 1982: 72; O'Followell 1908; Steele 2001). This would have been seen by women as a legitimate practice, due to the laws of the time (Blackstone 1765, p. 388) that stated that life began not at conception, but at the "quickening," the time at which the woman felt the fetus move inside her. Conscientious use of the corset in the period before the quickening to self-abort would not at all have been frowned upon by many women, for a woman who did not wish to fulfill her womanly duty to the family quite yet.

---

[3]For full timeline, see Appendix A.

Such tactics are also mentioned in the fictional writings of Guy De Maupassant, in *La Mère aux Monstres* (The Mother of Monsters) (1883), which details the story of a woman who, upon once accidentally bearing a disabled child due to corseting, develops a scheme to prostitute herself to create more such children to sell to the freakshows of the day, and to keep her shapely figure at the same time. As with the discourse in Chapter 2, such stories should be viewed with a lens that corrects for male bias and the collective cultural horror felt about a woman who controlled her own sexuality and fertility.

The purpose of underbust corsets, which were uniformly stand-alone garments, was to form and support the waist. Sometimes called waist cinchers, they fit over a larger garment to gather it in and create a fashionable focal point. They could be as simple as wide reinforced belts, or as complex as T.95-1949, a blue velvet underbust corset edged with white lace, which was able to be laced closed in the front and back. The top and bottom of the corset come to points, and frame the bust and the mons veneris. It is an elegant statement piece, meant to emphasize a tiny waist (54 cm or 22 in in circumference), and to draw attention to the fullness of the attributes above and below it.

Within all of the above possibilities, there exist corsets that **can** be laced closed, and those that **must** be laced closed in order to function properly. Corsets can be constructed of between one and four panels. If a corset is one panel, with only one area of closure, and if it is built into a garment, then it is most likely to function only if laced completely closed, with no space between the two ends of the panels. An example of this is T.854-1974, a brocade ball gown with built-in boning and stays, that laced up the back. Examining this gown, there is no allowance for a space between the lacing holes, no modesty panel to expand the garment, and no other panels present—it is meant to be laced completely closed, and the circumference of the garment (48 cm/18.9 in at the waist) is an absolute dimension.

However, other corsets are meant to be worn in various ways as determined by the comfort of the wearer. T.53-1960 is made of two panels, a right and a left, that join together with hook and eye clasps in the front, and lavender silk ribbon in the back. The ribbon is laced in such a way that it would show the skin of the wearer. It is well worn, and very decorative, containing lavender embroidery and garter clips for stockings, indicating that it was an undergarment rather than worn over clothing. As with modern corsets of this construction, the back laces could be loosened for ease of undressing, and then pulled tight by the woman herself when she put it on. This, and the fact that weight gain or loss could be accommodated by the laces, gives agency to the wearer, allowing her to be in control of how she wore the corset.

The other type of control exerted was that of the ability to create and patent new types of corsets. While men were tailors in England and France during this time, and the social area of high fashion was seemingly reserved for them, women held the positions of seamstresses, both officially and unofficially (Bruna 2015; Salen 2008; Swanson 2011). Particularly during the latter half of the nineteenth century, women of the working and lower classes, needful of respectable employment, turned their specialized knowledge of corset creation to the ever-expanding consumer market, filing patents, fighting for them in court, and winning the right to profit from their prowess (Swanson 2011). This control is particularly notable in light of our earlier discussion of the idea of Separate Spheres—here we see women stepping into the public sphere, making money independent of male control, and doing so very successfully.

These dual controls, that of how the corset was worn and that of how the corset was made, indicate that women were active participants in the social and cultural processes that formed their bodies. It highlights how women had multiple vectors of agency, and within those vectors, made choices that expressed their various subjectivities and their internalized bodyscape, as shown in Chapter 2 by the analysis of the discourse surrounding corsets.

Female Purchasing Power: Class and Corseting

Before we continue to look at the corsets themselves, we must pause for a moment to discuss socioeconomic class, women's work, and the purchasing power that women possessed during this time. Incomes varied wildly, from the richest of the rich (those with knighthoods, peerages, and the like), to the poorest of the poor (the indigent and destitute, to paraphrase Dickens' "A Christmas Carol" 1843). Obviously, those at the lower end of the scale had less choices when it came to clothing themselves, and less buying power in general, needing to make do with second-hand items, "turned" items that were made over into fresh fashions, patched and mended clothing, and garments worn long past the time when they were out of style.

What must also be taken into account is the sheer mass of London's population—hundreds of thousands of people in the 1770s, and almost 2 million in the 1840s, according to estimates (Demographia 2019), in just a few square miles. London was host to thriving markets of all kinds, including second-hand stalls, at which garments could be had for pence (Smith 2002). Yet, it is extremely difficult to look back through the years and understand what that means; what we consider pence today (pennies, or 1/100th of a dollar or a pound sterling) are not the same as pence before the United Kingdom went on the decimal system. Prior to the decimal system (in which one pound is worth 100 pence, and there are various coin denominations which make up various pence amounts), one pound was equal to twenty shillings, and one shilling was equal to twelve pence, meaning that one pound was equal to 240 pence.

So, what did an "average" or "comfortable" salary look like? What could be comparable to today's lower-middle, middle, and upper-middle classes? One rather informal study aggregates wages from various professions in the 1700s, and shows that occupations which we currently see as middle class (clerks, skilled laborers, police, etc.) were paid between 18 and 50 pounds annually for their labor (Bonenfant 2019). This study does actually mention the primary occupation of the parishioners of St. Bride's, listing it as "skilled in printing trades" (ibid.), and showing the average annual salary at 43 pounds in 1710, and rising to 67 pounds in 1797 (ibid.). This is correlated by a periodical from later in the time period—the Publisher's Circular (1891), which showed that salaries continued to rise concordantly with the standard of living. Page after page of advertisement for businesses which did bookbinding, printing, stationery sales, and other types of publishing show that it was a profitable enterprise, with guaranteed profits between 300 and 1800 pounds annually.

Women were, at the time (and are currently) paid less on average, and many times such payments were unofficial—passed through husbands, as part of supporting the husband's work, or given as a shopping or household allowance. If not "employed" through their spouse, much employment that women were seen as qualified to do, such as being part of the servant class, or being a governess or a teacher in a girls' school, came with housing and meals (room and board). Servants were paid decently—it was the done thing for non-impoverished households to have domestic help, and such positions were seen as very respectable—so women were often employed as maids, cooks, housekeepers, and the like, with wages between five and 20 pounds (Bonenfant 2019). So, let us surmise that women had between one- and 10-pounds discretionary income, if they were employed and/or married, and if they were part of the lower-middle, middle, or upper-middle class.

What could be done with that money? In 1770, when the St. Bride's Lower Churchyard opened, sixpence was the equivalent of five pounds 43 pence in today's money (this entire section by the inflation calculator at "In 2013 Dollars" 2019). One pound was 180 pounds 87 pence, and ten pounds the lordly sum of 1808 pounds 75 pence. When it closed in 1849, sixpence was 37 pounds 80 pence, and one pound was 126 pounds in today's money.

To return to our fictional example, Bob Cratchit, clerk to Ebenezer Scrooge, is paid 15 shillings a week (Dickens 1843), or .75 pounds per week, in the year 1843 (94 pounds 50 pence per week, in 2019's money). That would make his yearly salary 39 pounds, or 4914 pounds 10 pence in today's money, a sum that had significantly more buying power than it does today. Bob Cratchit was solidly lower-middle class, as a clerk in an accounting firm.

One ad for a brand new, patented corset from 1870 shows the price for between 21 and 42 shillings, or 123 pounds 95 pence to 247 pounds 89 pence in today's money (The Family Recorder 2011). This is quite a lot, actually, and various corsets, such as certain American corsets were considerably cheaper. From 1902, an advertisement lists a corset as being $1.50, which is $44.86, or 33 pounds 63 pence in today's money (Maryland Historic Society 2019). We can see by this example that, although a family-like Cratchit's was squeezed tight at the seams, a smaller family might have done quite well on such a salary, and a man could definitely support a wife and keep her in, definitely not the newest fashions, corsets at the second-hand stalls where prices were pence on the pound, on these wages. They would be even better set if she handmade her stays, as was often done, as shown earlier by Styles (2007). All this is to say: a very poor woman could have anything from the simplest of stays, if she made them herself, to the most elaborate of corsets, if she got them as a gift or through aftermarket means. This has given us a basis on which to examine the museum collections of corsets, based on fineness, materials, and wear.

The Corset Collections: Victoria and Albert, Fashion Museum Bath, St. Fagans, and the National Museum of Scotland

In order to be able to comment on the use of corsets in not only London, but the majority of the United Kingdom, I looked at four collections: The Victoria and Albert fashion annex, the Fashion Museum in Bath, St. Fagans Museum in Cardiff, and the National Museum of Scotland in Edinburgh, leaving out only collections in Ireland and Northern Ireland, due to distance, time, and a dearth of materials. In total, I examined 148 corsets.

The large variety of materials, styles, and colors in the museum collections exemplify the diversity of choices over the long period of corset wearing. Corsets with specific purposes exist in the collections, as well as a large range of "general" corsets. This can be seen in such examples as a "wedding" corset (T.90-1928) and a nursing and pregnancy corset (T.95&A-1984) both in the Victoria and Albert collection, and the pregnancy corsets in the Fashion Museum in Bath collection (I.27.1) and the National Museum of Scotland (N.P. 05-984/A.1905.984).

There were many distinct variations on the shape of the corset, as shown by the garments in the collections, from the completely structural full corset created of Aertex[4] cotton and meant to be worn either against the skin or over a light chemise (T.233-1968, V&A), to the extremely decorative underbust corset meant to be the top layer of a multilayer outfit (T.95-1949, V&A), to the inbuilt structural boning that created the form of a larger garment such as the "golden wedding dress" at St. Fagans (65.81/21). All of the corsets were measured and evaluated for their materials and dimensions, regardless of their purpose.

The collections contain corsets made of leather, wool, linen, silk, and cotton or variations of cotton such as canvas, twill, and jean. Of these, leather and wool are the least common as both materials were more often used for outerwear, leather being too stiff and completely unbreathable, and wool often being itchy despite how finely it was woven. Cotton and silk were much more common, comprising 41% and 49% of the primary materials respectively, with linen at 7% and wool at 2% (breakdowns of the materials by decade can be seen below). Primary material was determined by examination of the corset to see what material made up the body of the garment, and all garments contained one primary material.

Many contained secondary materials, often the lining of the garment would be another type of material, among which silk and cotton were still most prevalent. I expected to find that silk increased in prevalence over time, and that cotton decreased. This would be due to silk prices falling with various rebellions on the European continent, particularly the 1831 and '34 *revolutions des canuts*, with rioting by Lyonnais silk makers. Additionally, cotton prices increased due to the changing structure of the Indian and American cotton markets, as India came more firmly under British rule and America established tentative trade customs with her former colonizer (Interview at Maison des Canuts 2012,

---

[4]Aertex is a patented type of cotton fabric, created in the late 1880s by the company of the same name. It is a light but strong fabric of loose weave, which allows for air to flow across the body as moisture is taken away.

and pers. corrs. with curator Virginie Varenne). However, trends in the shifting of fabric seemed to go decade by decade regardless of which collection the garments came from, with silk increasing in prevalence steadily until the 1800s, and cotton remaining largely stable throughout. This could be explained by many things—cost, availability, trade, weather seeing as silk and cotton are both plant-based crops, and the ever-shifting nature of fashion itself. Most of the corsets were boned with either steel, or whalebone, or a combination of both, although there were a few that were not. The trend in boning did shift, predictably, from whalebone to steel after cold rolling became the norm during the latter period of the Industrial Revolution (Bruna 2015; Steele 2001), however, I did not quantify that particular shift as many of the corsets did not have their boning type recorded and were not worn through enough for me to be able to tell by eye.

In regard to the boning, as mentioned earlier, the function of it is to stiffen various parts of the garment and it can technically be made of anything that serves that purpose. However, certain materials are ill-suited to the stresses of use in a corset, which is why wood—which can be inflexible—and stiffened cardboard—which can be way too flexible—are rarely seen in the records, be they written accounts of women's experiences, advertisements, or patents. The two expected structural materials, therefore, are whalebone from the throat cavity of the baleen whale, and steel—either non-augmented steel or spring steel, and these were both represented in expected times during the trajectory of the corsets which had information, or in which the materials could be clearly seen. Additionally, one corset was stitched in such a way that the firmness of the canvas material became its own structure, negating the need for whalebone or steel, and one had leather boning.

Social and cultural factors influenced not only what fabric was available at the time but what was in style, the ability of the woman to purchase, or not to purchase new clothing, and an element of comfort and fit (Bruna 2015; Steele 2001; Summers 2001). This could make quite a difference in certain stylistic elements, for example, before the invention of the artificial fuchsia or magenta color in 1859, any pinks or brilliant purples would have been the result of natural dyes and as such would have been expensive to produce and thus the purview of the

Photo 3.4   F.73-129/2 (Photo by author, used with permission from St. Fagans Museum, Cardiff)

extremely rich. However, after 1859, the aniline dye became all the rage and women would have been hard-pressed to find fashionable clothing without some sort of aniline color, particularly the fuchsia that was so in fashion (Bruna 2015).

Various corsets in the collections, such as F.73-129/2, 36-244/1, and 46-424/5, all from St. Fagans, contained a particular bright green called Paris Green which was synthesized out of an arsenic-copper compound, and was both strikingly beautiful and incredibly toxic. This luminous color was created in 1814 and became all the rage for coloring everything from clothing to wallpaper, despite its additional use as rat poison. Also still in use at the time, although less popular, was Scheele's Green, a less stable arsenic-copper compound, which was similarly toxic and yet used to color candies and other foods (Photos 3.4, 3.5, and 3.6).

Thus, the purchasing of such clothing, or the decision to seek out another color, makes a rhetorical statement about the bodyscape of the day, and whether or not the woman chooses to accept or reject the current fashions. However, is that statement accurate?

Photo 3.5   36-244/1 (Photo by author, used with permission from St. Fagans Museum, Cardiff)

Photo 3.6   46-424/5 (Photo by author, used with permission from St. Fagans Museum, Cardiff)

A Brief Word About Museums

Here we must pause for a moment to ponder the "museum quality" paradox, which has two parts: (1) If something ends up in a museum, usually that thing is determined to be of interest—it is unique, or a prototypical example of its type, or it is beautiful or stands out in some way and (2) museums emphasize preservation, so objects that find their way to museums are either durable, or able to be stabilized enough to withstand handling, storage, and display.

These two factors tend to create a general shape or feel to museum collections. They increase the number of artifacts that represent the higher levels of socioeconomic status, and deemphasize that which is considered "normal" or "everyday." Yet, paradoxically, that which is normal and everyday is more likely to survive through time in order to be included—often being more durable and rugged, and thus better preserved and better able to take being handled during collection acquisition. What then becomes a museum's collection are the artifacts that are unique but well-preserved examples of materials that are fine enough that people will come see them, but durable enough that they exist to be collected in the first place.

What does this mean in terms of corsets? We can expect to see silk overrepresented in the collection—silk is objectively prettier and more valuable than cotton or linen. However, that representation may conversely take a dip because silk is also far less durable, prone to shredding, laddering, and being devoured by moths (before collecting, not after, of course). We can expect to see brighter colors, more creative patterns, and greater extremes of decoration, due to the uniqueness factor, with things that are ordinary or plain in the minority. If a corset or dress has been mended, we can expect those mends to be discrete, or if they are not, then it is likely that the corset will not spend much time on display, residing in an archival box in storage, waiting for a researcher to come along. Many museums have storage that stretches larger than the display areas, and contains hundreds of artifacts that are rarely seen, and only displayed if there's a special need for them. We can also expect a greater quantity of recent corsets to be found in the sample, with very few from the seventeenth century and early eighteenth century.

The collections do all contain corsets of various fineness and expensiveness, with perhaps the most expensive being a silk jacquard ball gown in the Victoria and Albert collection (T.854-1974), and the least being a linen chemise from the same collection (T.233-1968). Both garments, and everything in between, made personal statements at their time of purchase, and again at their time of either reuse or of donation. While one can speak to the upper level of wealth that would be necessary to buy a particular garment, one can only speak indirectly of its life or use value after its initial purchase. For example, the silk ball gown could only be purchased by the very wealthy. The amount of fabric, the fineness of the weave, the intricacy of the design, all speak to the fact that it would have been extremely costly to produce, and would have been out of reach to the lower echelons of society. However, once bought it may have been gifted to a poor relative. Once worn, it may have been passed on to a servant, or found its way to a second-hand store. Even the finest of things has the ability to make it into the hands of the poor, via informal or formal trade, which ruled over the garment districts of the city of London.

Furthermore, value is a relative trait—while often defined by the materials the corset is made of, like the jacquard silk, value can also be measured by the age of the garment, with older garments gaining their worth from the scarcity of examples from their time periods. Thus, a corset like 1935.772/A.1935.772 from the collection of the National Museum of Scotland, described as "Woman's stays of cream colored material, lined with white linen and stiffened with flat whalebone wires, and made to lace in the front, Scottish, mid 18th century," which has ties at the bottom for a decorative busk, though that busk is not in evidence, is valuable historically, and most likely to its original owner, but not made of valuable materials. It is well worn, and quite discolored, showing that the woman who wore it did so often. It is one of the everyday garments that are distinguishable from the fine gowns, and may (or may not, as we can see below) represent a woman from a lower socioeconomic class, though its donor has been lost to time.

What Corsets Are Represented in the Collections…

While several of the garments have donor names attached to them, history has forgotten many of the details associated with the individuals. However, three donors are able to be traced somewhat from records held by the Victoria and Albert fashion annex: Mary Ethel Burns, Viscountess Harcourt; London socialite Miss Heather Firbank; and a Russian immigrant to London corsetiere Myer Yanovsky. Harcourt donated the corset T.33-1965, a plain cotton corselet, which demonstrates the principle that one cannot assume poverty based on the spare nature of the garment. She is most well known by her connotation with her husband "Loulou," Lewis 1st Viscount of Harcourt, who was a noted roué among adults, and an assaulter of both sexes of children (Parris 1997, pp. 83–85). Firbank donated the dress T.33-1960, a full gown with boning and waist tape ribbons included in the internal construction. Other clothing donated by Firbank is also held at the Victoria and Albert but was not included in the corset collection (Victoria and Albert Museum 2015).

The tendency for materials to be handed down is shown most convincingly by certain corsets in all the collections which show aftermarket additions, for example those which have been augmented by hand-sewn lace and ribbons, an addition that covers some of the lacing holes and would not ordinarily have been a feature of a new corset. A specific set of these corsets, some eight in number in the Victoria and Albert collection, were all donated by the family of Myer Yanovsky (Victoria and Albert Archives 2012–2019). It is possible that these donations were of his own creation. However, based on their extreme wear, and the aftermarket additions, it is equally possible that they were used by women in his household, and donated after his death in his memory.

Conversely, the linen chemise could have been within reach of the poorest of women, but may have been purchased by a rich woman due to the fact that it is comfortable, readily available, and easy to don singlehanded, having only one set of buttons running down the front.

Many of the garments also showed evidence of being patched or mended. This can speak to several different impulses: frugality out of habit, the urge to preserve a loved garment, frugality out of need, or a sudden plunge from a state of financial stability to one of uncertainty are only a few. However, at each stage in the garment's life cycle from creation, to use, to mending, to discarding, the woman chooses and either reifies or rejects the garment, and thus the social meanings of it.

There were 148 total corsets available for examination in the four collections. They varied in date from the 1700s to the early 1900s, and were composed of four main materials, silk, cotton, linen, and wool. There were no synthetic materials, and low prevalence of linen (which was cold for the English climate), and wool (which would make an itchy and dense undergarment). There was also no clear pattern in individual collections—none of the non-London collections skewed one way or another in terms of material used, or size represented by the corset dimensions, so all corsets will be analyzed together, and all corsets are dated to the earliest possible date recorded in their accession data, regardless of where they fell in their decade (Graph 3.1).

As shown in Graph 3.1, the above discussion of trends in materials did correctly anticipate the museum quality paradox—the two most prevalent materials were silk and cotton, with silk potentially overrepresented in terms of the relative prevalence of socioeconomic classes in the living population. We also see sparse artifact distribution in the majority of the eighteenth century, with representation picking up after the 1810, and peaking in the 1880s and '90s. Part of this is due to the fact that the move away from baleen whalebone as a main structural component gave the garment more stability, which allowed individual examples to survive longer, and part is because two of the museums were established close to this time as well (Victoria and Albert in 1852, and the National Museum of Scotland in 1866) and thus providing many early garments, with the other two in the mid-1900s, giving rise to the prevalence of the later garments (Graph 3.2).

The type of primary closure also shows differentiation based on time period, with lacing being the sole closure type until the 1800s. Again,

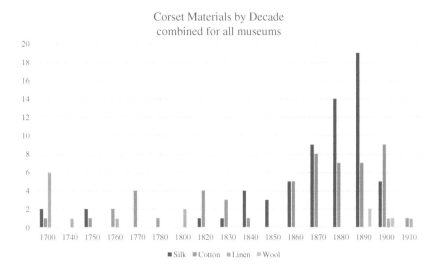

Graph 3.1 Main material of each corset, broken down by decade of manufacture

Table 3.1 Average bust to waist to hip ratio broken down by decade of manufacture

Decade or century	Average ratio (bust:waist:hips)
1700	1:.81:.63
1740	1:.94:.90
1750	1:.88:.84
1760	1:.81:.80
1770	1:.82:.78
1780	1:.74:.67
1800	.96:.68:1
1820	1:.78:.98
1830	1:.83:.95
1840	1:.85:.87
1850	1:.77:.97
1860	1:.82:.97
1870	1:.79:.97
1880	1:.77:.96
1890	1:.70:.88
1900	.97:.87:1
1910	.90:.73:1

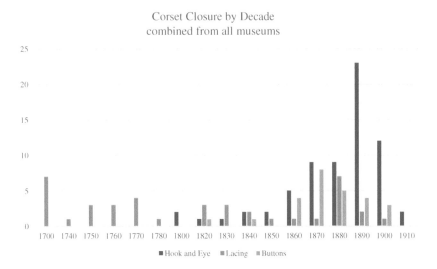

Graph 3.2   Closure material broken down by decade of manufacture

this is because of the industrial revolution—hook and eye closures were introduced as steel became cheaper and easier to procure, and as women were more often expected to be dressing themselves, rather than being dressed. This last point takes us back to our discussion of socioeconomic class—there are ways to construct a fully laced corset that allow for a woman to dress without assistance, but the hook and eye closure clinched it for women of all means.

We have discussed that corsets may have one-to-four panels, which make up the garment. Single panel corsets—which were most prevalent in the eighteenth century, or as corsets built into dresses at any time period—required the help of another person in order to wear them. They almost universally closed in the back, and women were often hand-sewn into the garment by maids or husbands. Very occasionally, a one-panel garment buttoned in the front. If so, it was generally made either very simply, or with very detailed patterning so that the corset could be handled by a woman who was pregnant or nursing.

Two-panel garments, consisting of a left and a right panel, can have matching lacing closures, or a laced back and a hooked or buttoned front. Similarly, there were three-paneled garments (solid back or solid front, connected to left and right front or back panels, depending on orientation) and four-paneled garments (two back panels and two front panels connected at the sides). Any front lacing type of two-to-four-paneled garment can be worn by a woman without assistance—it is simply a matter of lacing the back loosely first, wrapping the corset around the body, hooking, buttoning, or lacing the front closed and tightening the back laces to the appropriate tension. I, myself, have two types of corsets—those that have double laces, and those that have laces in the back and hooks in the front—and they are both easy to wear comfortably and well fitted, so long as the back laces are long enough to ensure flexibility of the initial fit when donning the garment.

Here we can see that the structural components of the garment changed both with the fashion, and with the changing expectations on women. As it became **slightly** more acceptable for women to participate in the public sphere, and as the class system of the 1700s, which was built on agriculture and trade and in which women worked mostly inside the home, fractured into the industrial system of the 1800s where women worked outside the home as often as not, the hook and eye came to replace the front laced corset.

…and What That Representation Tells Us

To look at what the representation of various corsets in the collections tell us, we must examine two categories of data: their dimensions and the repairs made to them. Far beyond the materials, which can only represent the women at the point of purchase, the size of the corset at its disposal and the manner in which the corset was cared for can give us a history. Combined, these data sets help us bust more of the myths around corseting—that women who wore them were disproportional to "normal" size standards, and that corseting was used by the very rich. I have addressed both these above, however, more remains to be demonstrated in regard to these prevalent ideas about corsets.

First, it is important to look at what silhouette women wanted during this time—virtually an insurmountable task if not taken decade by decade, as the fashionable proportions between bust, waist, and hips changed with each new style. For a clear timeline summarizing these changes, see Appendix A. In her book "How to Read a Dress," Lydia Edwards (2017/2018) takes us on a journey through what is fashionable for each decade between 1550 and 1970. We must only trouble her for some of that data—the years of this study, between 1700 and 1900. To briefly summarize, corseting gave women a slender waist, which was contrasted with the emphasized bust and hips, in almost all of those 200 years. The exceptions were neoclassical fashions of the late eighteenth century and early nineteenth century, which began with the shift-dresses of the 1790s and lasted through the whole regency period until the eighteen teens. In such fashions, the waistline crept upward until the skirts of the garment fell from directly beneath the bustline. In looking for a fictional example, one can do no better than the Ang Lee dramatization of Sense and Sensibility (1995), in which Emma Thompson and Kate Winslet were dressed in neoclassical styles, which draped elegantly from empire waists.

However, going with that example, their host for much of the movie, Mrs. Jennings (played by Elizabeth Spriggs) was not wearing regency fashions. Her outfit contained a distinct waist at the natural waist, via a corset. This illustrates a further point that muddles things when discussing corsets and fashion—not every woman changed with the prevailing style of the time. Women who were set in their ways, or who could not afford to update their wardrobe, would often wear what they wanted, or what they had. Additionally, while women may have desired the newest silhouette, they may not have been physically capable of attaining it, due to diet, genetics, or other factors that led them to be less hourglass than apple shaped. This led to a diversity of styles all circulating at once, as well as a diversity in the ratio of bust to waist to hips.

So, what do the corsets tell us about that ratio? In all decades apart from one, in which all three measurements were present for at least one garment, the average ratio is closer to an uncorseted woman than a tight-laced woman. For the purpose of this comparison, I am defining a tight-laced woman's waist as falling below 1:.70:1. This is slightly larger than the modern "ideal" ratio (36:24:36, or 1:.66:1) that Sir Mix-a-Lot did not desire in "Baby Got Back" (1992). The fact that women were individuals, and individuals have their own sizes and do not conform to

Table 3.2   Average, minimum, and maximum of bust, waist, and hips dimensions

	Bust (cm)	Waist (cm)	Hips (cm)
Average	81.5	59.8	74.4
Minimum	38.0	41.0	36.0
Maximum	119.0	94.5	122.0

a pattern, is evident in the average measurements of the corsets, seen in Table 3.1.

However, waist size itself among the 148 examples, rather than ratio, still trended very small. All dimensions were taken from all corsets that were identified as being adult, rather than child-sized, regardless of how small (Table 3.2).

On this level, one can clearly see that corseting did make a difference in the size of waists, but that not all women were tight-laced into oblivion. This correlates with the skeletal data that will be discussed in subsequent chapters. However, to return to the discussion of the physical makeup of the garments, many of the corsets show signs of aftermarket additions, repair, and alteration, demonstrating that women were extending the use-life of their corsets beyond the first tear or stain.

Aftermarket additions can be divided into three categories—decorative, mending, and wear and tear. Decorative additions found in these collections include lace stitched across the top, colored silk ribbons, and embroidery. These are both expressions of individuality, and representations of prevailing fashions, and like the corsets themselves, able to perform as multiple signifiers (Barthes 1967). They indicate both a distancing from and a conforming to the bodyscape of the time—a way to make the garment one's own, while not standing out too far from the accepted norm. Ribbons, embroidery, and lace would all add a touch of prettiness to a plain garment, and would serve to make a mass-produced garment feel like one's own (De Certeau 1984).

They also serve as a social equalizer, being equally available to the wealthy and impoverished alike. Embroidery and lace-making were thought to be quite civilized and ladylike, a mark of conformity to domesticity and one of the ways women were taught to be useful to their homes (see Wollstonecraft 1793, and also any antique store with both doilies and samplers). Women of the lower classes could, and often did, spend their spare time in the creation and decoration of their garments, including in embroidering patterns and tatting lace for cuffs, collars, and corsets. Similarly, ribbons could be had at second-hand stalls, and could be used to disguise stains, scuffs, tears, or worn patches.

The two other types aftermarket additions go hand in hand, and are also multiple signifiers—the mending done on certain corsets, and the wear and tear shown by others. Mending can show the care felt by a person in regard to a garment, but the need for a garment to be mended can also come from lack of care. Additionally, mending can be done from necessity, in order to extend the wear-life of a garment that one cannot afford to replace, rather than a personal/emotional desire to keep the garment. Here we can look at a few examples of mended garments and speak to what may be their significance.

T.38-1968 is a canvas corset with whalebone and wood boning, which has seen extensive mending. The whalebone is poking out in various places, most likely because it was donated before that could be mended. The mending is done from the interior, in tiny somewhat random stitches, with thread that matches the thread used to construct the garment. The corset itself is utilitarian looking and contains a ribbon strap on the front which may have served as a chatelaine holder.[5] From an objective standpoint, this corset is not pretty and does not look comfortable to wear. I would surmise that the mending was done for a practical reason, to extend the life of a needed garment, rather than to enhance and retain the beauty of a loved garment. It was donated by Miss G. Pettybridge. Conversely, the next garment is very fine in manufacture but shows almost no mending whatsoever.

Given by the Honorable Mrs. Tyser in memory of the Dowager Lady Remnant, T.429&A-1990 is a full silk ball gown, pale blue, with lace capped sleeves, and an internal corset structure. It has pointed busks

---

[5]This loop or hook would hold a lady's chatelaine—a pendant made of metal, with a decorative top and a hooped bottom. The hoop acted like a charm catcher, to hold various household implements, sewing notions, scissors, pencil and paper, and keys. It was a work-around for the regrettable lack of pockets designed into garments and the impracticality of carrying a purse around the house.

and back boning, with hooks at the top of the skirt portion to hook the bodice and skirt together. Overall, the dress is not in the best of shape—the lace is yellowed, the bottom ruffs are dirty, and the lacing holes are pulled tight and frayed at the edges. This was quite obviously used over and over until parts of it fell into disrepair. That it remained un-mended could indicate a few things—perhaps the Dowager Lady did not fancy it; perhaps she had fallen on hard times, as her husband had predeceased her—certainly it was well out of fashion by her own death in 1944; perhaps it was used well until she outgrew it, but then she held on to it for sentimental reasons. Regrettably, there are no available photographs of the Dowager Lady Remnant to speak to her sense of style or to her care for her belongings. As is often the case in the records of the British peerage, she has become a footnote to her husband.

Other worn and mended garments abound: the total from all four collections that showed more than a few stitches of mending includes 15 garments, and those worn, torn, or stained number 68 (Photos 3.7, 3.8, 3.9, and 3.10).

Not much is known about many of the donors, however, the internal ribbons which hooked around the waist of the woman wearing the garment often were printed with the name of the manufacturer. These show that women from as far away as Cardiff and Edinburgh were buying London and Paris fashions, as well as making use of the seamstresses and dressmakers in their own towns.

These examples also address the issue of who creates the museum collections, as women outnumber male donors by significant amounts. In analyzing the donors, I noted each donor listed, male or female. If the donor's sex could not be determined, due to use of initials or for other reasons, I left them out of the analysis. I only listed donors once, even if they donated more than one item in the collection. Of the 49 corsets or sets of corsets that had donor names attached to them, 45 were donated by women, and only four by men.

The fact that women outnumber men as donors over ten to one indicates that not only were women instrumental in the composition of the collection, they were instrumental in the fact that there is a collection to begin with. They defined the parameters on an individual level, leading

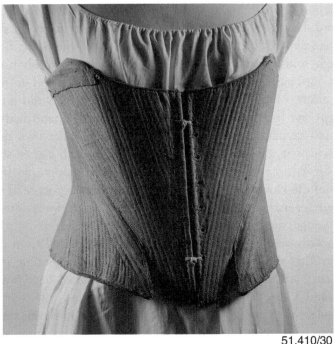

51.410/30

Photo 3.7 51.410/30, closed, exterior, front view (Photo provided by St. Fagans Museum, Cardiff)

to the ability to enter "corset" into the electronic database and get these specific results. They determined what was worthy of inclusion, and while that determination was not teleological—it had no endpoint in mind at the outset—the result is a collection that has a diverse set of garments, from fine to utilitarian, from cherished and mended to well worn and discarded.

In summation, the corsets had waist sizes that were overall smaller than those of today, though they trended larger and larger as the decades went on. Many showed use wear, sweat stains, rust from steel boning, ink, mended parts, or dirt from the bottoms of dresses being dragged over the street by women wearing them. Several of them had aftermarket additions, lace where none was originally, ribbons sewn on

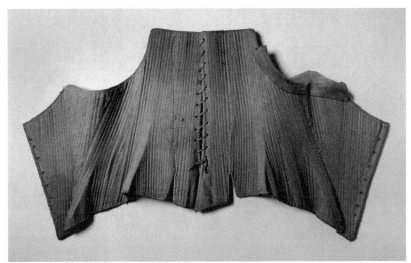

51.410/30

Photo 3.8 51.410/30, open, exterior view (Photo provided by St. Fagans Museum, Cardiff)

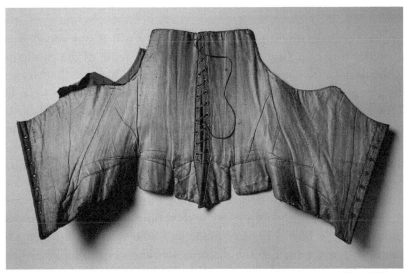

51.410/30

Photo 3.9 51.410/30, open, interior view (Photo provided by St. Fagans Museum, Cardiff)

53.119

Photo 3.10   53.119, open, exterior view (Photo provided by St. Fagans Museum, Cardiff)

to make a plain garment pretty, or embroidery which was added later. The ability to lace tighter or looser, the use and reuse of the garments, and the decision to change their decorativeness, all indicate that women both accepted and rejected the bodyscape of the time they were in, acknowledging that fashion was more than just what was available at the moment—that they could exercise their own agency in how they used the corset.

However, what about the idea that women were negatively impacting their health? We saw in Chapter 2 that women often defended the corset, from an aesthetic standpoint, and here in this chapter that the corsets were indeed multiple signifiers with various cultural overtones—as demonstrated by how they were made and who was wearing them. In Chapter 4, I will return to the discourse around corsets, looking more closely at the idea of clothing, health, and specifically dress reform, which worked both in concert with and against the writings of doctors of the day.

Bibliography

Barthes, R. (1967). *The Fashion System* (Ward and Howard, Trans.). Berkeley, CA: The University of California Press.

Bates, A. (2008). "Indecent and Demoralizing Representations": Public Anatomy Museums in mid-Victorian England. *Medical History, 52*(1), 1–22.

Bendall, S. (2014). To Write a Distick Upon It: Busks and the Language of Courtship and Sexual Desire in Sixteenth- and Seventeenth-Century England. *Gender & History, 26*(2), 199–222.

Blackstone, W. (1765). *Commentaries on the Laws of England.* Chicago, IL: University of Chicago Press.

Bonenfant, P. (2019). https://www.pascalbonenfant.com/18c/wages.html.

Bruna, D. (2015). *Fashioning the Body.* New York, NY: Bard Graduate Center, Yale.

Colmer, M. (1980). *Whalebone to See-Through: A History of Body Packaging.* Cranbury, NJ: A. S. Barnes and Co., Inc.

Cox, M., & Scott, A. (1992). Evaluation of the Obstetric Significance of Some Pelvic Characters in an 18th Century British Sample of Known Parity Status. *The American Journal of Physical Anthropology, 89,* 431–440.

De Certeau, M. (1984). *The Practice of Everyday Life.* Berkeley, CA: The University of California Press.

De Marchi, M., et al. (1976). True Hermaphroditism with XX/XY Sex Chromosome Mosaicism: Report of a Case. *Clinical Genetics, 10,* 265–272.

De Maupassant, G. (1883). *La Mère aux Monstres.*

Demographia. (2019). http://www.demographia.com/db-lonuza1680.htm.

Dickens, C. (1843). *A Christmas Carol.* London, UK: Chapman and Hall.

Dickinson, R. (1887). The Corset: Questions of Pressure and Displacement. *New York Medical Journal.*

Edwards, L. (2017/2018). *How to Read a Dress: A Guide to Changing Fashion from the 16th to the 20th Century.* London, UK: Bloomsbury Academic.

Fitzgerald, P., et al. (1979). A True Hermaphrodite Dispermic Chimera with 46, XX and 46, XY Karyotypes. *Clinical Genetics, 15,* 89–96.

Fontanel, B. (1992). *Support and Seduction: A History of Corsets and Bras.* New York, NY: Harry N. Abrams Inc.

Fowler, O. S. (1870). *Sexual Science; Including Manhood, Womanhood, and Their Mutual Interrelations; Love its Laws, Power, etc., Selection or Mutual Adaptation; Married Life Made Happy; Reproduction, and Progenal Endowment, or Paternity, Maternity, Bearing, Nursing, and Rearing Children;*

Puberty, Girlhood, etc.; Sexual Ailments Restored, Female Beauty Perpetuated, etc., etc. as Taught by Phrenology. Philadelphia, PA: National Publishing Company.

Gazette. (1904). https://www.thegazette.co.uk/London/issue/27691/page/4189/data.pdf.

Gülekon, I., & Turgut, H. (2001). The Preauricular Sulcus: Its Radiologic Evidence and Prevalence. *Kaibogaku Zasshi Acta Anatomica Nipponica, 76*(6), 533–535.

Hiley, M. (1979). *Victorian Working Women: Portraits from Life.* London, UK: The Gordon Fraser Gallery Ltd.

In 2013 Dollars. (2019). https://www.in2013dollars.com.

Inskip, S., et al. (2018). Evaluating Macroscopic Sex Estimation Methods Using Genetically Sexed Archaeological Material: The Medieval Skeletal Collection from St. John's Divinity School, Cambridge. *The American Journal of Physical Anthropology, 168*(2), 340–351.

Karsten, J. (2017). A Test of the Preauricular Sulcus as an Indicator of Sex. *The American Journal of Physical Anthropology, 165*(3), 604–608.

Kunzle, D. (1982). *Fashion and Fetishism.* London, UK: George Prior Associated Publishers Ltd.

Lee, A. (1995). *Sense and Sensibility.* Devon, UK: Columbia Pictures.

Lord, W. B. (1868/1870). *Freaks of Fashion: The Corset and the Crinoline.* London: Ward, Lock, and Tyler.

Maison des Canuts. (2012). *Personal Correspondence with Museum Curator Virginie Varenne, Regarding the History of the 1831 and '34 Revolutions.* Lyon, France: Person.

Maryland Historic Society. (2019). http://www.mdhs.org/costumeblog/?page=4.

Niu, D., et al. (2002). Mosaic or Chimera? Revisiting an Old Hypothesis About the Cause of 46, XX/46, XY Hermaphrodite. *The Journal of Pediatrics, 140*(6), 732–735.

O'Followell, L. (1908). *Le Corset: Histoire, Médicine, Hygiène.* Paris, France: A. Maloine.

Parris, M. (1997). *Great Parliamentary Scandals.* London, UK: Robson Books.

Salen, J. (2008). *Corsets: Historical Patterns and Techniques.* London, UK: Batsford.

Seleshanko, K. (2012). *Bound and Determined: A Visual History of Corsets 1850–1960.* Mineola, NY: Dover Publications.

Sir Mix-a-Lot. (1992). *Baby Got Back,* Def American.

Smith, C. (2002). The Wholesale and Retail Markets of London, 1660–1840. *The Economic History Review, 55*(1), 31–50.

Smith, N. (1827, July 24). Remarks on the Injuries Resulting from Confinement of the Chest by Dress. *Boston Medical Intelligencer,* 5(10), 153.

Steele, V. (2001). *The Corset: A Cultural History.* New Haven, CT: Yale University Press.

Styles, J. (2007). *The Dress of the People: Everyday Fashion in Eighteenth-Century England.* New Haven, CT: Yale University Press.

Summers, L. (2001). *Bound to Please: A History of the Victorian Corset.* Oxford: Berg.

Swanson, K. (2011). Getting a Grip on the Corset: Gender, Sexuality, and Patent Law. *Yale Journal of Law and Feminism, 23*(1), 57–115.

The Family Recorder. (2011). http://thefamilyrecorder.blogspot.com/2011/04/shopping-saturday-mrs-addley-bourne.html.

Victoria and Albert Archives. Accessed (2012–2017). http://collections.vam.ac.uk/item/O355213/corset-unknown/.

Victoria and Albert Museum. (2015). *London Society Fashion 1905–1925: The Wardrobe of Heather Firbank.* London, UK: Victoria and Albert Museum.

Wollstonecraft, M. (1793). *A Vindication of the Rights of Women with Strictures on Political and Moral Subjects.* Dublin, Ireland: J. Stockdale.

4

The Corset as Civilization: The Debate on Clothing and Women's Social Wellbeing

To begin this chapter, I would like to draw your attention to two skeletons of note from the Musée de l'Homme collection, as we continue to contemplate the use of the word "civilized" in relation to women's bodies. I was able to make certain distinctions for most of the skeletons I examined in Paris, dividing them first into the categories of "European" and "non-European," based on the location of origin recorded in the Musée de l'Homme records. These were then further subdivided into "Europeanized" and "non-Europeanized," based on their known location of origin and the level of colonization of that location at their recorded or estimated year of death. These details, scant though they are, allow me to tell you a (possible, and plausible) story about two of these skeletons.

For example, one skeleton's location of origin was "Bombay" (now called Mumbai), a location that has been controlled by Europeans—first Portuguese, then British—since the late 1500s, until India's independence in 1947. This control and its duration would allow plenty of time for the diffusion of clothing customs across all levels of society—a mark of "civilization"—including to the "domestic servant" who eventually journeyed to the European mainland and died in a hospice in Paris, in the case of the skeleton labeled as "Indian" and from "Bombay,"

© The Author(s) 2020
R. Gibson, *The Corseted Skeleton*,
https://doi.org/10.1007/978-3-030-50392-5_4

MNHN-HA-784. This skeleton can then be contrasted with another from "Bengal,"[1] a territory which was also under British control at the time of her collection, between the years of 1818 and 1820. Unlike Mumbai, however, the British only took control of Bengal in the mid-1700s, and by the time of skeleton MNHN-HA-810's death, the fashion may not have disbursed as widely in a territory that was claimed but held a minimal British presence (Photo 4.1).

This relevant distinction between Europeanized and non-Europeanized assisted in determining whether or not the individual would have worn a corset when living. I applied the same concepts as in the London sample: English, French, and other western or middle European women would de facto have worn corsets during their adult life, where Europeanized women from non-European countries would have been likely too as well, and non-Europeanized women would not (Encyclopedia of Clothing and Fashion 2010; Gruber 2016; Hall 2002, pp. 45–46).

This idea comes from the broader "fashion system" to which I have previously referred (Barthes 1967; Entwistle 2000), which indicates that the availability of materials, the trendiness of designs as well as their cultural diffusion, and the relative industry of the area (Entwistle 2000, p. 32) all contribute to the adoption and continuation of patterns of dress. Countries without a strong European presence would be categorically unlikely to adopt the boned, fitted, European style corset. You can see from the photo above that the skeleton from Mumbai exhibits deformation from corseting, with a cylindrical rib cage where the bottom ribs have been rounded inward toward the center line and small-angled spinous processes (see Photo 4.2), showing strong cultural diffusion of ideas across the "civilized" world, and ensuring that women who came under that métier had the proper shape. This contrasts with the skeleton from Bengal, which exhibits a rib cage that flares gently outward toward the bottom like an inverted V, as do virtually all anatomically normal human rib cages, barring other congenital malformations. But was this change in the shape "healthy"?

*   *   *

---

[1] Bengal, in this case, is really Bangladesh, which is in the far north-eastern interior of the Indian subcontinent.

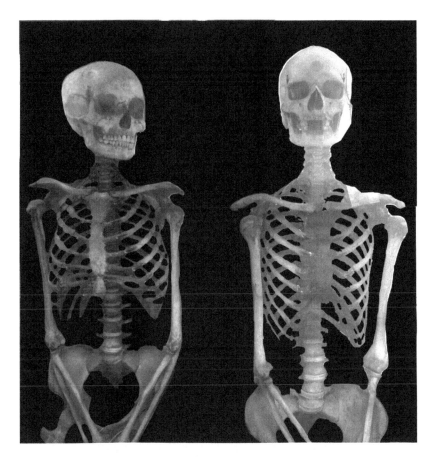

Photo 4.1 At left: MNHN-HA-810, from Bengal/Bangladesh. Coronal dimension: 20 cm. Sagittal dimension: 15 cm. Ratio of coronal to sagittal dimensions: 1:.75. Age at death, >46. Notes on accession data: Bengali (Bangladeshi) died at the *Cape de Bonne Esperance* (Cape of Good Hope), "collected" with the help of the naturalist Delaland fils, during his journey of three years to the Cape and *"Cafrerie"* (from kafir, or land of the infidels), in the years of 1818–1820, and given to M. Cuvier at the Musée de l'Homme. At right: MNHN-HA-784, from India. Coronal dimension: 19.5. Sagittal dimension: 17. Ratio of coronal to sagittal dimensions: 1:.87. Age at death, 36–45 (Notes on accession data: Indian from Bombay [Mumbai], a domestic servant who died under home care at the l'hospice Beaujon, in Paris, in 1839. Photo taken by author and used with permission from the Muséum National d'Histoire Naturelle)

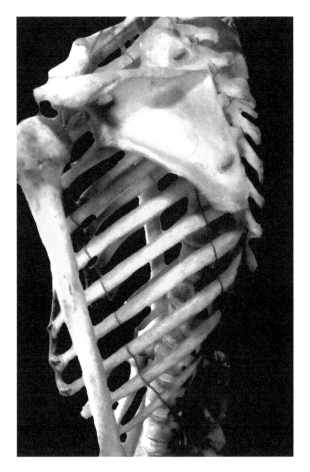

Photo 4.2   Downward pointing spinous processes from skeleton MNHN-HA-784
(Photo taken by author and used with permission from the Muséum National
d'Histoire Naturelle)

Civilized, Healthy, and in Proper Shape: The Evolution of the Corseted Woman

This chapter will deal with the second of our discourses around corseting: the widely held idea that health and civilization were tied up
in the corset. Doctors certainly contributed to this discourse, but as

we will see in later chapters, they had their own take on the matter. Instead, this chapter will look at Freud's ideas about hysteria and at nonsurgical opinions on what the corset did to women's health. This discussion surrounding women's place in civilization is one that must be approached with nuance. To illustrate the various opinions on the subject, I will draw from multiple sources to tease out the various strands of that discussion as it intersects with corsets, tight clothing, and the dress reform movement of the 1890s and 1900s. As seen in Chapter 2, women's relationship with their corsets and other clothing as arbiters of social standing and defense against penetrations (both real and symbolic) was deeply ingrained, yet also contested from both men and women from this time. Health and morality were deeply linked in the minds of the public, with ill-health and/or the poverty that occasionally caused such ill-health being seen as moral failings rather than failings of the flesh.

Through this time, we see a change and a conflict in this narrative, one from the public-facing authors railing against the tight stays of earlier times, to women creating their own dress reform movement to remove tight/hot clothing and release the burden on women's waists. We also see the incorporation of the work of the concept of "hysteria"; that women were troubled and unhealthy because their wombs wandered throughout their body and disturbed their minds. This led to ideas about the corset as a manipulator of the body, rather than just a killer, and about tight clothing being unhealthy and causing problems both mental and physical.

The Freudian/Hysterical Narrative on Corseting

To outline how the Freudian/hysterical discourse was established, we must discuss the source—Freud's work on hysteria. Written in 1893, Freud gives several case studies of hysterical women and girls, describing how repressed trauma from their pasts manifests itself in physical symptoms of unexplained origin (Freud 1893). From headaches (ibid., pp. 57, 59) to gastrointestinal disturbances (ibid., pp. 25, 88–90) to "virginal anxiety" (ibid., p. 62), almost any symptom or ailment that did not have an immediate known physical cause could be explained by being mental. The problems with this are myriad. We must recall that this is a span of time when arsenic was used as a beauty aid, mercury was used to set hats, match tips were constructed from molten phosphorous, and the idea that male fecundity was controlled by homunculi was just a few decades removed from having been the standard explanation for pregnancy (Abou-Nemeh 2013).

As mentioned, the Freudian/hysterical discourse was established over the course of the late twentieth and early twenty-first centuries, after Freud's work on hysteria strove to connect the inner workings of the immaterial mind with the outer manifestations of physical illness and disorders of the body (Freud 1883). With dozens of symptoms, many of which overlapped with corseting (ibid.; O'Followell 1908), attributed to women (and only women) being over- or under-sexualized, the connection of such a discourse to that of corseting seems almost teleologically destined. Emphasizing the idea of Separate Spheres ideology (Marsh, n.d.), the division of male and female work, male and female gazes, and male and female medical diagnoses into categories was logical, and supports the ideas outlined by Freud—that mental trauma caused by sexual assault or deprivation would be mapped onto the body, and that the sources of all such trauma could be understood via the erotic/exotic component of people's daily lives.

However, Freud's emphasis on the idea that all the trauma stemmed from too much or too little sex was an attractive idea, both at the time, and now. As discussed, sex sells, and because the corset is such an easily sexualized garment, the prevalence of the idea that corset wearers or tight-lacers focused on the exotic/erotic component (Kunzle 1982; Steele 1996, 2001; Summers 2001) was not seen as outside the realm of possibility. Yet, as shown in Chapter 2, giving that idea weight tends to deemphasize the "ordinary woman" who would wear a corset as an everyday undergarment, without necessarily thinking about the sexual component. To this end, I have already discussed the theoretical position of embodiment and agency, which can include sexuality but is not necessarily defined or delimited by it. Freud was not a huge proponent of the idea of female agency and had embodiment theory been a thing in his time, his theories would have been directly contradictory to it due to the components of the theory that emphasize conscious action and agentive choice.

Rather than seating the source of physical problems in the mind, as Freud was wont to do, embodiment theory encapsulates existence distinctly in the physical. The mind is not discounted but rather situated as the location of one's identity, which is then mapped upon the body in the form of the bodyscape of the day (Geller 2009). This allows for a person to act with agentive behavior, which is determined not by the subconscious, but by decisions based in the purposeful reification[2] of self, influenced by their cultural surroundings, and then masked onto the physical.

This idea of a purposeful creation of identity grants women a rich and distinct inner life—one in which they are aware of cultural norms and their part in upholding or diminishing those norms. This tracks much more closely with what we recognize today as the way in which we interact with our culture and with other people. While the world of the twenty-first century is certainly more decentralized and global, which contributes to one's cultural awareness, there are other ways in which that awareness could be internalized and was internalized in the time between 1700 and 1900, including one which we have already discussed; socioeconomic class. Dressing up or down to one's class (based on clothing, manners and mannerisms, and accent), and the fact that doing so is a common literary trope of the time, demonstrates just as varied an internal landscape as one could care to require for the creation of identity.

Identity within the body can still encompass a sexual aspect, but it is not ruled by it or defined by it, as a Freudian/hysterical discourse is. Women make their own choices with regard to their corsets to reify or to disidentify with the prevailing bodyscape of the time (de Certeau 1984; Pêcheux 1975; Geller 2009). These choices are necessarily limited by resources, location, and a woman's own desires. Before we get to those choices, what exactly was hysteria?

---

[2]The mapping of the abstract, such as the cultural construct of "self," onto the physical, such as the body.

Wandering Womb Syndrome: Corsets and Hysteria

A way in which corseting, health, and morality were linked was the notion of madness and/or hysteria. To be mad, to have a mental illness or to be hysterical, was to have an automatic cultural "out" from needing to wear a corset. Because the womb was said to wander, and constriction by corseting was largely blamed for that, we should look carefully at the symptoms attributed to hysteria:

Hallucinate, neuralgias, anesthesias, contractures, paralyses, epileptiform convulsions, which every observer has taken for real epilepsy, petit-mal and tic-like affections, persistent vomiting and anorexia...refusal of nourishment...visual disturbances...visual hallucinations....tongue clicking [p. 25]; crying...acts of revenge... [p. 27]; delirium [p. 28]; convulsions [p. 29]; fidgeting [p. 30]; lost perception of [real] smell... subjective sensations of smell [p. 31]; depression and lassitude, analgesia without tactile impairment [ibid]; vertigo, anxiety, faintness [p. 33]: hyperalgesia of the skin and muscles [p. 39]; ... peculiar expression nearer pleasure than pain [at stimulation of sore areas of the body] [ibid]; feeling of womanly weakness [p. 47]; irritable and unapproachable [p. 51]; splitting of consciousness [p. 53]; choking and tightening sensations in the throat, being unable to close her opened mouth, fainting [p. 54]; prickling sensation in the fingertips, jerky movements [p. 55]; periosteal and the neuralgic pains of the teeth, headaches which originate from so many different sources...rheumatic pains of the muscles [p. 56]; facial neuralgia...of the second and third branches of the trigeminus...excess of urates in the urine... [p. 57]; hallucinations, pains, convulsions, and long declamations, feeling of a slap in the face, 'violent pain in [her] right heel' [p. 58]; ...whole series of physical sensations, which were otherwise looked upon as organically determined, were of psychic origin...accompanied by a piercing sensation in the region of the heart ['I felt a stitch in my heart']. The piercing headache of hysteria was undoubtedly, in her case, to be interpreted as mental pain ['something sticks in my head']... the sensation of the hysterical aura in the throat...ran parallel with the thought, 'I have to swallow that.' [p. 59]; hypochondria, sexual neurosis [aversion or intensity of desire] [p. 61]; virginal anxiety [62]; nervous cough [p. 67]; persistent pain in [her] abdomen [p. 69]; excessive feelings of guilt...phobia of uncontrolled urination...suicidal ideation [p. 85]; general irritability, anxious expectation, anticipation of death, palpitations, asthma like attacks, perspiration, night-sweats, trembling, increased appetite/dizziness, diarrhea, vertigo, conjestions [sic] and paresthesia, night terrors, nausea and vomiting [pp. 88-90]; virginal fear, newlywed fear, fear of premature ejaculation or impotence in partner, anxiety over coitus interruptus or congressus reservatus, sexual fear in widows, fear of sexual climax [pp. 90-93]; ...masturbation in itself is more frequently the result of abuse or seduction than one supposes, [p. 98]. (Freud 1893/1952)

That the wearing of corsets was seen to cause this, and that the women were seen as responsible for that choice, emphasizes the contradicting nature of the discussion of women's agency, while simultaneously reinforcing the view that hysterical behavior was all in their heads. Speaking to this effect, Freud lists the causes of hysteria as:

Unrequited love [pp. 43-44]; repressed erotic idea [p. 52]; "such incompatible ideas originate in the feminine sex on the bases of sexual experiences and feelings" [p. 82];

And:

"insufficient [sexual] gratification" [p. 94]; sexual traumas of early childhood [97]; "We can, moreover, understand the disproportionately greater frequency of hysteria in the female sex, as even in childhood this sex is more subject to sexual assaults," [pp. 97-98]. (Freud 1893/1952)

As these ideas do contradict each other, it is important to work with them carefully. We can see that they are tied together by the ideas of identity and civilization. To be a (European) (White) (English) woman during this time was to focus on family and home—to remain tidily in the private sphere, tending to one's husband and children. To do so, one must be fulfilled in love and sexual desire—love for one's children, love and sexual desire for one's husband. To not have these things would create unrequited love, insufficient sexual gratification, repressed erotic ideas. However, propriety demands that one not be **too** sexual, therefore if they were then too much sex—from previous experiences or assaults—must be the cause. Women's identity must be culturally civilized, and therefore must be contained, ideally within the corset. And one way in which identity, both personal and cultural, is reflected in the physical realm is through body modification, such as by the corset, which molded the body to a more civilized shape.

Change Your Body, Change Your Identity

There are deliberate and incidental modes of body modification, as well as a distinction between modifications that people choose for themselves, and modifications that are done to them. As the name suggests, a body modification is a change to the body, and discussions of such usually surround those modifications that are permanent—tattoos, piercings, foot-binding, and the like. Corseting creates a bodily modification; the changes in the ribs and spinal structure detailed throughout this book. Prevalent trends in current thought (Kunzle 1982; Steele 1996, 2001; Stone 2012) indicate that the modification of corseting is both an unwanted imposition upon women, and a violence to them—specifically a patriarchal violence, reinforced by the overarching social structure, and enforced on female children by their female parents. Particularly it is compared to foot-binding (Stone 2012), which does demonstrably impair the mobility of the bound woman (Brown et al. 2012). I agree completely that a permanent, irreversible restriction in the mobility, both physical and social (recall that the ability to move downward in social class, in this case by going without a corset, is still social mobility), of a woman is to be considered a form of patriarchal violence. However, it is necessary to differentiate between that type of restriction and nonviolent changes in the skeletal structure.

Furthermore, the term violence implies intent—that harm was intended by the practice. Yet not all change is harmful, despite pain associated with that change. To compare corseting to another form of body modification, also imposed upon children by their parents, we can look at orthodontia (Ackerman 2010). This practice takes a functional skeletal system, in this case the teeth, and changes it to a more culturally appropriate shape. Corseting did the same for the ribs and vertebrae. No violence is intended via the change in the shape of the mouth, nor do men and women with orthodontically straightened teeth see it as such as adults, despite the fact that, as pointed out (ibid.), most braces are completely unnecessary.

However, as in orthodontia, parents who choose corseting make the decision for their children, based on their best knowledge at the time. This knowledge does, necessarily, reflect hegemonic ideology and good subjectivity, and certain parents do choose to go against it or allow their children leniency in the application of the device (bad subjects, who cannot afford to or "don't know any better," or disidentified subjects, who actively choose not to or who view braces as a tool of the hegemony). And as a child grows to an adult, they are more likely, and more culturally and mentally able to purposefully accept or reject that ideology, for their own reasons. Those reasons can be anything from a change of fashion, to a will to rebel against their own parents' ideologies, to indifference to their children's choices, reflecting again the fact that identity creation is a nuanced thing. Thus, change to the body does not imply violence, trauma, or pain, either structural or immediate.

Health, Civilization, and Morality—An Upright Woman Is a Moral Woman

As previously discussed in the opening vignette to this chapter, the ideas of civilization and morality went hand in hand with the idea of clothing—literally the longer a place had been under European or so-called "civilized" influence, the more likely that place was to have readily available European fashions. "Clothes make the man," a statement attributed to Erasmus' Adagia—a list of 500 proverbs—holds equally true for the woman, particularly if that woman were corseted. In the case of corseting, the body is quite literally remolded into a different shape. Ludovic O'Followell, in his 1908 treaty on the corset, states that the corset "moule le plastique féminine" (p. 13), which translates literally to "mold the female wax" but is metaphorically referring to the fact that the body was seen as something to be formed, something unfinished, and in need of disciplining. A "molding" of the form of femininity. This refers back further to the ancient Greek story of Pygmalion and Galatea, where the sculptor forms the perfect woman, and the gods breathe life into her, rewarding him for his work. In this twentieth-century case, the sculptor is the maker of the corset and the woman is touched not by the gods but by the art of the clothier. Furthermore, it explains why corseting began so early in the life of the woman; children were seen as closer to nature and needed to be shaped/molded away from nature to civilization. Thus, women are seen as more childlike than men, as their shaping process has not finalized yet.

By looking at the ideal bodyscapes of the day (Edwards 2017/2018; Geller 2009), we can see that overemphasized femininity, and uprightness of the body, was the goal of that shaping. This was reflected in cultural attitudes toward femininity, as well. Best shown in Mary Wollstonecraft's 1793 work "A Vindication of the Rights of Women with Strictures on Political and Moral Subjects," women were charged with seeing to the moral and physical growth of their household. Despite being seen as needing to be shaped themselves, they were meant to shape their children.

That the physical, cultural, and moral were conflated can be seen in mores surrounding poverty. We have examined how women could conceivably own a set of stays or a corset regardless of her socioeconomic class, however, the words often used to describe women who were not taking care to demonstrate the trappings and manners of their proper station in life—slovenly, slatternly, loose, wayward, public, etc.—are often connected to this idea of poverty and of whether or not they were deserving or undeserving poor. We will come back to this discussion as it specifically relates to the St. Bride's parish in a later chapter, however, it is worth pointing out now that work has indeed been done to show that, in the eyes of the English in the 1700s and 1800s, morality and wealth shared their contributions to civilization.

For example, in "Slumming," his work on the wealthy practice of poverty tourism in the Victorian period, Seth Koven gives us a dire picture of poorhouses, discussing exposés performed at the time, in which undercover reporters showed them to be places of degradation, lice, licentiousness, disease, and cruelty. Often, the prisons and workhouses shared the same property and the same overseers (Koven 2006), and the emphasis of incarceration was on the reformation and rehabilitation of the "undeserving poor," or those who were unworthy of individual charity and thus made the responsibility of the state. Personal property was confiscated when a person entered the workhouse, and often lost, and there were restrictions on how much currency you could have in order to be truly considered "poor" and thus needing a place in the house, therefore it was very difficult to leave once you entered, or to maintain both a job and a place to live.

Synthesis: Ideas About Corseting and Morality

To synthesize the above—that corseting was a moral imperative but overuse could cause immorality; that corseting was indicative of civilization, but also caused madness; that corseting formed the woman, but it could also malform her—is to accept that human beings are complicated, nuanced, and often contradictory. It also indicates that a paradigm shift in ideas about corseting is necessary. Corseting is not the issue at hand—the corset is used as a stand-in for what is "wrong" with being female. Were the corset not the fashion of the day, something else would have been the apex of moral goodness and the nadir of women's descent into madness and uncivility. Let us take these dichotomous pairs one at a time.

First: An upright woman is a moral woman/tight-lacing was sexy and immoral. Here we see fear of a woman's control of her own sexuality. Much of the cultural context of this time period was focused around the idea that women's sexuality was necessarily under the control of her male relations—fathers, brothers, husband, and to a lesser extent, sons (Davidoff and Hall 2002; Fowler 1870; Freud 1893/1952). A young woman, pre-marriage, was meant to be chaste and pure, only setting out to attract a suitable husband (as opposed to attracting an unsuitable husband, a lover who would not marry her, or a same-sex partner) (ibid.). She could signal that chasteness and purity by way of her dress and manner, being appropriately dressed and properly corseted, but not flaunting her figure or behaving in ways that were flirtatious and sexually desirous.

After marriage, her sexuality was meant to be contained to her husband, and him alone, and then subsumed by her devotion to her children (ibid., and also Wollstonecraft 1793, though Wollstonecraft was notoriously anti-marriage herself, and only married William Godwin under pressure). As she became pregnant and bore children, her use of corsets would have been good (use of a supportive, expanding pregnancy corset) or bad (use of the regular corset throughout pregnancy and confinement, or use of the corset to self-abort). Here we have the same action, corseting, with two very different views and/or outcomes. To retain her husband's attention, a woman properly remained corseted. To bear and care for the children, she modified her practice away from the desired silhouette, away from the desire of her husband, and toward the physically safe and healthy use of the garment. Thus, her use of the garment was moral, but any potential overuse or disidentification type of use was immoral.

Second: Corseting showed civilization/corseting led to hysteria. Two misconceptions of early scientific fields are at work in this dichotomy—scientific racism, and the lack of medical knowledge about the human body/human psyche. Scientific racism, as previously discussed, put white European-derived men at the top of the hierarchy, with their women coming just below them, and then continued downward through the so-called races. Because white European women who corseted were still white Europeans, they "necessarily" had to have a place above the so-called inferior races, and the way this was distinguished was through dress. Non-European, and non-Europeanized, women did not corset. They did other forms of constricted body modification (neck stretching, foot-binding, and the like) but they remained largely uncovered, and thus uncivilized. The civilized woman showed very little skin, particularly below the torso, did not bare her breasts (actually a change from European women of only a few centuries before this time, many of whom were painted with breasts out [Ribeiro 1986/2003, p. 92]), and wore the corset. In fact, when tea gowns (a type of loose, flowing afternoon dress that a woman would wear at home) became the rage, they were decried as a sign of uncivilized, "loose" morality (ibid., p. 142).

The judgment on clothing, and therefore people, being uncivilized was not limited to non-Europeans, however. In as late as 1904, American machinist Edwin Balch wrote "The costumes of semi-civilized peoples are not always the best, however. The Highland kilt seems principally adapted to kill off the weaker specimens of the canny Scot" (p. 324). He goes on to remark upon the corset:

> The human animal breathes with his entire skin....Arrest this process entirely for a few hours and you kill the man; arrest it partially and you produce more or less sickness....Similar unhygienic results are obtained by lining waistcoats with canvas, by corsets, by the abuse of starch... (ibid., pp. 326–327)

Continuing, he states:

> Civilized peoples have achieved two deformities of the human body, both of which are practically unknown among savages. The first of these is the crushing in of the ribs and the displacement of the lungs and the abdomen, often caused in the female sex by the misuse of the corset and by tight-lacing. The evils of this practice are universally known among medical men. Apparently such a custom is found among savages only in New Guinea, where Mr. Octavius C. Stone saw *men* [emphasis in the original], not women, constricting their waists so tightly with a stiff bark belt, that in one case where the waist measured about 53 centimeters the flesh above and below it bulged out to about 70 centimeters. (ibid., p. 329)

Thus we can see that European women retained their civilization, as did their clothing, despite what was perceived as harm to their bodies.

The lack of medical knowledge, both within and outside of the medical field, was due to two factors: the dearth of internal surgery (as distinct from amputations) done in general, and the tendency to see women as little more than men who bore children. As shown by various historical scholars (Aptowicz 2014; Fitzharris 2017; Montillo 2013), surgery was most often a last-ditch effort to save the life of a person, or to remove a viable fetus from a nonviable woman. In order for it to become more than that, medical science had to advance to an understanding of germ theory and use of anesthesia, both of which would allow patients to better survive the procedures and the days and weeks of hospital confinement that came after. It is here where we also find our third paradox: in general, people do not go to the doctor unless something is wrong, or abnormal. Therefore, most patients are not presenting without abnormalities, and combined with the lack of overall understanding of the workings of the female body, doctors distributed some very odd notions about women during this time.

One such notion was that of hysteria, which spread from Freud's writings to common and medical parlance very quickly. If we grant their belief that the uterus can wander about the body (it cannot, but let's humor them for a moment), then it might very well impact all the systems, as shown above in the list of symptoms. However, most of those symptoms are either physically unconnected to a uterus, wandering or not, or they are psychologically attributable, meaning that while it was "all in their heads," it was not without just cause or without a reasonable explanation other than hysteria.

You will notice that a good number of the symptoms enumerated in the above section on hysteria have to do with things that would have, at the time, been considered uncivilized—that is, out of the control of society and/or the women's male relatives (to circle back to the first dichotomy; they are all connected). Hallucination, irritability, weakness, headache, revenge fantasies, fear, anxiety, and masturbation, among others, have social as well as physical reasons for their appearance in an otherwise healthy woman. Particularly, one might point out, masturbation. While the rest are either recognizable as mental illness, or as physical illness that could happen to anyone regardless of sex, masturbation is seen as particularly problematic as it is a woman taking control of her own sexuality. Thus, while the corset civilized, it also uncivilized.

Third: Corsets molded women to the standard of the day/corseting malformed women. This particular point is difficult, because both sides of the dichotomy are accurate—that molding was the idea, and that the molding led to malformations of the skeleton, as I have demonstrated above and will quantify in later chapters. However, while I am using malformation in a dispassionate way, to indicate that the bone has formed in a way that is other than anatomically normal, people of this time period were using it in a pejorative manner. They meant that using the corset made women ugly, deformed, unappealing.

In the case of O. S. Fowler, a quasi-doctor, writing in 1870, hyperbole seems to be his style, as he thinks very little of women who corset, and spares no words saying so:

> If it merely injured the female body, prevented and killed offspring by millions annually, and rendered many that are borne too weakly to live, even then it should rouse and arm all civilization against itself; but when, besides, it perverts the female character from its pristine loveliness into a bundle of artificial appearances, physically and mentally, leaving man's heart desolated for want of a genuine woman to love and live for; when it even profanes the temple of female chastity; when most who sacrifice their virtue offer it up on this gaudy altar, and all, except those wholly uncultivated are prostituted in *spirit* [emphasis in the original text], from inexpressible loveliness to practical deception, what words are sufficient for its adequate condemnation? (Fowler 1870, p. 177)

This passage contains a lot to unpack, primarily, that he believes that corseting to an extreme is a moral flaw, rendering women no longer lovely, genuine, or pure, and creating in their very essence the impurity and corruption of a sexually incontinent being, the lowest of the low, a prostitute in spirit. Artifice and deception, words that are often associated with legal matters that constitute fraud, are assigned to the woman, making following fashion her crime.

No responsibility is assigned to the man to understand what a corset does, and he is seen as the wronged party, a victim of the deceit, which then turns him off his wife for good: "Besides, as far as dress itself awakens masculine admiration, of course laying off the dress must kill the admiration. If a false form captivates a man, his discovering the real facts in the case must necessarily disgust him" (ibid., p. 179).

Again, we have the idea that the garment can do more than one thing. The corset both lifts up a woman and brings her down. It allows her to express her true femininity, while also being deceptive. It is the ultimate in multiple signifiers and the ultimate in scapegraces—where society wanted to blame the woman herself, the instead blamed the clothing that she wore. However, the fashion did not last forever—dress reform followed on the heels of Fowler's words.

The Dress Reform Movement and the "Health" of Tight Constricting Clothing

The idea of dress reform centered on the relative "health" of garments— tight restrictive clothing was seen as unhealthy, although not for reasons that we might assume, given the scope of this book. Much of reform concentrated on two things: the relative temperatures of different zones of the body, and whether the shoulders, waist, or hips took the bulk of the weight of the garments.

Beginning during the 1850s, and continuing until the early 1900s, the dress reform movement did not start with the notion of abolishing the corset, although that eventually did occur. It began as a pushback against a very certain **type** of corseting, tight-lacing. Although I have mentioned the practice before, I will define it now, roughly, as the practice of reducing one's waist by more than two inches by use of the corset. No argument was made against shaping the waist, structuring a garment with a corset, or staying fashionable. Instead, the reformers sought to change the fashion to include garments that were less constricting, allowed for greater range of motion (to accommodate the changing acceptance of participation of women in the public sphere), and that equalized temperature and weight across the frame of the body. Notably, they were also against dresses that were sleeveless or backless— this was not about increasing sexual freedom, or immodesty. Most dress reformers still wanted to see women clothed from neck to wrists to ankles (and even wanted her to wear corsets!) they just wanted her to be of moderate temperature and not carrying all the weight of the dress on her hips.

Quoting a reformer, historian Stella Mary Newton remarks upon the continuous (unfavorable) comparison of the tight-laced woman to various classical Venus sculptures (1974, p. 44). This is reiterated, over and over and over again, by writers of the day, including one who penned a piece for the aforementioned journal "Knowledge" titled "Stays and Statues" (1883a, p. 23). In this case, the author went so far as to place a corset *on* a Venus figure statue, resulting in much ridicule and laughter. Yet, emphasizing that the reform movement still aimed for propriety for the most part, Newton goes on to remark upon a few women that did not—women who cut their hair short, or women who adopted mannish pants instead of the more feminine split skirts (1974, pp. 152–153). Our current feminists would not have recognized those of the day, who wanted only limited freedoms indeed.

Others, both male and female, were for reform, because once having tried stays, they found themselves wanting to keep them, and also found that desire to be dangerous. In another "Knowledge" article, a man named Richard Proctor tried a month-long experiment in using stays. Proctor is the author of a series of articles for this journal, regarding proper and judicious corset wearing. In one called "Stays and Strength" he states

> …I laughed at myself as a hopeless idiot, and determined to give up the attempt to reduce by artificial means that superabundance of fat on which only starvation and much exercise, or the air of America, has every had any real reducing influence. But I was reckoning without my host. As the Chinese lady suffers, I am told, when her feet bindings are taken off, and as the flat-head baby howls (so Dr. Leigh informs me) when his head-boards are removed, so for a while was it with me. I found myself manifestly better in stays. And now, perhaps, 'An Observer' will see what I meant when I said that if a man finds himself better in stays it shows that stays are weakening.…I would as soon have condemned myself to using crutches all the time, as to wearing always that beast of a busk. But for my one month of folly I had to endure three months of discomfort. (1883, pp. 50–51)

Still, others disagreed—a letter from the same journal, from the previous year, rails against the prejudice of anti-corseting reformers, stating that they "…despise history and personal experience and the results of daily observation, for every one now can see for himself the truth of what several other doctors wrote a dozen years ago, that in spite of all theory, 'tight lacers are generally active and healthy people,' and the best riders and walkers…" (Anonymous 1882, p. 415). Regrettably, this author (one of the only identifiable woman authors) did not name names, so I cannot check to see if those reports still exist.

Toward the end of reform, "Some Remarks on Corsets" was published in the "Massachusetts Ploughman and New England Journal of Agriculture"[3] (1904). This epitomizes the reform argument, and I will highlight in bold that which makes this reform, rather than anti-reform:

> W. E. Frothingill says that the modern woman wears heavy skirts, the weight of which is supported by bands around her waist—that soft portion of the body that is protected by no body walls. How is it possible to wear around this portion of the body bands which support the weight of numerous and often heavy garments? The answer is, by means of the corset. The garment forms a bridge connecting the firm chest wall with the firm pelvis. The use of the corset is to transmit the pressure of the skirt bands to the hips and the ribs, and so protect from their pressure the organs in the region of the waist. The conclusion is that so long as skirt-bands are fastened round the waist, corsets should be worn....The front should be quite straight, and **the waist measurement should be at least as large as the wearer's waist, measured over a single, soft garment. The abuse of the article consists in employing it as a means of compressing that which it was meant to protect from compressing, namely, the soft, middle portion of the body.** (p. 6)

While we cannot go back to over a hundred years ago and ask women what they thought of this advice, I can say from personal experience that a corset measuring larger than one's natural waist is legitimately painful—corsets that are not laced at least a little tightly have a tendency to rub and chafe, causing skin irritation and, if worn long enough, blistering. I can only imagine that this would increase with the dependent weight pulling on the corset. However, it does adequately demonstrate one point that is rarely mentioned: the reform movement was not entirely for the removal of women from their corsets.

Additionally, early twentieth-century mother and wife D. O. Teasley lays out specific ways in which she believes dress should change in a monograph, decrying tight-lacing, and insisting that a better way for women's clothing to be approached is to hang the weight of it from the shoulder,

---

[3]Showing exactly how every single person, regardless of profession or station in life, had an opinion on the topic at hand…

rather than the waist (Teasley 1904, p. 108). This was in response to the fact that heavy skirts, multiple petticoats, and large crinolines sat upon the bottom of the corset, adding weight to that aspect of the garment.

It is telling that Teasley's book is a series of lectures from a mother, to mothers and daughters, using the "appeal to authority" form of a logical fallacy. The final section of her book bemoans what might happen for future generations, generations which are "…rushing into almost every business in the world, in many cases taking the place of men, and the female organism is continually going downhill" (Teasley 1904, p. 109). She goes on to say that two generations previously, simple outdoor exercise improved women and that "those…occupied in sedentary employment and confined indoors most of the time can not [sic] possibly have the strength and vigor of those who get more fresh air" (ibid.). She appears to be forgetting that in her grandmother's time, tight-lacing was all the fashion, as was staying inside to improve one's pallor, and laws were on the books regulating women's right to use bicycles, let alone other sorts of physical activities.

Still, corsets were on their way out, with or without the sanction of the reformers. Fashions toward the end of the nineteenth century were less heavily boned, and some women eschewed corsetry and stays altogether (Cunningham 2003, p. 81). One in particular writes that she has taken them off completely and states "I may mention that I am eighteen, and have worn corsets (owing to my height) since I was twelve. Since I have left them off I have never missed the support, and would not, on any account, wear them again" (Knowledge, 1893, p. 347). So now that we have established what the corset is, what it was meant to do, and what women and others thought about it, we will take a look at a third discourse in Chapter 5—what doctors thought about the corset, and the actual physical manifestations of changes due to corseting.

Bibliography

Abou-Nemeh, S. (2013). The Natural Philosopher and the Microscope: Nicolas Hartsoeker Unravels Nature's "Admirable OEconomy". *History of Science, 51*(1), 1–32.

Ackerman, M. (2010). Selling Orthodontic Need: Innocent Business Decision or Guilty Pleasure? *Journal of Medical Ethics, 36*(5), 275–278.

Anonymous. (1882, November 24). Anti-corset History and Philosophy. *Knowledge, 2,* 415–416.

Anonymous. (1883a, January 12). Stays and Statues. *Knowledge, 3,* 23–24.

Anonymous. (1883b, March 16). The New Skirt. *Knowledge, 3,* 162–163.

Anonymous. (1883c, June 8). Rational Dress. *Knowledge, 3,* 347.

Anonymous. (1904). Some Remarks on Corsets. *Massachusetts Ploughman and New England Journal of Agriculture, 63*(18), 6.

Aptowicz, C. (2014). *Dr. Mütter's Marvels.* New York, NY: Penguin.

Balch, E. (1904). Savage and Civilized Dress. *Journal of the Franklin Institute of the State of Pennsylvania, for the Promotion of the Mechanic Arts, 57*(5), 321–332.

Barthes, R. (1967). *The Fashion System* (Ward & Howard, Trans.). Berkeley: University of California Press.

Brown, M., et al. (2012). Marriage Mobility and Footbinding in Pre-1949 Rural China: A Reconsideration of Gender, Economics, and Meaning in Social Causation. *Journal of Asian Studies, 71*(4), 1035–1067.

Cunningham, P. (2003). *Reforming Women's Fashion, 1850–1920: Politics, Health, and Art.* Kent, OH: Kent State University Press.

Davidoff, L., & Hall, C. (2002). *Family Fortunes: Men and Women of the English Middle Class 1780–1850.* Oxon, UK: Routledge.

De Certeau, M. (1984). *The Practice of Everyday Life.* Berkeley: University of California Press.

Edwards, L. (2017/2018). *How to Read a Dress: A Guide to Changing Fashion from the 16th to the 20th Century.* London, UK: Bloomsbury Academic.

Encyclopedia of Clothing and Fashion. (2010). http://angelasancartier.net/colonialism-and-imperialism.

Entwistle, J. (2000). *The Fashioned Body.* Malden, MA: Blackwell Publishers.

Fitzharris, L. (2017). *The Butchering Art: Joseph Lister's Quest to Transform the Grisly World of Victorian Medicine.* New York, NY: Macmillan Publishers.

Fowler, O. S. (1870). *Sexual Science; Including Manhood, Womanhood, and Their Mutual Interrelations; Love its Laws, Power, etc., Selection or Mutual Adaptation; Married Life Made Happy; Reproduction, and Progenal Endowment, or Paternity, Maternity, Bearing, Nursing, and Rearing Children; Puberty, Girlhood, etc.; Sexual Ailments Restored, Female Beauty Perpetuated, etc., etc. As Taught by Phrenology.* Philadelphia, PA: National Publishing Company.

Freud, S. (1893/1952). *Selected Papers on Hysteria, in Great Books of the Western World* (Vol. 54). Chicago, IL and Freud: University of Chicago Press and Encyclopedia Britannica, Inc.

Geller, P. (2009). Bodyscapes, Biology, and Heteronormativity. *American Anthropologist, 111*(4), 504–516.

Gruber, K. (2016). *Slave Clothing and Adornment in Virginia, in Encyclopedia Virginia.* Retrieved from http://www.EncyclopediaVirginia.org/Slave_Clothing_and_Adornment_in_Virginia.

Hall, C. (2002). *Civilizing Subjects: Metropole and Colony in English Imagination 1830–1867.* Chicago, IL: University of Chicago Press.

Koven, S. (2006). *Slumming: Sexual and Social Politics in Victorian London.* Princeton, NJ: Princeton University Press.

Kunzle, D. (1982). *Fashion and Fetishism.* London, UK: George Prior Associated Publishers Ltd.

Marsh, J. (n. d.). http://www.vam.ac.uk/content/articles/g/gender-ideology-and-separate-spheres-19th-century/.

Montillo, R. (2013). *The Lady and Her Monsters: A Tale of Dissections, Real-Life Dr. Frankensteins, and the Creation of Mary Shelley's Masterpiece.* New York, NY: HarperCollins Publishers.

Newton, M. (1974). *Health, Art, and Reason: Dress Reformers of the 19th Century.* London, UK: John Murry Publishers Ltd.

O'Followell, L. (1908). *Le Corset: Histoire, Médicine, Hygiène.* Paris: A. Maloine.

Pêcheux, M. (1975). The Subject Form of Discourse in the Subjective Appropriation of Scientific Knowledges and Political Practice. In N. Harbans (Trans.), *Language, Semantics, and Ideology* (pp. 155–170). New York: St. Martins Press.

Proctor, R. (1883). Stays and Strength. *Knowledge, 3,* 50–51.

Ribeiro, A. (1986/2003). *Dress and Morality.* London, UK: Berg.

Steele, V. (1996). *Fetish: Fashion, Sex, and Power.* Oxford, UK: Oxford University Press.

Steele, V. (2001). *The Corset: A Cultural History.* New Haven, CT: Yale University Press.

Stone, P. (2012). Binding Women: Ethnology, Skeletal Deformations, and Violence Against Women. *International Journal of Paleopathology, 2*(2–3), 53–60.

Summers, L. (2001). *Bound to Please: A History of the Victorian Corset.* Oxford: Berg.

Teasley, D. (1904). *Private Lectures to Mothers and Daughters on Sexual Purity: Including Love, Courtship, Marriage, Sexual Physiology, and the Evil Effects of Tight Lacing*. Moundsville, WV: Gospel Trumpet Company.

Wollstonecraft, M. (1793). *A Vindication of the Rights of Women with Strictures on Political and Moral Subjects*. Dublin: J. Stockdale.

5

The Corset as a Killer: Did Corseting Negatively Impact Longevity?

Rather than focus on one example for the opening vignette of this chapter, I will focus on a group of women: the elderly women of St. Bride's parish. The myth that corseting killed women persists to this day. To counteract that myth, we can turn to evidence from the St. Bride's collection, FAO90. The Museum of London's Centre for Human Bioarchaeology aged all the skeletons in the FAO90, and divided them into age groups of <18, 18–25, 26–35, 36–45, >46, and unclassified. The overall breakdown of skeletons that I examined was thus (Table 5.1).

This is approximately the same general distribution as that of the "all adults" column from the entire excavation, as shown here, and also highly comparable to the female column, meaning the results that I got were approximately those that I should have gotten (Table 5.2).

However, I must say a brief word about the age groups used in assessing this sample, which I will come back to in detail later in Chapter 7. This type of age range (starting with the truncated 18–25, signifying that the skeleton is not a juvenile (under 18), and then every ten years after) is not standard. I do not know why the Museum of London's team decided to create this new scale, nor why they stopped at the age of 46. This is atypical in terms of creating age ranges, which are usually

© The Author(s) 2020
R. Gibson, *The Corseted Skeleton*,
https://doi.org/10.1007/978-3-030-50392-5_5

Table 5.1 Age at death of St. Bride's FAO90 skeletons, in four age categories

St. Brides: category	Number	Percentage
18–25	2	2.7
26–35	13	17.8
36–45	20	27.4
>46	37	50.7
Unclassified	1	1.4
Totals	73	

Table 5.2 Percentages of ages at death from entire St. Bride's FAO90 sample

All adults	%	Male	%	Female	%
18–25 years	10	2.7	5	2.9	4	3.2
26–35 years	44	11.9	22	11.3	21	16.8
36–45 years	88	23.8	54	27.8	30	24
>46 years	162	43.9	88	45.4	64	51.2
Unassigned Adults	65	17.6	25	12.9	6	4.8
Total	369		194		125	

determined by looking at skeletal populations with known ages, then assigning a 0–3 or 0–4 ranking based on the various age-related traits, such as is done in cranial suture fusion, with 0 being no change/open cranial sutures, and 4 being obliterated sutures. These ranges are often much larger than 10 years, due to human variation—considerably closer to 25–30 year ranges. Those ranges are also often constrained to ages that suggest two states: "has passed young adulthood" (19–28-ish), and "has hit middle-age" (over 46, as seen in the Museum of London's ranges), due to the fact that once the sutures close and/or obliterate, no more change usually occurs. Or, rather, the change that does occur has not been studied or codified into standard ranges. However, it is what they did, so it is what we have to work with.

Of the 73 skeletons that met evaluation criteria—they had vertebrae, or vertebrae and ribs, for evaluation—and of those that had skulls that were in good enough preservation to examine ectocranially,[1] 23 of the skulls put them at the far end of the age at death spectrum

---

[1]Ectocranial examination is considered only a middling-good predictor of age at death, particularly without adding in endocranial suture fusion. However, as the skulls were intact, I was only able to access the ectocranial sites, and I am working with the data that is available to me.

(though I revised some of those ages downward based on other skeletal elements, creating a more robust age range). In particular, seven skulls showed evidence that the women died between 40 and 60, with some potentially much older. Here is the complete profile of one of those women, FAO90 1637: Listed as over 46 years at death, FAO90 1637 showed complete ectocranial obliteration of the coronal suture, both squamous sutures, and the sagittal suture, with partial-to-complete closure of the lambdoid suture. She also showed extensive tooth loss, and near-complete resorption of the empty mandibular and maxillary alveoli. Her ribs show distinct rounding, with coronal (dividing the ribs into front and back) and sagittal (dividing the ribs into right and left) dimensions within four centimeters of each other. Her largest rib circumference is 66 cm, not accounting for any flesh that might have added to the measurement. Her spinous processes show extreme distortion from the anatomical normal of 45°, with T4–T8 measuring 38.66°, 35.75°, 23.61°, 18.25°, and 19.43°, respectively (Photos 5.1, 5.2, 5.3, 5.4, 5.5, and 5.6).

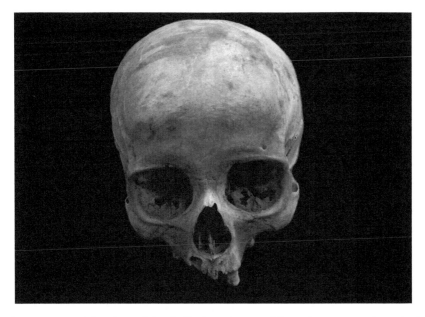

Photo 5.1   Anterior view of the skull of FAO90 1637 (Photo © Museum of London)

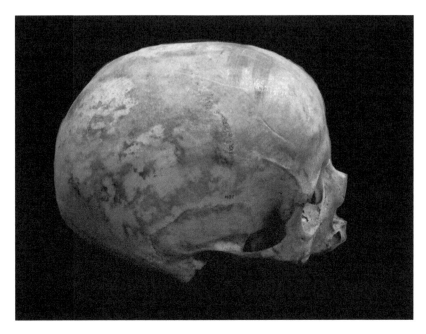

Photo 5.2 Right side view of the skull of FAO90 1637 (Photo © Museum of London)

Being conservative and putting her age at 60 (though she could be much older than that based on the sum totality of skeletal markers…), she might represent any number of women in the St. Bride's death and burial records. While I will do an in-depth analysis of these records in Chapter 6, let us look at a few examples now. On February 2, 1783, Hannah Hubbard was buried in St. Bride's Lower Churchyard, after dying at age 88. On March 26, 1786, Susannah Powell of Parson's Court was buried, having died of a fever at age 62. On December 31, 1792, Jane Burst was buried, having died of asthma at age 70. On December 19, 1823, Ann Gilbert of New Street Square was buried at age 61 after having hanged herself. On November 4, 1838, Hannah Rapson of Water Street, whom we have more data for and will meet in detail in Chapter 6, was buried after dying of decay at age 80. And these women are typical of the data found in the St. Bride's archives. That these women were older when they died, and that the general age at

Photo 5.3   Posterior view of the skull of FAO90 1637 (Photo © Museum of London)

death for St. Bride's which will be discussed in detail in Chapter 6, was quite old, does indicate that the discussion around corsets and lifespan was skewed by the prejudices of the medical community.

*   *   *

Why Did Doctors Hate Corseting So Much?

The idea that corseting was bad for your health was not a new one, nor were the arguments, as used by dress reformers and shown in the last chapter, unique. Most arguments were merely a rehashing of the unsubstantiated medical claims which trickled their way outward from the medical community—the bisected livers, drastically decreased breath capacity, consumptive pallor, displaced uteri, and increased mortality of corseting lore. When examining the downfall of the corset, modern

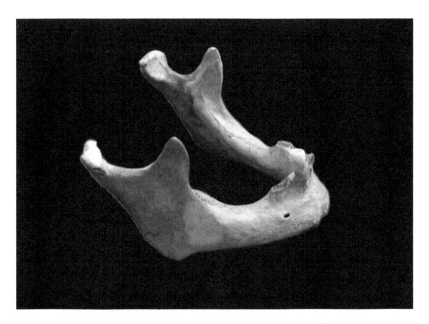

Photo 5.4   Right side view of the mandible of FAO90 1637 (Photo © Museum of London)

researchers cite such problems as the main claims of the dress reform movement (Summers 2001, p. 113), which then compressed them into general complaints about the "health" of the garment. Many of these complaints can be attributed to inaccurate anatomical knowledge from the medical community itself. For example, the complaint of uterine prolapse is rarely discussed in regard to women who had not had children. Given what we now know about gestation and parturition, and acknowledging that contraception was rare and back-to-back pregnancies frequent during this time, it is much more likely that uterine prolapse was not caused by the corset, but rather by many childbirth experiences with no recourse to anesthetic, surgical intervention, or aftercare. Furthermore, livers are naturally bisected, into large and small lobes. As many surgeons of the time had not been exposed to either living patients for surgery, or legal autopsies (Aptowicz 2014; Montillo 2013), it is entirely possible that the reports of such corset related injuries were…exaggerated.

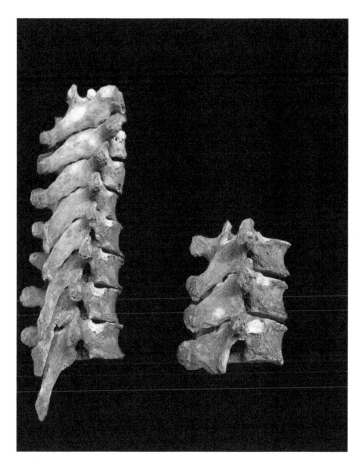

Photo 5.5   Right side view of vertebrae T1–T8 and T10–T12 of FAO90 1637 (Photo © Museum of London)

The third and final type of discourse I will discuss in this book is created by the privilege mistakenly granted to medicine and doctors by European peoples of the time, and their American descendants. In modern Euro-American discourse, authority figures, most particularly doctors, are automatically given higher credence than their patients. This begins with the expectation that years of study, explicitly the study and knowledge of the internal workings of the body, implies that their interpretation of symptoms and disorders is of a more pure and

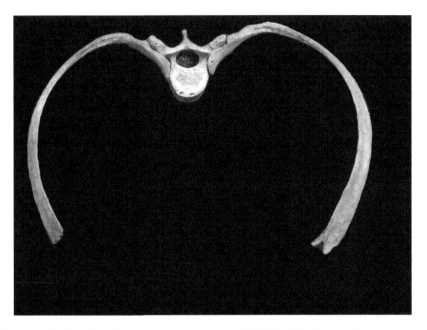

Photo 5.6   Vertebra T4 and associated ribs of FAO90 1637 (Photo © Museum of London)

unbiased nature than the knowledge or interpretation of the patients. However, that expectation is not necessarily a rational one, particularly in the case of doctors during the time period of 1700–1900. Medicine was just moving out of the barber shop and into the university at the beginning of this time period. Whatever their faults, however, doctors did know more about the technical side of things than nondoctors.

Many doctors were taught anatomy by men who bought the demonstration corpses from grave robbers, and who were still using Vesalius' illustrations of the uterus which had dual protrusions, or "horns." Human uteri do not contain these structures, but Vesalius was not dissecting humans—he drew his illustrations from dogs or pigs, who do indeed have bifid uteri. This functional lack of understanding about female anatomy over several hundred years eventually led to a Freudian type dismissal of women's problems as "hysterical," and indicates that we need to take a closer look at any medical literature about corseting that was produced during the time. One work in particular stands out among the many that exist: that of Ludovic O'Followell, which was written at the tail end of the time period, 1908.

O'Followell's full length book on the evils of corseting begins by detailing the 46 symptoms of corseting, many of which have considerable overlap with Freud's symptoms of hysteria, showing their common origins in the misunderstandings of the female physiognomy. Yet, several of the symptoms which O'Followell outlines have no basis in their potential ability to have been caused by a corset. He follows that list with a demand for laws to be passed in regard to women who corset, outlining fines and other punishments, including jail time. Finally, he deconstructs the female body, taking a system-by-system approach to the damage done when she chooses to corset. He does not explain his experimental parameters, nor does he have a control group, and his book is bracketed on either side by advertisements…for corsets.

To finish this chapter, I push back at just one of his notions—that the corset regularly kills its wearer. While it is impossible to gain the life-history of all the women whose skeletons I have examined, it is possible to create an age profile for each of these skeletons, and to say a few things about that age profile and what it shows about longevity. Despite the osteological paradox (more on that momentarily) longevity is one marker of health, specifically of health-resilience—the ability to bounce back from injury and/or illness. Many of the women had skeletal markers of pathologies though few had more than one or two, and many had other indicators of old age, such as osteoporosis. Had the corset been a killer, the St. Bride's population would have skewed much younger, demographically.

Doctors and Their Anti-Female Prejudice

To understand the origin of certain highly prejudicial ideas about corsetry, one must look back to Ambroise Paré, who used metal corsets in his medical practice "to amend the crookednesse of the bodie" (Cotes 1649,

p. 582, as cited in Steele 2001/2011, p. 5). Used on men and women both, as corrective devices for problems with the back (most likely scoliosis), Paré also believed that tight clothing could create deformities where none had existed before. It is in his work where we see what may be the first distinction between medical corseting and fashion corseting, and the concept that what can cure may also cause.

It is also through Paré that we first see the idea that the corset can kill. Quoting his Case Reports and Autopsy Records (in Steele 2001), he writes of a woman "…bound and compressed in her wedding dress, came from the altar after having taken bread and wine in the accustomed manner, thinking to return to her place, fell rigidly dead from suffocation…" (ibid., p. 13). Paré was a contemporary of Vesalius, the legendary anatomist of the 1500 s who created illustrations of the human body that were used for centuries to come. Medical knowledge of the day was not standardized or formulized (Fitzharris 2017), and did not become so until after teaching hospitals were established in the mid-1800s. Before then, two types of doctors were sought to treat or cure what ailed people: apothecaries, and surgeons.

Apothecaries, the precursors to pharmacists, dealt in the powder and tincture realm of medicinal treatment. You would visit one for herbal or chemical treatments, and for things that were not obviously surgical in nature—what we currently understand as viruses, certain bacterial infections, inflammations, and skin complaints, mostly. Surgeons, on the other hand, were used to remove limbs and diseased organs if either were potentially deadly, or to perform Caesarian sections to potentially save a child. Their track record for actually healing a person was…not great (Aptowicz 2014; Fitzharris 2017). I have outlined the reasons for this above, but they are worth restating: anesthesia was not widely understood or used before the late 1800s, and doctors who expressed the radical idea that surgeons should clean their instruments between dissecting corpses and operating on living humans were laughed out of their operating theaters (ibid.). People can and do die from shock caused by pain, and between that and the rampant infections caused by non-sterile conditions, the injury or disease had to be life-threatening already before a surgeon was consulted.

However, that is not to say that doctors, surgical or not, did not possess specialized knowledge. They definitely did, and while consulting a surgeon may have been the last resort, it was still an option pursued by many and respected by most. This two-hundred-year period saw the development of medical and surgical theory grow by leaps and bounds, with the likes of Joseph Lister's development of cleaning techniques, and Thomas Dent Mütter's adoption of anesthetic, as well as his invention of plastic surgery—the techniques he developed to treat burn victims are still used today. These developments and others like them allowed people to survive surgery much more frequently, as well as allowing surgeons to gain understandings of female anatomy that were not possible by the mere study of corpses and Vesalius' drawings.

What makes the use of cadavers for anatomical study particularly problematic? Partially, the fact that women were used as cadavers far less than men. This stemmed from the history of anatomical studies in England. Historically, there were three main ways to acquire anatomical cadavers for use by hospitals and medical schools: donation; deaths of those who had in some way forfeited their claim on burial, be that via dying intestate with no relatives or being sentenced to death by the state (Dwight 1896); or grave robbing.

Donation was not a popular option. Although philosopher Jeremy Bentham (Jenkins 2011, p. 107) did will his body to an anatomist, he stated that he did so to show that rich people as well as poor had contributions to make to medical science. Instrumental in creating the Anatomy Act of 1832, he was also a religious outlier for the time, being a nonbeliever in anything resembling an afterlife. Christian belief in heaven and/or hell made people less likely to donate their bodies, seeing that certain teachings required the body to be as intact as possible for bodily assumption into heaven. Bentham wished his body to be studied, and then preserved and displayed in the halls of University College London, which it was for a while, until pranks from students led to the museum temporarily removing it from display (Doughty 2017). Bentham has since been restored to his place in the halls, after a specially designed display was built to hold the remains and ensure that they are undisturbed by high-spirited students (UCL 2020).

The second way that people became medical cadavers was also unpopular, and happened much less frequently to women: the death penalty. With anatomy laws creating this as a "legitimate" way to acquire cadavers, and therefore knowledge, the demographics of dissection skewed to the male. Women simply did not commit capital crimes in large numbers, despite gaining great notoriety when they did (Flanders 2011; Walkowitz 1992).

Finally, grave robbing was a definite way for women to end up on the cadaver dissection table, yet doctors were often unconcerned with creating a balanced number of sexes in their studies. This became a recursive cycle, with lack of knowledge of the anatomical differences between men and women creating the idea that those differences are immaterial, which then in turn created a lack of desire to work on women as a subject separate from men (Aptowicz 2014; Fitzharris 2017). Yet, eventually, women's medicine did become a specialized subject, and J. Marion Sims is known as the father of modern gynecology (ibid.). It should be noted, however, that Sims began practicing in 1835, almost ¾ of the way through our period under consideration.

To bring the data on doctors and their views on corseting to the late 1800s, the medical paper by Robert Dickinson, a doctor of obstetrics in New York, titled "The Corset: Questions of Pressure and Displacement" (1887) discusses the distinct physical effect of the corset on the body. What immediately stands out about this work is that he did not take photos of his subjects, but instead used shadows and projections to make drawings of women both in and out of their corsets. While I understand the lack of x-ray, used heavily after its invention by O'Followell, but unavailable in 1887, I do not understand why there are no photographs at all in this work. Drawings are, because of the fallibility of the human hand and eye, unreliable and inconsistent. These drawings, along with later ones by O'Followell and Witkowsky, are stylized and generic, showing what he believes would occur to the organs of a corseted woman. Unlike O'Followell, however, Dickinson does not appear to have done his own autopsies to discover what, if any, organ displacement actually occurred.

O'Followell and His Treatise on Corsets[2]

The bulk of my analysis is focused on Ludovic O'Followell's 1908 treatise on corseting. Used in two of the three main cultural histories of corseting (Kunzle 1982; Steele 2001), and referenced in countless popular culture circles, O'Followell is considered the go-to resource on what corseting does to a body, and as he published at the end of our time period, he can be considered the culmination of medical knowledge. His work borrows from and summarizes much of the other opinions, knowledge, and illustrations used by other physicians before him. Written in 1908, his textbook is assumed to be in the common domain (although it is not), and thus assumed free to use for illustrations, leading his x-rays and drawings to be spread across the internet. There are several problems with this distribution and its use by corseting scholars, however: although the written text has also been digitized and put on the internet, it is rarely referenced; the photos, drawings, and x-rays are mostly, for various reasons, inaccurate or misleading; O'Followell's disdain for women who corseted veritably bleeds from the text, rendering the illustrations even more suspect; and the overall book is sandwiched between advertisements for the very product the book is devoted to lambasting—fashionable, tight-laceable corsets.

O'Followell outlines each section of the body and how the corset affects it. However, it is impractical to make a full survey of all the above. I will instead concentrate on three facets for analysis: the verbs associated with the women who corseted vs. the corset itself, and how he perpetuates the idea that the women lack agency; his list of symptoms of corseting damage, which share considerable overlap with the symptoms of hysteria; and extreme dimensions suggested by the advertisements and how they differ from the dimensions of women who actually corseted.

---

[2]Regrettably, due to French copyright laws, O'Followell's works are not yet in the public domain, and so all illustrations from Le Corset have been described rather than shown. the author sends her apologies, and a promise to release a second edition pending demand when the copyright is lifted.

In O'Followell's (1908) opening information and first chapter, five main areas stand out as needed for analysis: (1) Page 13, which contains a list of symptoms of corseting damage. (2) Collocations (words used in proximity to a chosen word) of violent verbs, adjectives, and adverbs near the word corset or its cognate stand-ins throughout the preface and body of Chapter 1 (Preface—16). (3) The use of metaphor and agentive behavior when speaking about the corset, as illustrated by a passage on page 13. (4) A proposed law regarding the use and sale of corsets on page 14. And finally, (5) the advertisements for corsets that bracket the body of the book. It is in this portion of the book that O'Followell sets the tone for the entire book and gives the reader some much needed information about his attitudes toward corseting and toward women. First, I examine what he believes corsets do to the female body:

Example 1: Symptoms of Corseting Damage

A scary picture again, but the author would have been even darker if he had read the page of Bouvier with which he was unconcerned, it is true, with those who wear bad corsets: slices near the armpits, difficulty with the venous circulation of the upper limbs, accidents resulting in the compression of the brachial plexus, flattening, crumpling of the breasts and diverse maladies of the lymph nodes or the mammary glands, extreme difficulty of certain movements, weakening and atrophy of compromised or inactive muscles, pressing down and permanent overlapping of the lower ribs, restriction of the lower part of the thorax, reduction of the cavities of the chest and the abdomen, repression of the diaphragm, compression of the lungs, the heart, the stomach, the liver, and the other abdominal viscera, above all after a meal, more or less difficulty with breathing and speech, and at the very least aggravation of the lungs, disposed to coughing up blood, palpitations of the heart, syncope, circulatory difficulty returning the blood to the veins of the heart, embarrassment in the circulation of the head and the neck, frequent congestion in the upper genitals [Ed. note: I am not certain what this refers to; maybe absent periods…], difficulty using the muscles which have become languorous, digestive lesions (ulcers), indigestion, nausea, vomiting, slowness and easy interruption of the matter in the shrunken intestine, deformation, displacement of the liver and swelling in the vertical dimension abutting the iliac fossa, reduction of the other senses and depression moreover in substance, difficulty in abdominal circulation, prolapse of the uterus, troubles menstruating and, in the enlarged state (pregnancy), disposition towards abortion (miscarriage), with uterine hemorrhage, etc., etc. Such is the incomplete picture of the harmful effects that one can produce with the same corsets of today, badly constructed and badly applied. (1908, p. 13)[3]

This list, which O'Followell sees as incomplete, contains 46 individual symptoms associated with corseting. One line, however, seems more significant than all the symptoms combined, the attribution of these problems "qu'au port de mauvais corsets" (1908, p. 13). If there is a mauvais (bad) corset, there must be a salutaire (beneficial) or utile (useful) corset. And in this case, the responsibility is not on the doctor who treats the woman, or on the corsetier who dresses the woman, but the woman herself, those women "qu'au port de mauvais corset." Here we see a creation of the women into bad subjects, people who are in effect harming themselves by badly expressing their womanhood.

---

[3]Tableau effrayant déja, mais que son auteur aurait pu assombrir encore s'il avait lu cette page de Bouvier qui ne s'applique, il est vrai, qu'au port de mauvais corsets: excoriations au voisinage des aisselles, gène de la circulation veineuse des membres supérieurs, accidents résultant de la compression du plexus brachial, aplatissement, froissement de seins et maladies diverses de ganglions lymphatiques ou des glandes mammaires, affaissement, déformations ou excoriations des mamelons, difficulté extrême de certain mouvements, affaiblissement et atrophie des muscles comprimés ou inactifs, abaissemet et rapprochement permanent des côtes inférieures, rétrécissement de la bas du thorax, reduction des cavités de la poitrine et de l'abdomen, refoulement du diaphragme, compression des poumons, du coeur, de l'estomac, du foie et des autres visères abdominaux, surtout après les repas, d'où la gène plus ou moins grande de la respiration et de la parole, aggravation des moindres affections pulmonaires, disposition à l'hémoptysie, palpitations de coeur, syncopes, difficulté du retour du sange veineux au coeur, embarrass dans la circulation de la tête et du cou, congestion fréquet aux parties supérieures, efforts musculaires difficiles ou langereux, lesions des fonctions digestives, gastralgie, nausées, vomissments, lenteur et interruption facile du cours des matières dans l'intestin rétréci, deformation, déplacement du foie augmenté dans son diameter vertical et repoussé vers la fosse iliaque, réduit dans les autres sens et déprimé en outre dans da substance, gene de la circulation abdominale, abaissement de l'utérus, troubles de la mentruation et, dans l'état de grossesse, disposition à l'avortement, aux hémorragies utérines, etc., etc. Tel est le tableau incomplet des effets nuisibles que peuvent produire même les corsets d'aujourd'hui, mal construits ou mal appliqués.

The mauvais corset was a choice, and so they could choose not to wear it, and so they were both liable for their own health problems, and crazy for continuing to wear something that so harmed them. This reinforces the perceived connection between corseting and hysteria—a tight-laced woman was a woman who was not in her right mind. Furthermore, if the woman miscarried, it was implicitly her own fault, because it was publicly known that tight corseting caused disposition à l'avortement, aux hémorragies utérines. And that word, "caused," needs more unpacking. The corset, a garment, was said to cause the woman to have such a predisposition. This is not the only attribution of agency that O'Followell gives to the corset, as shown by the next example.

Example 2: Violent Verbs

This section contains the list of all verbs collocated ± 8 words from "corset":

abuse (2), accuse (2), atrophy, attribute, constrict, conserve, consider, cry, critique, be the cause, degenerate, destined, determine, become, direct, against, drive (2), envelope, harm, excoriate, existe, function, rail against, need, reform, play, fall ill, watch, die (2), mold, not dangerous, cannot be, permit (2), lose, wear (5), press, produce, recommend, make, reproach (2), continue, apply to oneself, will be (punished) (2) (1), if she is pregnant, if she is wearing, succumb, surveil, tolerate. (ibid.)[4]

Here we can see what the corset does: atrophies, constricts, conserves, is the cause of, causes degeneration, determines, trains, envelopes, is

---

[4]abuser (2), accuser (2), atrophier, attribuer, constricter, conserver, considerer, crier, critiquer, être la cause, dégénérer, destiner, determiner, devenir, diriger, contre, entrainer (2), enveloper, néfaster, excoriater, exister, fonctioner, fulminer (contre), falloir (2), reformer, jouer, maux, montre, morir (2), moule, n'est pas dangereux, ne pouvent etre, parmi (2), perdre, porter (5), presser, produire, recommander, render, reprocher (2), rester, s'applique, sera (puni) (2) (1), soit à la grossesse, soit au port, succomber, surveiller, tolèrer, (cause de maladies a) revenir.

harmful, excoriates, functions reforms, plays a role, molds, is not dangerous, presses, produces, renders, causes maladies of circulation. And here we can see what women do: abuse, cry, degenerate, are destined to, have ailments, die, lose, carry, apply, are punished, have pregnancies, wear, succumb.

Of the 45 individual verbs located near "corset" in the preface and first chapter of O'Followell's work, 29 are violent or harmful. These verbs can then be broken down into two categories, actions by the corset, actions by women, and what people say in regard to the corset. In these categories, 13 verbs relate to harmful effects of the corset, 8 verbs relate to self-harmful actions by women, 7 verbs relate to O'Followell or others speaking against the corset, and finally 2 relate to keeping watch on the corset. In terms of giving agency to the corset, it is interesting to note that 60% more verbs deal with what the corset does than with the women who wore it. Additionally, as a percentage of the total amount, 65% of the verbs which deal with the corset are violent or harmful, and 61% of those which deal with women are as well. Clearly, O'Followell and Dr. Lion (author of the preface) both ascribe considerable agency to the corset, and a lack of the same to the woman. To continue that discussion, it is necessary to look at a specific passage on page 13.

Example 3: Agency and Metaphor

It is believed, since there have been four hundred years of the corset molding the form of femininity, the most gracious half of the human race has degenerated to the point that [the artifices of the clothiers are] rendered indispensable the artifices of the clothiers are [rendered indispensable] to conserve the appearance of beauty. The corset, it atrophies the articulations of the vertebral column, giving most of their contemporaries a round back, inelegant shoulders, and making them swing their hips at home, the "[duck] march" that Schopenhauer saw as characteristic of villains of the beautiful sex. According to one statistic given by Monsieur P. Maréchal, regarding 100 young women wearing the corset: 25 will succumb to illnesses of the lungs (consumption); 15 will die during their first childbirth and 15 more will acquire in their first childbirth mortal injuries; 15 will suffer diverse illnesses, and only 30 will preserve their health intact. (1908, p. 13)[5]

In regard to agency, the corset, an inanimate object, is given agentive powers—it molds the form of the woman. This has the effect of also partially removing agency from the woman. She is acted upon by this garment which she has put on, and that choice, to wear the corset, leads to the degeneration of the entire sex. Furthermore, in subsequent lines the corset agentively conserves the appearance of beauty in women. And yet, it also takes that away, by atrophying the vertebrae, rounding the back, making the shoulders inelegant, and making the woman duck walk. Yet even when the women's health, rather than the corset, is under discussion, they are not agents—instead, non-agentive verb forms are used: They "will succumb," "will die," "will acquire," and "will suffer," all things that happen to them rather than them playing an active role. The only agentive verb form is slightly disingenuous, as they "will preserve their health intact," which seems to imply "despite wearing the corset." Thusly, women need to be protected from the corset—protected from themselves—by a law.

Example 4: A Proposed Law

First article—it is forbidden for all women thirty years or younger, to wear the corset, the waist-cincher, or the bustier or overbust corset. All women convinced to put on such clothing will be punished with one to

---

[5]A l'en croire, depuis quatre cents ans que le corset moule la plastique feminine, la plus gracieuse moitié du genre humain a dégénéré au point de render indispensables les artifices des couturiers pour conserve quelque apparence de beauté. Le corset, en atrophiant les articulations de la colonne vertébraie, donne à la plupart de nos contemporaines un dos rond, des épaules inégales, et provoque chez elles ce déhanchement, cette "marche en canard" que Schopenhauer regardait comme une des vilaines caractéristiques du beau sexe. D'après une statistique, donnée par M. P. Maréchal. sur 100 jeunes filles portant corset: 25 sont destinées à succomber des maladies de poitrine; 15 mourront pendant leur premier accouchement et 15 autres garderont de ce premier accouchement des infirmités mortelles; 15 souffriront de maladies diverses, et 30 seulement pourront conserver leur santé intacte.

three months in prison; the power of the punishment will be raised to one year if the delinquent is pregnant. If the delinquent is a minor and lives with her parents, they will be, moreover, be charged a fine of 100 to 1.000 francs.

Second article.—All women over thirty, at the date of the passing of the present law, raised wearing the corset in whatever manner they please, may continue to do so except during pregnancy.

Third article.—The selling of corsets will be rigorously regulated; all vendors are required to note the name, age and address of the buyer in a special register, statutory, they're required to be presented at the request of the authorities. If the age of the buyer inscribed in the statutory register is reported as younger than the legal age aforementioned above, the vender will be punished by the confiscation of the corsets contained in their shop and a fine of 100 to 1.000 francs. In the case of recidivism an additional penalty of the same size will be inflicted upon them, they will be incurring a punishment of 15 days to three months in prison, and they will be forbidden to make their living in the same industry and from selling corsets. (16)[6]

While O'Followell never specifically condemns or condones this potential law, it fits rather well into the overall structure of the preface and first chapter. It is the creation of the good subject by force of the justice system, the creation of the woman who corseted like she should (either after 30, when she was done with childbearing) or not at all. In the opinion of this proposed law, women of childbearing age needed the

---

[6]Article premier.—Il est interdit à toute femme âgée de moins de trente ans, de porter corset, ceinture-corset, ou cuirasse-corset. Toute femme convaincue d'avoir d'endossé un de ces appareils sera punie de un à trois mois de prison; la peine pourra être élevée à un an si la délinquante est en état de grossesse. Si la délinquante est mineure et habite chez ses parents, ces derniers seront, en outre, condamnés à une amende de 100 à 1.000 francs.

Article 2.—Toute femme âgée de trente ans révolus, à dater du jour de la promulgation de la présente loi, pourra porter un corset de tel modèle qu'il lui plaira, hors cependant durant l'état de grossesse.

Article 3.—La vente du corset sera rigoureusement surveillée; tout vendeur devra noter le nom, l'âge et l'adresse de l'acheteuse sur un register special, réglementaire, lequel devra être présenté à toute requisition des autorités. Si l'âge de l'acheteuse inscrit sur le registre réglementaire était constaté inférieur à l'âge legal précité ci-dessus, le vendeur sera puni de la confiscation des corsets contenus dans ses magasins et d'une amende de 100 à 1.000 francs. En cas de récidive, en outre des mêmes peines qui lui seront infligées, il sera puni de quinze jours à trois mois de prison, et il lui sera interdit de se livrer par la suite à l'industrie et à la vente des corversets.

law's protection, while the law stopped caring once the woman reached the age where she was considered past interest.

This age was marked as "over thirty, at the date of the passing of the present law," (ibid.), and indicated that any woman who grew up in the tradition of the corset would be able to continue using it if she were over 30, unless she were pregnant. This shows that protection of fetal life, rather than the comfort of the woman, was the object of proposing the law. Data is unavailable on the topic of average age of menopause during this time. However, as with the rest of the "female problems" approached by doctors, menopause was only beginning to be studied, medicalized, and pathologized, (Lock and Nguyen 2010, p. 51).

The assumption, potentially based on average life expectancy (Our World In Data), which will be shown to be problematic in the next chapter, and on false notions about the potential for fertility after a certain age, may have been that a woman would experience a sharp drop in both at 30, so who would care if she corseted? O'Followell views the corseted women as merely misguided, albeit unwomanly, women (bad subjects), who need to be educated in the ways of not lacing themselves too tightly, for look what it does to their children and their body (in the next 14 chapters of his book!)

This patronizing attitude is then reinforced in the final lines of Chapter 1, where he states: "I think, in effect, that this book is not written only for doctors, and I do not wish to again see all the female doctors setting up corset shops, because I think that would oblige all corset makers to frequent doctors" (1908, p. 16).[7] Specifically, the use of "les femmes-médicins" (female doctors) connotes sarcasm and the hegemonic patriarchal ideology for which this time period is famous, but also the phrase "livre n'est pas écrit seulement pour des médicins" shows that he intends women to read this book, and, as they should learn to be better women thereby. It does not appear to occur to him that women who pursued the practice of medicine might be attempting disidentification, only that they were bad subjects.

---

[7] J'estime, en effet, que ce livre n'est pas écrit seulement pour des médicins, et je ne souhaite pas plus voir toutes les femmes-médicins s'installer corsetières, que je ne songe à obliger toutes les corsetières à se faire recevoir médecins.

Example 5: Advertisements for Corsets

If, as we see in the previous parts of the document, O'Followell and Lion are contemptuously patriarchal toward women who wear their corsets tight-laced, that they give the corset agency considerably more than the women, and that their use of metaphor shows that women are both childlike, and in need of being shaped by the corset away from nature and toward a more culturally acceptable form, what then are we to make of the advertisements, which are situated directly after the frontispiece at the beginning of the book? The drawn corseted women have approximately the same aspect ratios when comparing bust or hip size to waist size—1:.41. Today's modern "ideal" ratio is 1:.7 as mentioned in Chapters 2 and 3, and the average of the corsets I examined was much closer to the ideal.

Additionally, the only photograph in the advertisements, on the ad for the new and improved medical corset, has the 1:.7 aspect ratio. The 1:.41 ratio would mean that a woman with a 24-inch waist, or a slender but anatomically normal build, would have to have 58.5 inch bust and hip measurements, in order to be accurately represented in these drawings.

There are two advertisements which specifically mention medical corsets, only one of which shows the anatomical model. The other shows four corsets, each which is purported to treat a certain malady—corset "le rêve" (en bandes de tissue élastique); corset "Ophélia" (Affections de l'Abdomen); corset "le radieux" (Coupe anatomique); corset du D'Namy (Maladies de l'Estomac). While these are vouched for by a doctor in the ad, the pictures with them, showing the unrealistic and extreme tight-lacing, are targeted toward women's egos.

Yet the medical advertisement seems to actually want to help women with scoliosis or other spinal problems. Looking at the accompanying text, the corset "employés...au traitement," (employs as a treatment). It "n'exerce qu'une pression péripherique" (doesn't' exert peripheral pressure) on the organs, and, "à leviers," (with levers) it moves the body into proper alignment. In the eyes of this advertiser, the only good corset is a mechanical one, active, and lever based. And the only good subject is one who employs a good corset.

The good majority of the rest of the advertisements either mention fashion (mode), price (prix), or that they are "l'Orthopedie Dernières Élégances" (the last word in orthopedic elegance). Finally, one ad's illustration does not match the product it sells; it shows a woman in Greek drapery, rather than a corset. The French carried a romanticized ideal of their Greek and Roman roots, demonstrated by stylized visions of the French state represented by their female champion "Marianne," which every shopper would certainly recognize as a visual cognate when viewing this ad. Furthermore, this comes closer to a feminine ideal, as the illustration implies that their corsets are looser, closer to nature, but still stylish and womanly. It is the Venus de Milo all over again.

One caveat remains, however. I am unfamiliar with publishing practices of early twentieth-century Paris, but I am somewhat familiar with those of today. Potentially, O'Followell may not have had complete control, or any control, for that matter, over the advertisements used to bookend his work. Therefore, I am not claiming that the oddness of the aspect ratio, the allusion to Greco-Roman origins, and the heavily medicalized final ad were his idea or were added with his knowledge or approval, merely that the audience for this book was both financially empowered women, and male medical students, and that the advertisements and the text are in disaccord with each other.

Other Physicians

Overall, the literature shows that doctors saw women as passive dupes of fashion, giving agency to the corset and, if any at all was ascribed to the women, limiting the women's participation to the idea that she was wont to follow fashion without comprehending what unnatural things it wrought on her body. Literally said to mold her (O'Followell 1908) or straighten her body to culturally appropriate dimensions (Paré in Kunzle 1982), the corset served a dual role—that of the appropriate civilized form, creating proper womanhood, and that of the tight-laced scourge of female health. And this was not confined to O'Followell and Paré.

In 1875, French physician Paul Vaissette completed his doctoral studies on the topic of "L'Usage Prématuré et Abusif du Corset"

(Vaissette), a 43-page discussion on using corsets too early or wrongly. William B. Neftel, MD, ascribed a greater tendency to tuberculosis to women who corseted in his essay "Some Considerations on the Pathogenesis of Disease in Women" (1887). "Le Corset: Être Physiologique et Pratique" by Dr. Gaches-Sarraute (1900) has much of the same illustration as O'Followell's book—the main difference between them is that O'Followell lends an historic angle to his study, whereas Gaches-Sarraute does not. Also, O'Followell is widely used today, whereas I had to do some digging to find Gaches-Sarraute's text, showing how history is created by those documents that survive.

Were I to enumerate upon every single study found on the effects of corseting on the liver, lungs, stomach, and uterus, this would quickly become a laundry list of such works. There are so many that they can be divided into categories:

For imprecations about the corset in general: (Anonymous 1829b, 1741, 1887; Dickinson 1887; Gaches-Sarraute 1900; Nottingham 1841; Smith 1827; Vaissette 1875).

Doctors decrying the practice of tight-lacing in general: (Anonymous 1829b, 1890a, 1890b; Carter 1846; Fowler 1844; 1870; Sherry 1871; Young 1860).

Effects on the liver: (Collins 1888; Corbin 1830; McWhinnie 1861; Murchison 1877).

On the stomach: (Anonymous 1829a; Chapotot 1892; Corbin 1830).

Correlation of tuberculosis and other diseases: (Klebs 1909; Neftel 1887).

Death under chloroform: (Anonymous 1890c).

And problems with the uterus and ovaries: (Cleland 1880).

And this was by no means an exhaustive list—of the 74 articles, chapters, opinion pieces, and books mentioned as being created by doctors and listed in O'Brien's helpful bibliography of dress and health, these were the ones that I could access from various libraries. These are the ones that survived. But they do not tell the whole story. The story told by the above sources is one in which doctors are seen as the ultimate authority, and they believe in their own authority, but discount the lived experiences of women. If we look only at the doctor's words on corseting, we will see women as in constant internal agony, as living short lives of silent suffering, all of which can be tied to the corset.

While we cannot reach back into time and ask the women themselves, we can deconstruct the symptoms that were listed. To return to O'Followell, who is the most often quoted of these doctors and the most well known today (Kunzle 1982; Summers 2001; Steele 2001/2011), the symptoms at issue are these (in a cleaned repeat of the list above, divided by organ system):

Skin: cuts in the armpits; flattening of the breasts.

Lymphatic: diverse maladies of the lymph nodes or the mammary glands.

Circulatory: difficulty with the venous circulation of the upper limbs; compression of the heart; palpitations of the heart; syncope; circulatory difficulty returning the blood to the veins of the heart; embarrassment in the circulation of the head and the neck; difficulty in abdominal circulation.

Skeletal: pressing down and permanent overlapping of the lower ribs.

Nervous: accidents resulting in the compression of the brachial plexus.

Muscular: extreme difficulty of certain movements; weakening and atrophy of compromised or inactive muscles; difficulty using the muscles which have become languorous.

Pulmonary: repression of the diaphragm; compression of the lungs; more or less difficulty with breathing and speech; aggravation of the lungs; disposed to coughing up blood.

Digestive: compression of the stomach, the liver, and the other abdominal viscera, above all after a meal; digestive lesions (ulcers); indigestion; nausea; vomiting; slowness and easy interruption of the matter in the shrunken intestine; deformation, displacement of the liver and swelling in the vertical dimension abutting the iliac fossa.

Reproductive: frequent congestion in the upper genitals; prolapse of the uterus; troubles menstruating; in the enlarged state (pregnancy), disposition toward abortion (miscarriage), with uterine hemorrhage.

Mental: Substantial depression.

Miscellaneous: restriction of the lower part of the thorax; reduction of the cavities of the chest and the abdomen.

Basically, all but a few of these have multiple causes **other** than corseting. A few, as discussed above, are symptoms of tuberculosis, (though, recall, that was blamed on corseting too). Looking at a few systems, we now, in 2020, have diagnoses for these problems. Over-parturition accounts for uterine prolapse, extreme shifts in weight or malnutrition do the same for lack of periods, genetic issues, or a family predisposition can make someone more prone to miscarriage and hemorrhage. Malnutrition was rampant during this time, and it can also account for almost all the digestive symptoms, as well as muscle atrophy and heart palpitations. One possible explanation for much of the liver damage observed by the doctors is non-cirrhotic portal fibrosis, which comprised of both fatty liver degradation and of lobes and veins where they perhaps should not have been, and the biggest cause of the condition was low-level arsenic poisoning (Mazumder 2001). This type of liver disease was not isolated from its fellows until 1956 (*Gut* 1989). The lone skeletal symptom, the only thing on the list that is definitively corseting damage, is somewhat accurate, although in the Musée de l'Homme collection I saw only skeletal *cartilage* overlapping itself, not the individual ribs.

Even when women were able to move more into the public sphere and speak about their own health, their words were discounted, ridiculed, or decried as satire. Some saw Lord's (1868) long book on corseting and tight-lacing through history, in which he reproduced positive letters about the experience, as "shamelessly biased" (Kunzle 1982, p. 225). Yet why is a production of such kind any more biased than long monographs by doctors purporting to show the harm of corsets? O'Followell's book extolled the virtues of "modern" steel-boned corsets, while lambasting the practice of using older ones, and bias can be found on every page, whether he is comparing the natural female form to that of various Venus figures, or using x-rays to show how much less impactful "modern" corsets are to the figure. Furthermore, O'Followell, Paré, and Fowler do not use women's writings in their publications, nor do they make reference to what women report as their own experiences. Instead, they use scientific (or pseudo-scientific, in Fowler's case) examinations of what they see as physical trauma to speak for the woman, without considering that change to the body may not be traumatic.

However, if we harken back to the beginning of this chapter, we can ignore the doctors and their maledictions for a moment to discuss one biomarker of relative health—longevity.

But Did They Die Young?

To link this question to the skeletal research done for this study, it is necessary to look more closely at the relative age ranges of the women in both skeletal collections—the St. Bride's collection on which this book is focused, and the Musée de l'Homme collection to which I compared it. This runs into the osteological paradox—any indication of disease or disability that can be read in the skeleton is not necessarily an indicator of poor health, it can be either that, or it could conversely indicate resilience. After all, the person lived long enough to survive what ailed them, and for that ailment to leave skeletal damage. However, barring cases of disorders which prematurely age the skeleton (progeria type diseases), if a skeleton can be aged, then we can speak about the longevity of the individual.

While longevity is not the only marker for quality of life, and it is possible to live far past the age's life expectancy and be summarily miserable, it is one marker by which anthropologists, doctors, and the general public all identify that quality of life is present and/or has improved. When discussing things such as sanitation, pharmaceutical developments, air and water cleanliness, and other developmental factors that impact health, longevity is also discussed as a way to indicate that such factors have positively benefited humanity. It is also one of the only relatively reliable things which can be read in skeletal health. The presence of a de-fleshed skeleton by definition indicates a life-ending event, yet as the osteological paradox indicates, not every traumatic or life-changing event is life-ending, and one cannot truly discern life quality from life quantity. Yet it is possible to contrast what doctors say happened to women who corseted (in terms of life expectancy) to what the skeletal record shows. The next chapter will detail the longevity of the women in St. Bride's Lower Churchyard, and Chapter 7 will discuss the skeletal evidence of that longevity in detail.

Bibliography

Anonymous. (1741). Sur les Mauvais Effets de l'Usage des Corps a Baleine. *Histoire de l'Academie Royale des Sciences*, 76–77.

Anonymous. (1829a, September 15). Godman on Tight Lacing; Injurious Effects of Tight Lacing on the Organs and Functions of Respiration, Digestion, Circulation, etc. *The Boston Medical and Surgical Journal, 2*(31), 1–4.

Anonymous. (1829b, June 30). On the Pernicious, and Often Fatal Effects, of the Compression of the Female Waist by the Use of Corsets. *The Kaleidoscope; or, Literary and Scientific Mirror, 9*(470), 425–426.

Anonymous. (1887, December 10). Evil Effects Produced by the Corset. *Medical and Surgical Reporter, 57*(24), 786.

Anonymous. (1890a, June 14). Death from Tight Lacing. *The Lancet*, 1316.

Anonymous. (1890b, August 22). Death from Tight Lacing. *Science, 16*(394), 107.

Anonymous. (1890c, March 22). Experiments of the Hyderabad Commission on Tight-Lacing as a Cause of Death in Chloroform Anaesthesia. *The Lancet*, 662.

Aptowicz, C. (2014). *Dr. Mütter's Marvels*. New York, NY: Penguin.

Barthes, R. (1967). *The Fashion System* (M. Ward & R. Howard, Trans.). Berkeley: The University of California Press,

Carter, T. (1846, August). The Morbid Effects of Tight-Lacing. *The Western Journal of Medicine and Surgery, 6*(2).

Chapotot, E. (1892). *Déviations, Dislocations, Troubles Fonctionnels de l'Estomac Provoqués par le Corset*. Paris: J.-B. Bailliére et Fils.

Cleland. (1880, February). Tight Lacing, Venous Congestions, and Atrophy of the Ovaries. *Glasgow Medical Journal, 13*(2), 89–92.

Collins, W. (1888, March 17). The Effect of Tight Lacing upon the Secretion of Bile. *The Lancet*, 518.

Corbin, E. (1830, April 24). Des Effets Prôduit par les Corsets sur les Organes de l'Abdomen, et en Particulier sur le Foie. *Gazette Médicale de Paris, 1*(17), 151–153.

Dickinson, R. (1887). The Corset: Questions of Pressure and Displacement. *New York Medical Journal*.

Doughty, C. (2017). *Iconic Corpse: The Head of Jeremy Bentham*. https://www.youtube.com/watch?v=9FvYfuwZvyY.

Dwight, T. (1896). *Anatomy Laws Versus Body-Snatching in Forum*, 493.

Fitzharris, L. (2017). *The Butchering Art: Joseph Lister's Quest to Transform the Grisly World of Victorian Medicine*. New York, NY: Macmillan.

Flanders, J. (2011). *The Invention of Murder: How the Victorians Revelled in Death and Detection and Created Modern Crime*. New York, NY: Macmillan.

Fowler, O. (1844). *Fowler's Works on Education and Self-Improvement; Cultivation of the Memory and Intellect; on Matrimony; Hereditary Descent, Its Laws and Facts; Natural Religion; Temperance, and Tight Lacing. All Founded on Phrenology and Physiology*. New York, NY: Fowler.

Fowler, O. (1870). *Sexual Science; Including Manhood, Womanhood, and Their Mutual Interrelations; Love its Laws, Power, etc., Selection or Mutual Adaptation; Married Life Made Happy; Reproduction, and Progenal Endowment, or Paternity, Maternity, Bearing, Nursing, and Rearing Children; Puberty, Girlhood, etc.; Sexual Ailments Restored, Female Beauty Perpetuated, etc., etc. As Taught by Phrenology*. Philadelphia, PA: National Publishing Company.

Gaches-Sarraute. (1900). *Le Corset: Étude Physiologique et Pratique*. Paris: Masson.

Gut. (1989). Progress Report: Non-Cirrhotic Portal Fibrosis, *30*, 406–415.

Jenkins, T. (2011). *Contesting Human Remains in Museum Collections: The Crisis of Cultural Authority*. New York, NY: Routledge.

Klebs, A. (1909). *Tuberculosis: A Treatise by American Authors on Its Etiology, Pathology, Frequency, Semeiology, Diagnosis, Prognosis, Prevention, and Treatment*. New York, NY: D. Appleton & Company.

Kunzle, D. (1982). *Fashion and Fetishism*. London, UK: George Prior Associated Publishers.

Lock, M., & Nguyen, V.-K. (2010). *An Anthropology of Biomedicine*. Malden, MA: Wiley.

Lord, W. B. (1868/1870). *Freaks of Fashion: The Corset and the Crinoline*. London: Ward, Lock, and Tyler.

Mazumder, G. (2001). Arsenic and Liver Disease. *Journal of the Indian Medical Association, 99*(6), 311, 314–315, 318–320.

McWhinnie, A. (1861, January 5). Remarkable Case of Displacement of an Enlarged Liver from Tight Lacing; and on a Case of Obliteration of the Vena Porta. *The Lancet*, 5–6.

Montillo, R. (2013). *The Lady and Her Monsters: A Tale of Dissections, Real-Life Dr. Frankensteins, and the Creation of Mary Shelley's Masterpiece*. New York, NY: HarperCollins.

Murchison, C. (1877). *Clinical Lectures on Diseases of the Liver, Jaundice, and Abdominal Dropsy: Including the Croonian Lectures on Functional Derangements of the Liver Delivered at the Royal College of Physicians in 1874*. New York, NY: W. Wood.

Neftel, W. (1887, October 8). Some Considerations on the Pathogenesis of Disease in Women. *The Lancet*, 704–707.

Nottingham, J. (1841). Compression of the Female Waist by Stays. *Provincial Medical and Surgical Journal, 3*(6), 110–111.

Sherry, W. (1871, February 18). Death from Tight-Lacing, With Post-Mortem Results, etc. *The Lancet*, 256.

Smith, N. (1827, July 24). Remarks on the Injuries Resulting from Confinement of the Chest by Dress. *Boston Medical Intelligencer, 5*(10), 153.

O'Followell, L. (1908). *Le Corset: Histoire, Médicine, Hygiène*. Paris: A. Maloine.

Our World in Data. (2013). https://ourworldindata.org/life-expectancy/.

Steele, V. (2001). *The Corset: A Cultural History*. New Haven, CT: Yale University Press.

Summers, L. (2001). *Bound to Please: A History of the Victorian Corset*. Oxford: Berg.

UCL. (2020). https://www.ucl.ac.uk/news/2020/feb/jeremy-bentham-finds-new-home-ucls-student-centre.

Vaissette, P. (1875). *L'Usage Prématur et Abusif du Corset*. Paris: A. Derenne.

Walkowitz, J. (1992). *City of Dreadful Delight: Narratives of Sexual Danger in Late Victorian London*. Chicago, IL: University of Chicago Press.

Witkowsky, G. (1898). *Tetoniana: Curiosités: Médicales, Littéraires, et Artistiques sur les Seins et L'Allaitement*. Paris: A. Maloine.

Young, S. (1860). The Evils Arising from Tight-Lacing. *The New Orleans Medical and Surgical Journal*, 412–413.

6

Women's Experiences in Life, Death, and Burial: The St. Bride's Parish Records

While I do not have a direct primary source for what the life of a corseted woman from the St. Bride's Parish would have been like, I do have indirect sources regarding one of those lives: that of Hannah Rapson (née Fulford), the wife of a London publisher, Richard Rapson. During an extensive genealogy search by Rapson's descendent, Jodi Fuller, it was confirmed by curators at the Museum of London (Fuller 2012) that due to the date of her interment, and her prominence as a long-time St. Bride's parishioner, Fulford was indeed one of the female skeletons held at the Museum of London's Centre for Human Bioarchaeology. Based on historical documentation and in consultation with Fuller, I have pieced together a picture of Rapson's life.

Born in late 1761 or early 1762 in the cathedral town of Salisbury, Rapson married at the age of 19 or 20, about average for the time (Davidoff and Hall 2002). The Fulford family belonged to the Anglican church of St. Edmunds, where she was a volunteer with the needy—her natal family was of the middle class (Fuller 2015). Married in 1800, by certificate rather than a posting of banns, Hannah Rapson and her husband spent much time apart during their early years. Richard Rapson's printing business was lucrative, but it was also in London, hours away

© The Author(s) 2020
R. Gibson, *The Corseted Skeleton*,
https://doi.org/10.1007/978-3-030-50392-5_6

Table 6.1   Rapson/Fulford Baptism and Fertility table

Name	Date born	Date baptized	Months between birth and baptism	Months between children	Hannah's age at each birth
Hannah Rapson (née Fulford)		24/2/1762			
David Rapson	7/12/1784	31/8/1785	9		21/22
Charles Rapson	15/8/1786	30/5/1787	10	20	23/24
Phebe Rapson	9/8/1788	9/11/1788	4	25	25/26
Hannah Rapson	28/7/1790	30/8/1790	1	24	28/29
Edmund Rapson	25/6/1792	18/7/1792	1	24	30/31
James Rapson	6/8/1794	1/9/1794	1	27	32/33

from his wife and children. For the first three years of their marriage Hannah did not bear children, but beginning in 1784 she bore one every two years on average (Table 6.1).

Despite contraception being outlawed, the Fulford/Rapson family may have been using some sort of precautions, particularly as there were no family tales or rumours of miscarriages either before 1784 or between children.[1] Due to the fact that breastfeeding can temporarily halt ovulation if done exclusively and consistently (NIH 1985), it is entirely probable that such a method was used for both purposes, feeding and bonding with the children, and ensuring they were evenly spaced. Throughout this time, and the rest of her adult life, Rapson would have been corseted—it was what was done by middle-class, Christian, respectable publisher's wives at the time.

The family moved to London and the parish of St. Bride's just off of printers' row at Fleet Street in 1800. Richard Rapson was ten years older than his wife and died in 1825, thirteen years before her (Family Search 2015). Their in-laws, particularly the Clement family, were even more well off than the Fulford/Rapson family. William Innell Clement was a media tycoon, buying and selling various printing and newspaper businesses for upward of one million pounds equivalent in today's money

---

[1]Note: this is partially speculation, as neither myself nor my informant (Fuller 2015) had much in the way of fact to go on.

(National Archives Money Calculator). Although she had wealthy rel-
atives, and a caring parish, nothing stops the passage of time, and
Rapson died at the age of 77. Her cause of death was listed as "decay"
(Fuller 2015, verified by the St. Bride's Parish records).

In 1758, a few years before Hannah Rapson was born, life expectancy at birth in the United Kingdom was 36.2 years (Our World in
Data). This number is uncorrected for juvenile mortality. In 1848, the
year she died, maternal mortality rates were 600 per every 100,000
live births (ibid.).[2] In many ways, Rapson beat the curve, and did so
while leading a quite ordinary middle-class life, a life which would have
included daily corseting. Additionally, there are no family stories mentioning her, no legends of extraordinary illness or injury, no tales of her
being a "loose" or "mad" woman who did not wear a corset, no lore that
would indicate she was anything other than an unexceptional woman, a
mother of six, who lived and died as was expected of her (Fuller 2015).
Her ordinariness, though a single anecdote and not to be taken as hard
data, as well as the predominance of older women in both the St. Bride's
and the Musée de l'Homme samples, decries the idea that the corset
shortened life, impacted reproduction, or created hysterical women.

*   *   *

Before diving into the bulk of this chapter, however, I shall take a
moment to discuss the methods used to collect and analyze the data
I present here, and in the next chapter. In examining the skeletal collections, I focused on finding the place on the skeleton where I might
reasonably expect to find deformation away from anatomical normal.
Because the corset creates an unnatural waist, rather than the natural one created by the bottom of the rib cage in uncorseted women, I
posited that if corseting created a distinct deformation of the ribs and
spinous processes, then both the sixth rib and the T6 would show deformation in all cases of corseting, regardless of the shape of the corset,
even though it is not technically at the waist. All corset shapes, whether
underbust or overbust, produce pressure and constriction anatomically

---

[2]The most recent reported rate, in 1999, is 5/100,000.

directly inferior to the breasts, where the sixth rib meets the sternum. This, therefore, was the most likely area in which I could both record appropriate data, and compare those data with data from my control group of male skeletal remains.

However, in the St. Bride's collection, not all skeletons had one or both of their sixth ribs or T6. Additionally, it was often not possible to create multiple pairings of consecutive ribs in order to see the overall shape of the thoracic cage. Therefore, it was necessary to broaden my measurements to include all other existing vertebrae/rib pairs, which allowed me to recreate as much of the thoracic cage as possible. To create these pairs, I sided the ribs following White et al. (2011, p. 156), and using the articular facets at the head and neck of the ribs I determined matches between the ribs and corresponding articular facets on the transverse processes of the vertebrae (ibid.). I then noted which ribs had matches with one or both ribs, and stabilized them in trays of coarse sand. Making sure the sand supported the vertebral body, I aligned the vertebra so that the vertebral body was level and facing forward as it would be in the skeleton, if the skeleton had been standing up. I then rematched the ribs with the articular facets on the transverse processes, ensuring that the sand supported them in such a way that articulation was as accurate as possible. This method is not without its drawbacks, yet has been used by myself in the first study done on this material (Gibson 2015), and by Moore and Buckberry (2016) when looking at similar material.

After alignment, I photographed the matched pairs, and measured them in two directions with a pair of electronic digital calipers, accurate to the millimeter—across the sagittal plane and across the coronal plane. For the sagittal measurement, I measured from various landmark coordinates, following DiGangi and Moore (2013, pp. 326–346): these were from the rearmost part of the spinous process to a point directly between the two ends of the ribs, where the midpoint of the sternum would be, were the ribs articulated. Due to the uniform and consistent deformation on the ribs, this was less difficult than it would have been if the ribs had followed an anatomically normal curvature. However, as they did not, the midpoint of the sternum would indeed have fallen directly across from the vertebral body, thus making for an easy and

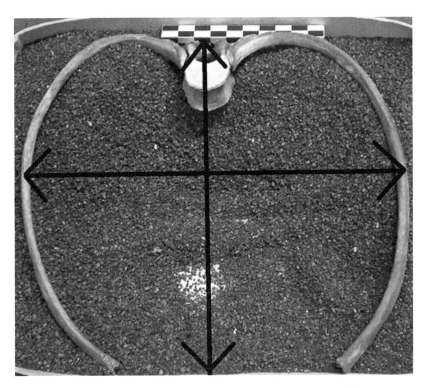

Photo 6.1 FAO90 1611—T6 and ribs, coronal dimension 21.6 cm, sagittal dimension 19.4 cm, spinous process angle 30.7 degrees. Arrows added to show coronal and sagittal measurements (Photo © Museum of London)

accurate measurement of bodily depth. The coronal measurement was achieved by, again, following DiGangi and Moore (2013, pp. 326–346) and finding the most lateral point on each rib and measuring from one to the other. If only one rib match was available, the coronal dimension was achieved by measuring from the lateral most point on the rib to the midpoint of the vertebral body and doubling that measurement (Photo 6.1).

To summarize, I considered T6/the sixth ribs to be an optimal pairing for determining deformation, but used other pairings as available when necessary. For both collections, I either measured the circumference at the sixth rib (Musée de l'Homme) or calculated the circumference using an online calculator for all available rib pairs (St. Bride's). I also measured the total dimension for both the coronal and sagittal aspects of all rib pairs. I further measured the angle of all extant spinous processes in both collections using ImageJ software, which measured the angles from both the 2D and the 3D images of the vertebrae. 2D images were taken using a Canon DSLR camera, and 3D images were captured with a Next Engine stationary scanner (St. Bride's images) and a Cubify Sense handheld scanner (Musée de l'Homme images only).

St. Bride's Lower Churchyard

Instead of looking at both skeletal collections in this book, for the purpose of cohesion and simplicity I am concentrating on the St. Bride's Lower Churchyard cemetery collection. St. Bride's off of Fleet Street in London has been a church since London was Londinium—recognized as a place of worship by the Romans in AD 43, it went through many permutations before the lower churchyard was opened in 1770. In this iteration, it was a Church of England, frequented by mostly printers, newsmen, publishers, and their families. In addition to the parish members, it was frequented by the nearby workhouse and prison.

This site is important because of its relative unremarkableness. It is exemplary of London cemeteries of its time in that there were burial fees that needed to be covered in order to be interred, the graves were marked but the markers were not necessarily durable or made of stone, and because of a limited amount of space, coffins were often stacked atop one another to conserve effort, maximize profitability, and better serve the parish. Because it was a parish cemetery, it is safe to reach a few conclusions about the people who were buried in it: they were unlikely to be transient, meaning their food, water, air pollutant, and disease vectors were likely to be similar; they were at least nominally Christian; and they may not have been wealthy, but they were wealthy enough to be buried and remain so in spite of grave robbers. Thus, they can be seen as a relatively cohesive population in terms of factors that would impact their skeletal health.

While the lack of grave markers and the haste with which the graves were excavated (a bomb was dropped on the church and cemetery during WWII, necessitating immediate archaeological recovery after the war) makes individual skeletal identification impossible, records of who was buried during the time have not disappeared entirely. The parishioners of St. Bride's during that time were generally printers of various types—newsmen, typesetters, booksellers, publishers, and their families (stbrides.com). Because of the demographic of the churchyard—local parishioners, and both men and women from the workhouse and from the prison—I can confidently state several things about the skeletal population. They were exposed to the same environmental factors: London sunlight, smog, air, water, and food. Being anywhere from upper-middle class to impoverished, they would have worn domestically and locally produced clothing, and followed local fashions, including, for the women, the use of a corset regardless of socioeconomic status. This removes certain variables from the question of their lived experiences, such as how corseting damage would be expressed on upper-class women's bodies who would most likely have had better/more consistent nutritional access, or how and whether it would be expressed on women from nonurban sites, where fashion often took a backseat to practicality in terms of corset use (Hiley 1979).

The collection of St. Bride's Lower contained not only parishioners, but also the remains of inhabitants of the Shoe Lane and Bridewell workhouses and Fleet prison. Shoe Lane and Bridewell were poorhouses, holding women and children, and governed by the same committees that were responsible for "Bedlam" or Bethlehem Hospital. In "Slumming" historian Seth Koven gives us a dire picture of poorhouses, discussing exposés performed at the time, in which undercover reporters showed them to be places of degradation, lice, licentiousness, disease, and cruelty. Often, the prisons and poorhouses shared the same property and the same overseers (Koven 2006), and the emphasis of incarceration was on the reformation and rehabilitation of the "undeserving poor," or those who were unworthy of individual charity and thus made the responsibility of the state. Personal property was confiscated when a person entered the workhouse, and often lost, and there were restrictions on how much currency you could have in order to be truly considered "poor" and thus needing a place in the house, therefore it was very difficult to leave once you entered, or to maintain both a job and a place to live. In his unpublished work on the excavation, Adrian Miles writes: "in the lower churchyard there was no differential [sic] by wealth and status, leading to it being the poorer members of the parish, lodgers and those who had not contributed to the poor rate who were mainly buried there" (Miles and Coheeney 2010).

In contrast, the Church of England parishioners of St. Bride's are easily traceable through marriage licensing and birth and baptism registries, which show that not all the high status/middle-class individuals were buried in the crypt as previously thought (Museum of London 2013; Fuller 2015). Archaeological evidence indicates that lower status individuals were most prevalent due to an abundance of simple wooden coffins and a distinct dearth of nameplates, however, this could also be a result of the large number of infants and children buried therein.

As the remains are of Christian individuals, whether that status is affirmed by their membership in the church or assumed based on the requirements of the poorhouses (Koven 2006). Common practice of the twentieth and twenty-first centuries would indicate the necessity of their swift reburial under church law in a Church of England owned crypt or unused church building (Lohman and Goodnow 2006, p. 86). However, in accordance with a compromise between church law and the interests of the scientific community of England, as represented by the Home Office, "[W]hen excavated human remains are more than 100 years old and have significant future research potential, deposition in a suitable holding institution should be arranged" (Lohman and Goodnow 2006, p. 88). While neither of the phrases "significant future research potential" nor "suitable holding institution" are defined, FAO90 is indeed significant for its comprehensive dates during the postmedieval period, and for the uniqueness of its composition.

The skeletons are currently held in the Rotunda at the Museum of London, a building specifically for preservation and sampling, and upon the renovation and upcoming move of the Centre, will be held in a new laboratory storage facility equipped for the same practices. Out of the 544 sets of remains in the St. Bride's lower churchyard collection, there were 369 adults (194 male and 125 female). The 125 female skeletons were broken down into standardized age at death groups, with four in the 18–25 group; 21 between 26 and 35; 30 between 36 and 45; 64 over the age of 46 at death; and six un-aged. As has been discussed in the previous chapter's introduction, certain remains in the >46 at death population showed age markers that put them considerably older than the minimum age in that category, indicating that those women who made it through childbirth and past menopause had a further tendency to outlast their projected age at death for the time (ourworldindata. com).

Sample Details: Who Is Represented in FAO90

Our World in Data (2013) has data on life expectancy in Britain for all of the period during which St. Bride's Lower Churchyard was in use. It did not fluctuate by that much. The first data shows that in 1773, three years after the opening of the Lower Churchyard, life expectancy at birth was 39.77 years, and at the end date in 1850 it was 42.77, a change of just 3 years (ibid.). The lowest point was 35.81 in 1783. Thus, one can see that women in the St. Bride's collection, regardless of if they came from the parish or from the poorhouse, did still exceed their life expectancy at birth. However, life expectancy at birth is calculated based on childhood mortality—this will be addressed in full later on in this chapter. Furthermore, the UK's office of national statistics shows that for women, the median age at death was 47 in 1841, and peaked at 48 in 1870, with the low point between the two being 40 in 1849 (Office of National Statistics) (Table 6.2).

Breaking that down further, over half the women in the St. Bride's collection were over 46 years of age at death, with the skeletal evidence of some (complete obliteration of cranial sutures, loss of all teeth and extreme mandibular and maxillary resorption, advanced vertebral friability) indicating lives that stretched on into their seventh or eighth decades or longer. Due to the fact that they, relatively uniformly, showed evidence of corset related deformation, as well as extremely small rib circumferences, the data does not support the doctors' claims that corseting shortened life for women. In effect, women expressed their multiple

Table 6.2 Male and female ages at death, St. Bride's FAO90 Skeletal Sample

Age range	Female N	Male N	Total
18–25	2	0	2
26–35	13	0	13
36–45	21	4	25
>46	37	5	42
Total	73	9	82

subjectivities in texts and in how they lived their life, and the length of those lives and writings about them directly contradicted what doctors predicted would occur.

The St. Bride's Parish Archives

Three aspects of the archived burial records of the parish of St. Bride's are worth attention—the ages at death, what the women were dying from, and the delineation of the parish boundaries. I will examine these individually in the next three sections.

Age at Death: Our Assumptions vs. the Data

We must return here to one of the myths that surround corseting—that corseting shortened lives, and that women were not living for that long regardless. If I asked you at what age the average woman died in the 1700s and 1800s, your answer would most likely be influenced, again, by popular culture. We hear such ideas in numerous ways throughout our lives, in many of the publications we encounter. It is often repeated by the media of the time, as shown above in the discussions of popular and medical views of the corset. And it is repeated in our time, by contemporary fiction authors, such as Edith Wharton, who wrote of May Archer (née Welland), "Yes, May might die—people did: young people, healthy people like herself; she might die, and suddenly set him free" (1920/1993, p. 296). And, yes, of course they did and still do sometimes. However, this is held up as the norm—but is it?

In a word, no. At least not for the St. Bride's population during these years. In many more words, the archival data simply does not support such a norm, particularly if one removes all juveniles from the sample. To investigate this, I pulled the St. Bride's Parish Burial Records for the years from 1770 to 1849, and isolated every woman over the age of 16 ($n = 3815$), regardless of whether or not she was buried in the lower churchyard. I did not make the distinction between churchyards because in reading the record, I discovered that the majority of the burials listed as L (lower yard) were not connected to any type of noted socioeconomic difference, and I therefore determined to examine all the data together, to create a more complete picture of the parish. Thus, I recorded name, age, date of death, burial location, and if the following information was listed, I also recorded street address at which she resided or died, and cause of death. Within these data, I isolated the ages in two ways: using the Museum of London's age classification, I categorized the data into four groups (1 = 16–25, 2 = 26–35, 3 = 36–45, and 4 = 46 and over), and I also categorized the data by a straight decade at death (1 = 16–19, 2 = 20–29, and so on). The two different methods had two corresponding reasons—I wanted to see if the preponderance of 46+ skeletons I had found in the FAO90 collection was indeed accurately representative, and I wanted a closer-to-life understanding of the age derivations than the Museum of London's grouping had given me.

In fact, the FAO90 collection slightly underrepresented the correct distribution of ages at death as divided into the four categories. In FAO90, as shown above, 36 out of 73 skeletons were in the fourth category, making them 49% of the sample, whereas in the parish records, the over 46 category made up 63% of the total sample. An average of approximately 18 women under the age of 46 died per year over the entire period that I examined, whereas roughly 30 were over that age at death. To put it a different way, in this cross-section of remains from the St. Bride's Parish, a woman was one and a half times more likely to live to age 46 or beyond than she was to die at any time before that.

However, continued use of this category system when one has more exact data can lead to confusion of the data itself—if one were to analyze the archival data and with it graph these four data categories (how

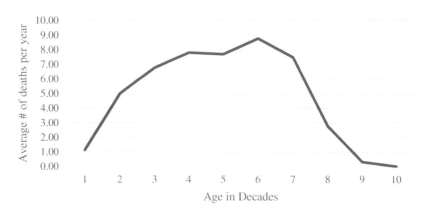

Graph 6.1   Average age at death in St. Bride's Parish records 1770–1849

many women died per year on average based on the four point scale) it would be an extremely clunky and uninformative graph. Rather than analyzing only the skeletal age data, a graph by average decade at death of the data from the parish archives will give us much more information, and a clearer picture of the average lifespan of all of the St. Bride's Parish woman during this time (again, the following using only the archival records, in an effort to not count people more than once via their representation in both the skeletal material and the archives).

As you can see from both the Graph 6.1 and the Table 6.3, recorded deaths among women in the St. Bride's Parish form almost a normal distribution, with fewer toward each end and a distinct peak at approximately age 60.[3] Relatively fewer died in their 20 and 30s, and

---

[3]Please note: The following presentation of data from the St. Bride's Parish archives reflects **only** a flat reporting of tabulations of women in each age category, not any type of advanced statistical analysis such as life tables or survivorship curves. For the advanced analysis, one need either rely on governmentally tabulated data (such as that found on OurWorldInData.com) or tabulate one's own results. The governmental datasets only go back to 1980, falling far short of the time period relevant to my above-gathered data. And to create an accurate picture of St. Bride's Parish in terms of life table projections or survivorship analysis would require far more data than was gathered for this study. Most life table projections assume a beginning cohort of 100,000 births, per year or cohort, and my entire dataset contains only 3815 individuals spread out over 79 years, or an average of just over 48 individuals per year. Thus, while the sample size remains large enough to demonstrate that women were not killed by their corsets and did not overall die at a young age in general once they reached adulthood, it is not generalizable to talk about their overall longevity as relates to the greater London population.

Table 6.3   Total and average deaths per year, St. Bride's Parish 1770–1849

Decade/years of life	Total deaths from 1770 to 1849	Average per year, 1770–1849
16–19	90	1.13
20–29	399	4.99
30–39	541	6.76
40–49	624	7.80
50–59	615	7.69
60–69	701	8.76
70–79	598	7.48
80–89	221	2.76
90–99	25	.31
100–109	1	.01
Total	3815	~48

relatively fewer lived to their 80s and beyond. Nearly three times as many women died past 40 as died before that age. If we take it back another decade, due to the "women died before their thirties" myth, it rises considerably—nearly seven times as many women died past 30 as died before that age.

These data confirmed two things to me—that the women in the FAO90 collection were not a fluke representation of the St. Bride's parish population, and that, for this population over this span of time, our popular culture representation of corseting had gotten it wrong. Women were certainly living far beyond what doctors and literature told us. Seeing corseting deformation on these skeletons, these women who lived into their 40s, 60, 90s, even, indicate that women were definitely being altered by the corset, but in this population, they were not being killed by it. However, the corset, being widely blamed for early death, must make an appearance somewhere else in the St. Bride's Parish data, as cause of death or contributing to death, right?

Causes of Death in St. Bride's Parish

Wrong. There are 109 listed causes of death, comprising some 2273 female deaths where the cause was both known and recorded. Corseting, tight-lacing, use of stays, overlapping ribs, and other things that are distinctly traceable to corseting and corseting alone, are not

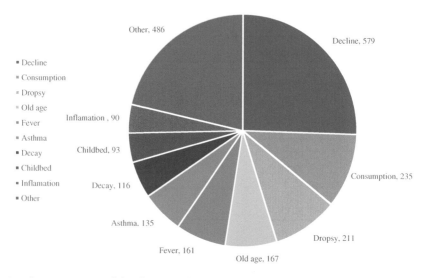

Graph 6.2   Causes of death, St. Bride's Parish 1770–1849

anywhere among them. Of the women with known causes of death, which comprise approximately 60% of the entire sample, none of them died of corseting. So, what did kill them?

Shown by the Graph 6.2, many of the causes were nebulous or undefined. Decline, the single biggest killer, can be approximately summed up as "we do not know why the body stopped working, but it stopped working." Similarly, decay, decay of nature, mortification, and sudden death, are all vague, though the first three were most likely gangrene or something similar. Some of the more interesting causes of death were below the threshold for inclusion into main categories, and so became part of "other," but deserve to be delineated for their uniqueness: two women hanged themselves, while two others died of unspecified suicide. Two died of a "Visitation of God," while two died of venereal disease. One was executed, one had a miscarriage. One died only of "Evil." One died of "Hydrophobia" (rabies), while one died of the unlikely cause of a dislocated shoulder. There was one case of measles, one case of dysentery, one was scalded to death, one fell out a window, and one was poisoned. One died after hard drinking, one burst a blood vessel in her throat while coughing, and one died of grief.

Additionally, it was possible to see a cholera outbreak begin, spread from workhouse to the surrounding areas and back again and then eventually slacken and pass out of the causes of death. The first death was Frances Parker in the workhouse on July 9, 1832, at the age of 60, then Ann Rowbottom and Mary Dibben on the 12th (aged 58 and 82), Hannah Woodford and Sarah Middleton on the 14th (aged 67 and 75). Mary Field, 40, of Bridge Street died on the 16th, and then three more women from the workhouse, Rebecca Moore (70), Mary Britton (66), and Charlotte field (49), a few days later. In the last week of July and the first week of August, Martha Hartill of Hancock Yard (49), Ann Nankwell (30) and Elizabeth Caldwell (42) of Dawes Ct., Elizabeth Wenson (50) of Fleet St., and Sarah Swindall (23) of Dove Ct., all succumbed. The outbreak paused for a few weeks before reemerging in Elizabeth Turner (80) of Peckham House, who died on August 22, and Phobe Wackett of Water Lane (41) on September 30. The next summer of 1833 saw another outbreak beginning in July, which eventually killed seven women in the parish, only one of whom was in the workhouse.

Another myth falls by the wayside from this data, too: Only 93 women of the 2273 whose cause of death was known died in childbirth or of childbed fever; a mere 4.1%. If we expand that to the whole sample, whether or not there was a cause of death recorded, that becomes 93 out of 3815, or 2.4%. In the last three years of this study, the maternal mortality rate for the entire United Kingdom was .59% in 1847, .61% in 1848, and .58% in 1849 (Our World in Data 2019). While 2.5–4.1% is very large in comparison, such rates still exist in the world today, in places where infrastructure and medical support are both lower than America and Europe (Our World In Data 2019), and it certainly is not the "tragic heroine who always dies in childbirth and leaves motherless children" story told of the time period. Women were not dying willy-nilly from the corset, or from childbirth, or from consumption (a significant, but not enormous, 10% of the known-cause deaths in St. Bride's). The biggest predictor of death was not age, parturition, or illness. It was poverty.

In many cases, location was listed in the burial record. While the next section of this chapter will go into detail about the various addresses of St. Bride's Parish, we must take a moment to discuss the prison and the workhouse. Out of the 2273 records which contained cause of death and/or location data, 32 women died in the prison, and 836 died in the workhouse/poorhouse, with 1405 dying at locations other than that (either unknown (or unrecorded) locations or ones with a street address other than the prison and workhouse). While nearly twice as many women died outside of the workhouse than inside of it, the fact that the workhouse was the single largest location of death is significant— it shows the vast structure of poverty in London at the time, and how impactful that was on both life and death. The largest medical category of cause of death was "Decline" at 579 women or 25%. Women who died in the workhouse, regardless of whether they were shown to have another cause of death[4], measure 37% of all deaths, 12% more than the top medical killer. If we add in prisons, that becomes 38% of all deaths. And as seen in "Slumming" (Koven 2006), prisons were often filled with debtors who could not pay their bills, or people who were arrested for things such as vagrancy, which often equated to homelessness. The biggest killer of this era was the fact of being poor.

The Bounds of St. Bride's Parish

As churches were (and are) abundant in London, each one could serve as small space as a few standard city blocks[5] in either direction. St. Bride's Parish, therefore, was roughly delineated in an uneven quadrilateral, with the north and south edges (top and bottom) measuring .28 miles and .17 miles, respectively, and west and east edges (left and right) measuring .28 miles and .45 miles. The north boundary was delineated by Shoe Lane, Snow Hill, and Holborn Road, and the south by Tudor Street. The east was delineated by Snow Hill, Fleet Place, and River Fleet, and the west by Fetter Lane and Bouverie Street. They buried

---

[4]In the column "cause of death" in the St. Bride's Parish Records, "Workhouse" or "Poorhouse" was occasionally listed instead of or in addition to a medical cause. This is a valid cause of death—people died in the workhouse and people died *because* of the workhouse due to the meagre food and poor living conditions, or from literally working themselves to death.

[5]…though whether there is such a thing as a "standard" London block is highly debatable…

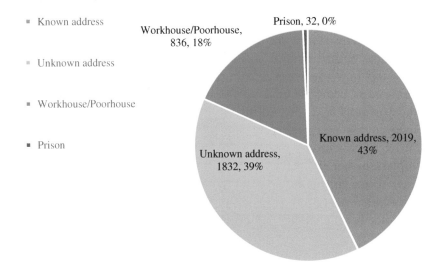

- Known address
- Unknown address
- Workhouse/Poorhouse
- Prison

Workhouse/Poorhouse, 836, 18%

Prison, 32, 0%

Known address, 2019, 43%

Unknown address, 1832, 39%

Graph 6.3 Population location, St. Bride's Parish, 1770–1849

approximately 50 women per year from these parish bounds. This area encompassed the church, the churchyard, the workhouse, and the prison, and was in very close proximity to the criminal courts and to the medical school at St. Bartholomew's, all of which can still be seen on modern maps. As previously mentioned, the main profession of the parishioners was printing, typesetting, bookbinding, and various types of publications, and the area is still known for this today, with printers, bookstores, and libraries in the various streets.

As shown in the Graph 6.3, 2019 of the women had known addresses, while 836 were buried from the workhouse and 32 from the prison. 1832 women either had unknown addresses, or their addresses were not recorded (there was considerable discretion when it came to which details were added, and it varied according to the curate of the time).

Of the known addresses, most of them were within or near the official bounds of the parish, and those who are not are often from near neighboring parishes, or from other churches which occasionally used St. Bride's as an overflow. There is nothing in the data to suggest that this burial ground was any more or less an ordinary church of its time, serving its parish and some Christians beyond the parish bounds, burying the impoverished dead from the workhouse and those who died in prison, and by all imports, a cherished local church.

This now returns us to the question, who was buried in St. Bride's parish, and how can we reconcile the discourse about corseting with what we now know about these women? You can find the entire data set in Appendix E at the end of this book, as there are way too many women to list everyone specifically here. To return to the opening narrative of this chapter, however, we can see Hannah Rapson as an exemplary of her time—a devout Christian woman, active in society, mother to six children, wife of one of Fleet Street's printers, she died on November 4, 1838 of decay, approximately at age 80. She corseted during her life, and is certainly one of the women of advanced age whose bones I will discuss in the next chapter. She was predeceased by her husband, Richard Rapson, who died on June 15, 1825 of paralytic fever, and a young child, presumably either a grandniece or a grandchild, Sarah Rapson of Cock Pit Ct, who died on July 13, 1825 of smallpox. The answer to this question seems to be merely ordinary women. A few from the upper-middle class, based on minor office holding by their husbands, as seen in the archives, but mostly middle- to lower-class women, with a significant portion of those who ended their lives destitute, but may not always have been so. Women who likely treated the corset as twenty-first-century women treat their bras and panties—not given much thought unless there's a reason to do so. The corset was changing their bodies, but not, necessarily, their lives. In the next chapter, I will show those skeletal changes, and discuss them in regard to what we have learned about these women so far.

Bibliography

CDC. (2019). https://www.cdc.gov/reproductivehealth/maternal-mortality/pregnancy-mortality-surveillance-system.htm?CDC_AA_refVal=https%3A%2F%2Fwww.cdc.gov%2Freproductivehealth%2Fmaternalinfant-health%2Fpregnancy-mortality-surveillance-system.htm#trends.

Davidoff, L., & Hall, C. (2002). *Family Fortunes: Men and Women of the English Middle Class 1780–1850*. Oxon, UK: Routledge Press.

DiGangi, E., & Moore, M. (2013). *Research Methods in Human Skeletal Biology.* Waltham, MA: Elsevier Ltd.

Family Search. (2015). https://familysearch.org/learn/wiki/en/Marriage_Allegations,_Bonds_and_Licences_in_England_and_Wales.

Fuller, J. (2012). http://www.wiltshire-opc.org.uk/Items/Salisbury/Salisbury%20-%20Hannah%20Fulford%20(St.%20Edmund)%201762-1838.pdf.

Fuller, J. (2015). Pers. Corrs.

Gibson, R. (2015). Examining the Morphological Effects of Long Term Corseting on the Female Skeleton: A Preliminary Morphological Examination. *Nexus: The Canadian Student Journal of Anthropology, 23*(2), 45–60.

Hiley, M. (1979). *Victorian Working Women: Portraits from Life.* London, UK: The Gordon Fraser Gallery Ltd.

Koven, S. (2006). *Slumming: Sexual and Social Politics in Victorian London.* Princeton, NJ: Princeton University Press.

Lohman, J., & Goodnow, K. (2006). *Human Remains and Museum Practice.* Paris, France and London, UK: UNESCO and The Museum of London.

Miles, A., & Coheeney, J. (2010). *A Post-medieval Population from London: Excavations in the St Bride's Lower Churchyard 75–82 Farringdon Street, City of London, EC4.* London: MOLA.

Moore, J., & Buckberry, J. (2016). The Use of Corsetry to Treat Pott's Disease of the Spine from 19th Century Wolverhampton, England. *The International Journal of Paleopathology, 14,* 74–80.

Museum of London. (2013). https://www.museumoflondon.org.uk/collections/other-collection-databases-and-libraries/centre-human-bioarchaeology/osteological-database/post-medieval-cemeteries/st-brides-lower-post-medieval.

National Archives Money Converter. (2017). http://www.nationalarchives.gov.uk/currency/.

NIH. (1985). *How Breast-Feeding Postpones Ovulation.* https://www.ncbi.nlm.nih.gov/pubmed/12314029.

Office of National Statistics. (2012). https://www.ons.gov.uk/peoplepopulationandcommunity/birthsdeathsandmarriages/deaths/articles/mortalityinenglandandwales/2012-12-17#trends-in-average-life-span.

Our World in Data. (2013). https://ourworldindata.org/life-expectancy/.

Our World in Data. (2019). https://ourworldindata.org/maternal-mortality.

St. Bride's (2019). http://www.stbrides.com/history/index.html.

Wharton, E. (1920/1993). *The Age of Innocence.* New York, NY: Macmillan.

White, T., Black, M., & Folkens, A. (2011). *Human Osteology* (3rd ed.). Burlington, MA: Elsevier Press.

7

The Corseted Skeleton: Skeletal Remains of St. Bride's Lower Churchyard

One female skeleton which showed precisely how early corseting deformation can occur, is the one labeled MNHN-NA-782 from the Musée de l'Homme collection. The skeleton is of unknown origin, and marked as 20 *ans,* or 20 years old at death, in the record. Regrettably, this is completely incorrect. Based on the absence of completed or partial epiphyseal fusion on the majority of the long bones,[1] the lack of her wisdom teeth, and the partial eruption of the second molars (also called "12-year molars" for when they usually come into the jaw), I reestimated the age at death as between 13 and 17. This does not necessarily take into account lack of skeletal development relative to age at menarche—we cannot determine whether any size difference in her body's development is related to having gone through the hormone

---

[1]This was based on aggregating the age ranges from all fused and partially fused bones, following Bass (1987), Byers (2008), and Ubelaker (1978), and using the lower end of the age range for unfused bones as a template for potential maximum age. Fused: Ulnar head and distal humerus. Partially fused: Humeral head, radial head, femoral head, greater trochanter of the femur, lesser trochanter of the femur, femoral foot, proximal and distal ends of the metatarsals, and proximal ends of the proximal phalanges. Unfused: Tibial head, first and second sacral vertebrae, iliac crest, sternal end of the clavicle, body segments of the sternum, and left transverse process of L5.

© The Author(s) 2020
R. Gibson, *The Corseted Skeleton,*
https://doi.org/10.1007/978-3-030-50392-5_7

167

surge during puberty—however, this probably would indicate only that she most likely had not started menstruation yet, nor hit that growth spurt, not that my aggregate skeletal assessment was incorrect (Lai et al. 2008).

Also note: the skeleton does not exhibit any signs of congenital dwarfism, or any other congenital or metabolic defect that could interfere with height and skeletal development. These needed to be ruled out in order to ensure that her diminutive size and lack of age-related skeletal markers were not due to "abnormalities." Congenital dwarfism is a genetic condition that results in shorter limbs and smaller bones in general. Metabolic defects or malnutrition may also effect stature, leaving adult skeletons looking smaller, more fragile, and more childlike than they would normally be. However, neither adults with dwarfism nor the malnourished would show the age-related markers on the body that indicate juvenile or subadult bones. Thus, she is simply a young girl with a correspondingly juvenile/subadult skeleton—her skeletal development indicates she was less than 18 years old at death. The reason for her inclusion as an opening vignette to this chapter, despite the very young age, and the apparent lack of skeletal development in keeping with that age, is that she has a rib-cage coronal to sagittal ratio of 1:89, which is a cross-body coronal dimension of 18 cm and a sagittal dimension of 16 cm, and clearly deformed spinous processes with extreme angles even for within the female sample. She has been corseted.

There are a few reasons that she would have been. As mentioned below, and in various preceding chapters, corseting often began in childhood in much of Europe during this time (Müller 2006, p. 104; Shrimpton 2016, pp. 49–50). However, there is no reason to think that this child was British, French, or even European. Because of the piecemeal makeup of the Musée de l'Homme, she could have come from any number of indigenous populations of North America, South America, or Asia. And because of her extreme youth, and the (most likely purposeful) overestimation of her age at death, there is every reason to suspect more nefarious origins. Two spring to mind—she may have been a daughter of a wealthy person of a Europeanized country who was included by accident and then her origins were covered up, or, which is more likely, she may have been a child prostitute. In this way, a child between 13 and 17 years of age at death might end up in a French museum collection, with no name or place of origin, and with the museum directors who originated and perfected human anatomization vastly overstating her age.

To that second point—the idea that she may have been a child prostitute—there is more likelihood than the first. Prostitution was not a hidden vice in this time period, but an openly accepted sexual practice. It was not condoned, necessarily, but it was not an offense for which men would have been ostracized, so long as they were on the "purchase" portion of the exchange (Matthew 2000, pp. 185–186; Walkowitz 1992, pp. 81–83, 100–102). Unmarried men without serious romantic attachments were understood to get certain needs met through the practice of prostitution (ibid.). Child prostitution was socially condemned, however, it still occurred, and the London advertisements for prostitutes would mention age through various euphemisms like comparisons to flowers, and references to freshness and innocence (ibid.). Indeed, many had opinions on the "Age of Innocence" (Müller 2006, p. 94), saying that at 7 years old, a girl became aware of her own sexuality and by 14 she is fully aware. From a twenty-first- century perspective, this is abhorrent, of course, and I in no way condone this behavior. However, just as we have seen civilization, race, gender, and corseting to be cultural constructs, so too is childhood—many cultures through the world, both now, and previously, define childhood as ending earlier than current Western or American/British moral and legal standards do.

Photos 7.1, 7.2, 7.3, 7.4, 7.5, and 7.6 illustrate not just the deformation of her spinous processes, which show that she corseted (as discussed below), but emphasize her extremely young age. This evidence demonstrates two things: that corseting as a practice began early for many women, and that the effects on developing bone began to show early.

Without knowing her origin, I cannot say more about whether this practice was of her own culture, or from the Europeanization of her location, however, that matters little to the overall discussion of corseting and civilization—she was corseted, and therefore either civilized or in the process of becoming so. As mentioned, many of the phrases we use for immorality or uncivilized behavior, particularly among women—to be a loose woman, a slut, or a slag, for example—tie back

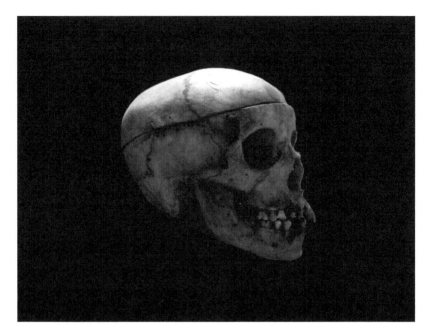

Photo 7.1 Right side view of the skull of MNHN-NA-782 (photo by author and used with permission from the Muséum National d'Histoire Naturelle)

to the use of corseting. A woman with loose corset laces could give easy access to her body, with the additional implication of vaginal "looseness" linguistically indicating that she had a lot of sex.[2] A slut or a slag was a person who did not keep themselves or their surroundings tidy, or who did not use (or did not "properly" use) a corset. Thus, the "civilized" woman corseted early and continued to do so. This young girl's skeleton, therefore, gives us a plausible story as to why, and how, she shows such changes at such a young age, and how she came to be in the Musée de l'Homme.

*   *   *

---

[2]This is not accurate; the amount of sex had, or not had, has nothing to do with the tautness of vaginal muscles.

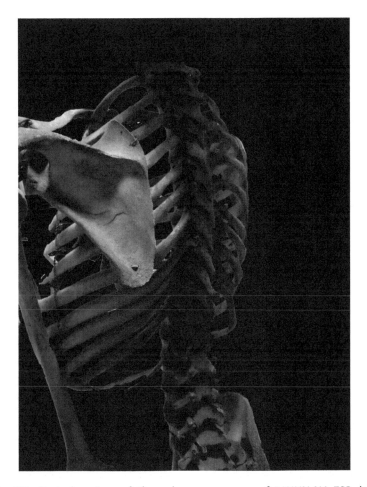

Photo 7.2 Posterior view of the spinous processes of MNHN-NA-782 (photo by author and used with permission from the Muséum National d'Histoire Naturelle)

The Skeletal Evidence of Corseting

The practice of corseting is as multifaceted as the symbolism of the corset itself, so how early the woman would have begun wearing a corset differed from area to area, class to class, and family to family. However, some women were corseted as little girls, occasionally as soon as they

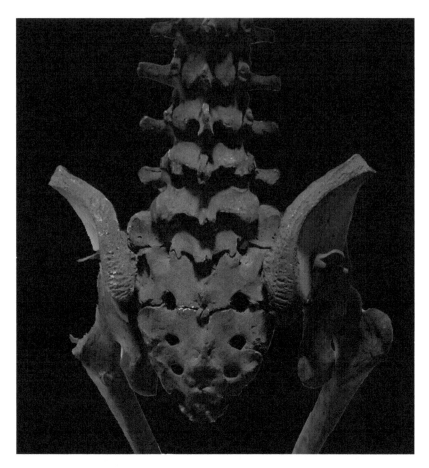

Photo 7.3   Posterior view of the pelvis of MNHN-NA-782 (photo by author and used with permission from the Muséum National d'Histoire Naturelle)

could walk (Müller 2006, p. 104; Shrimpton 2016, pp. 49–50). Others began the practice at puberty or pre-pubescence, to signify impending womanhood (Lord 1868, pp. 149–150). Skeletal changes would have begun occurring quickly once a corset was fitted to their body, and indeed have been seen on the above skeleton with an age range of 13–17 years at death.

In fashionable urban areas, corseting was the preferred way to shape the body of the child, as discussed in previous chapters (Anonymous

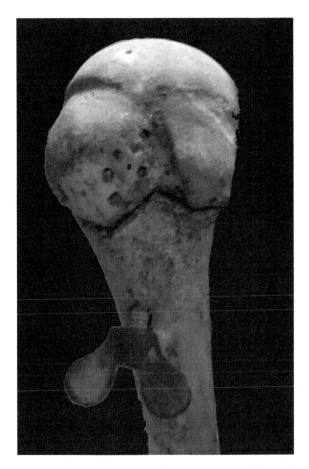

Photo 7.4 Head of the right humerus of MNHN-NA-782 (photo by author and used with permission from the Muséum National d'Histoire Naturelle)

1866, 1883; Balch 1904; Lord 1868/1870; Müller 2006; etc.). This idea was deeply imbedded in the consciousness of the time, with "Mademoiselle de Maintenon" writing to a French magazine ("Lettres"), in 1696:

> Letter to the Mistress General of St. Cyr—you were given the memoires of the high-class women, who had made note of the ages when young girls were dressed. It is not that there is nothing to change on the top,

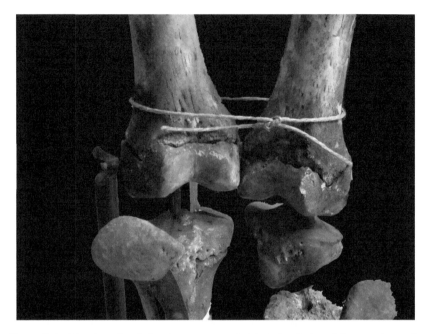

Photo 7.5 Distal ends of the femora, proximal ends of the tibiae, and patella of MNHN-NA-782 (photo by author and used with permission from the Muséum National d'Histoire Naturelle)

they wear the corset, when it is necessary, to conserve their size. Think of the wrong you are doing to the girl who becomes hunchbacked, it is your fault, and for this she will never be in a state to marry, be in a convent, nor find a good woman to take charge of her. Spare nothing for their soul, their health, and their size. (Waugh 2018, p. 43)[3]

This was not universally welcomed, of course. Shown by both the doctor's discourses, and the reformers, the changes to the body were acknowledged and decried. Emperor Joseph II of Germany wrote an edict against

---

[3]Lettre à la maistresse generale de Saint-Cyr—faittes vous donnes des mémoires par les maistresses des classes, qui doivent marquer le temps que les Demoiselles ont esté habillées. Ce n'est pas qu'il faille rien fixer là dessus, car il faut donner aussy souvent des corps, qu'il en sera besoin, pour conserver la taille. Songés au tort que vous faittes à une fille, qui devient bossue par vostre faute, et, par là, hors d'estat de trouver ni mari ni couvent ni dame qui vielle s'en charger. N'espargnés rien pour leur âme pour leur santé, et pour leur taille.

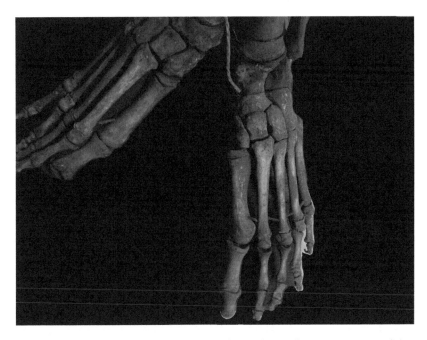

Photo 7.6 Dorsal view of the bones of the feet of MNHN-NA-782 (photo by author and used with permission from the Muséum National d'Histoire Naturelle)

the use of stays in 1800, asking the headmistresses and headmasters of boarding schools to refuse girls wearing stays (ibid., p. 127).

As discussed in Chapter 4, this is a deliberate form of body modification. But did the wearers see it as such? I contend that we must make a distinction between intended and unintended consequences. Corseting manifests on the skeleton in two ways, both of which are changes to the thoracic cage—the ribs and the vertebrae. Pressure over time is a demonstrated way to alter bone morphology, either deliberately in the case of intentional skeletal body modifications like orthodontia or foot-binding, or accidentally, through situations such as thumb sucking, unintentionally leaving babies immobile, or the wearing of improperly sized shoes. This can happen in adult bone, but is much more likely to occur on developing or immature bone, due to the fact that bone remodeling occurs on a much faster and more regular basis while the skeleton is still growing. Because corseting was used in such diverse ways, with childhood being the acceptable age, but adolescence to young adulthood being the most usual age, we cannot say that the wearers intended to alter the developing skeleton in the manner that they did, despite all their pontification about molding the wax of the woman. Most likely, the results were incidental to the main goal, which was the cultural change from child to young woman to marriageable woman.

So, what does that molding do? Corseting puts radial pressure on the rib cage, distorting the usual wide-oval shape (broader than it is deep) into a much more circular profile. For example, my own (current, and fully fleshed) dimensions are a rib cage circumference of 88 cm, with coronal and sagittal dimensions of approximately 36 cm and 17 cm respectively. This is a ratio of 1:.47, a wide-oval. These ratios are expressed in setting the coronal or left to right body dimension to 1, and the sagittal, or front to back body dimension, to a proportion of the coronal dimension. In contrast, one of the most round rib cages of the St. Bride's skeletons has a circumference of 64 cm, with the coronal and sagittal dimensions both measuring 20.2 cm, a 1:1 ratio or a perfect circle (FAO90 1703).

As you can see from Photos 7.7, 7.8, and 7.9, in FAO90 1703 when the 6th ribs are properly articulated with the T6 vertebrae, they form a circle. In anatomically normal ribs, the body of the rib moves laterally away from the vertebrae at a downward angle, curving around the side of the body, and ending with the sternal end angled downward, where it connects to the sternal cartilage. The sternal cartilage then angles upward and inward, toward the center of the chest, where it attaches to the sternum. In corset-altered ribs, the sternal rib ends begin to point forward instead of down, and the bodies of the ribs curve sharply inward, resulting in the whole rib making a stable, flat C shape, rather than the downward-slanting and highly torqued C that is a "normal" rib.

FAO90 1703, a woman between the age of 36 and 45 years at death, shows that the pressure of the corset rounded the ribs—Photo 7.1 shows the sixth thoracic vertebra and the associated ribs, which have coronal and sagittal measurements of 20.2 cm × 20.2 cm—they are a

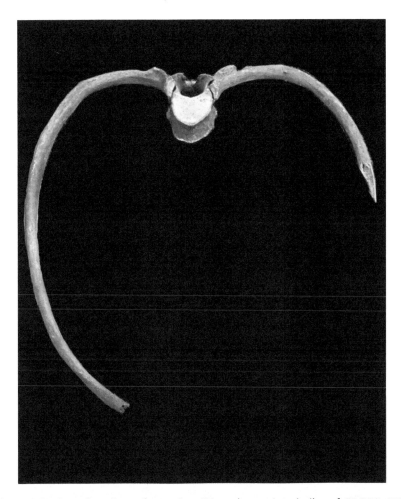

Photo 7.7 Superior view of vertebra T6 and associated ribs of FAO90 1703 (photo © Museum of London)

perfect circle. Photo 7.2 shows the seventh thoracic vertebra and the one remaining rib. As the paired ribs are bilaterally altered, I measured them as though the second rib was present, giving me a coronal and sagittal measurement of 21.4 cm × 21.4 cm. Neither of the examples of ribs retained the typical downward facing torqued C shape of anatomically normal ribs.

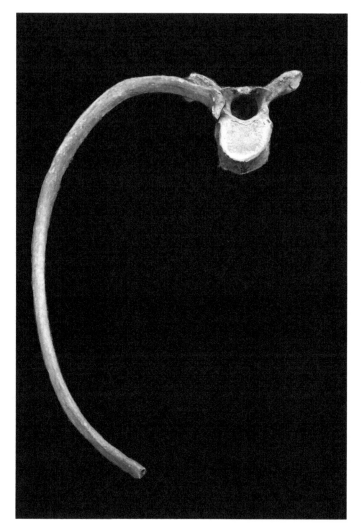

Photo 7.8 Superior view of vertebra T7 and associated rib of FAO90 1703 (photo © Museum of London)

Additionally, the thoracic spinous processes, normally able to be felt by hand if you run your fingers down your back, are diverted from their "normal" angles of about 45 degrees (measured from the body of the vertebrae), to extremely small angles between 10 and 30 degrees. This

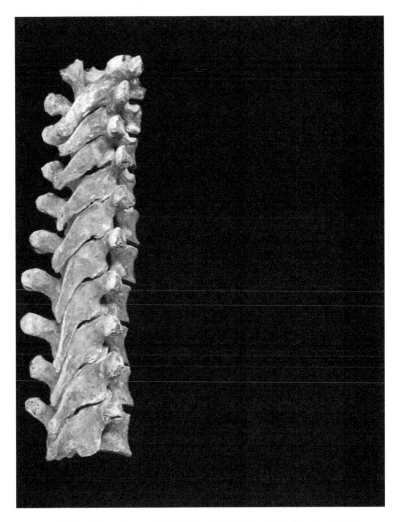

Photo 7.9   Right side view of T1-T10 of FAO90 1703 (photo © Museum of London)

causes the spinous processes to overlap, forming new articulation facets. It can create such distortion in the overall thoracic spine, that the
inward part of the S curve, at the mid- to lower-back, flattens out, and
the intervertebral disks atrophy.

Despite this modification, there are no concrete reports of this being traumatic, violent, or painful. Just as certain other forms of body modification show no adverse effects once the body acclimates to them, after temporary periods of discomfort or pain (braces, neck stretching), we must not assume that quality of life was diminished. As previously mentioned, the thoracic cages were not intact in the St. Bride's sample, therefore I set about reconstructing as many pairs of ribs as possible, and those pairs did not always include the standardized pair of sixth ribs and T6 which I measured in the Musée de l'Homme sample. Because of this, I used all existing pairs from the St. Bride's collection to ensure that the data analysis is as thorough as possible, and has as large a sample size as possible for both groups.

As briefly mentioned in the previous chapters, rib shape and vertebral spinous process angles do not usually display signs of being sexually dimorphic,[4] (for anatomical normal ribs and vertebrae, see Bass 1987, pp. 132–133; Byers 2008, p. 44; Evans 2015, pp. 96–97; White et al. 2011, pp. 153–158. For anatomical abnormalities of the ribs and vertebrae, see Brickley and Ives 2008; Ortner and Putschar 1981, pp. 273–274 and pp. 282–283, for a discussion of sexual dimorphism in ribs and vertebrae in anatomical textbooks, see the footnote). The extended citation just here in regard to what "anatomically normal" means is an unfortunately flawed stand-in for further research on the topic. To explain, I must digress for a moment.

We know, from text-based evidence—historical records, paintings, photos, and the like—that modern corseting began in the 1500s and continued until at least the early 1900s, at which point the practice fell out of favor. There were many reasons for this change. The Dress

---

[4]In this particular case, stating something so obvious is a bit like trying to prove a negative. The cited sources do not mention ribs or vertebrae in relation to sexual dimorphism, because ribs and vertebrae *are not* sexually dimorphic, therefore there is actually nothing to mention. However, they do mention other sexual dimorphisms of the human skeleton—femoral angles, mandibular angles and flare, pubic angles, sciatic notches, external occipital protuberances, mastoid processes, and the gracile or robust nature of the bones on average (ibid.), ergo were there something to be mentioned about the sexual dimorphism of the ribs, the researcher might reasonably suppose that such a thing would be mentioned. This is further complicated by the default anatomical illustration being that of the male skeleton, up to and including the model skeletons provided by replica skeleton companies such as Bone Clones and Skulls Unlimited. However, I digress.

Reform movement of the 1870s–1900s, the lack of materials to make full corsets which occurred during WWI, the shift in fashion to a less defined silhouette in the 1920s, and then the flexibility provided by a bra/girdle combination all contributed to the eventual downfall of the corset. But it is not as though there was a cutoff point after which wearing a corset was outlawed. Some women enjoyed the corset, or did not feel able to change with the fashion for whatever reason, and thus continued to wear it. We cannot, therefore, define a point at which we could expect to see completely "normal," uncorseted rib cages.

As an example, necessarily hypothetical as my data did not extend this far, imagine a woman who was born in 1880 and began corseting at age 13. Let us make her white, middle class, and Christian, to make her an exact cognate of the St. Bride's women. In 1893, fashions were still years away from the removal of the corset and the substitution of the bra and girdle. So, let us say she remained corseted until the era of the flappers (defined as between the mid-1910s to the late 1920s). That is thirty-ish years of corseting. Decidedly long enough to produce the effects in her skeleton. Now, even if she took off the corset, and lived to be 100 years old (dying in 1980), residual effects would be present on the skeleton—as they are in the modern body modification we do on a regular basis: braces. Additionally, this hypothetical woman would most likely not be in a skeletal collection. Even if we adjust her year of death to 40 years previously, and have her dying in 1940, we run into the same problem as before: her race, class, and religion would all be determining factors in her likelihood of being in a collection—white, middle class or above, Christian women remained buried, whereas women of color, impoverished women, and nonreligious women were more likely to be in collections. The largest skeletal collections in the United States, namely the Terry collection at the Smithsonian Institute, and the Cobb collection at Howard University, are skewed toward African American individuals of lower socioeconomic status. The good majority of people who died as recently as this also had relatives to bury them, and they remain buried. Were I to propose to excavate a cemetery of women who I could potentially guarantee had not corseted, I would need to begin with women born after 1940, and this is not a feasible proposition for the parameters of this study.

However, even if she were, there would need to be a researcher asking the question—general data about skeletal remains is recorded in various collections, but it is usually descriptive rather than research-question based. Apart from an abstract of an unpublished talk from 1985, there is no evidence that any researcher prior to myself has asked that question (Angel 1985). So, our hypothetical woman would not necessarily have had her ribs and vertebral angles measured or analyzed for the data to be available for comparison.

So, we have here two different issues when looking for data against which to compare rib and vertebral dimorphism: no one has bothered to look previously, therefore the question remained unanswered, and the inability to ask this particular question of modern datasets. While there is no way to retroactively fix the first problem, the second problem can be somewhat mitigated by using what comparisons **are** available, in this case comparisons between male and female sets of remains from the same collection (as I have done for the St. Bride's collection) and comparisons between skeletons from European and Europeanized, corset-wearing populations, and non-corset-wearing, non-European populations, as I have done with the Musée de l'Homme collection.

Two recent articles, however, delve deeply into the dimorphic potentials of vertebral body shape and size by looking at known-sex collections. Amores et al. (2014) looked at multiple dimensions on the 7th cervical and 12 thoracic vertebrae, and collected data each of these dimensions for 121 individuals. Notably absent from their comprehensive list, however, is the angle of the spinous process. This may partially have to do with the fact that the spinous process of the 12th thoracic vertebrae is rather stubby and not at all angular, being close in form to its neighbor, the L1, thus it would not make a good data point for their analysis.

Bastir et al. (2014) look at the sixth through ninth thoracic vertebrae of males and females, and conclude that the overall shape of the vertebrae differs between sexes. However, they do a comprehensive 3D analysis that also does not address vertebral angle. They do indicate that "In lower vertebrae the spinous process in males, systematically projects more caudally while in females this process is oriented horizontally" (ibid., p. 516), but no indication is given that this in any way contributes to a lessening of the angle the spinous process creates in relation to the vertebral body. The question remains: does this show that there is no difference between the two, or is this a lack of evidence that there **is** a difference? Because Bastir et al.'s sample size is small, but robust and representative, comprised of individuals between 20 and 42 years of age at death, I feel relatively comfortable saying that this shows that there is no difference between male and female spinous process angles. With such a meticulous study, and such clear 3D scans in the Bastir et al. paper, any deviation such as is seen in my populations would have been immediately identifiable.

Similarly, two recent articles address sexual dimorphism in rib shape and thoracic configuration. Garcia-Martinez et al. (2016) examines how rib structure influences respiratory depth, and shows that female rib cages from their sample individuals (female sample = 24 individuals, male sample = 18 individuals, total = 42 individuals) are less pyramidal shaped, and more downward facing (ibid.). Although the shape difference may appear to contradict my data analysis, the entirety of the shape must be taken into account, specifically that the ribs of my female populations are not downward facing at all, let alone displaying a pronounced downward orientation toward the sternum as Garcia-Martinez et al.'s sample shows. Furthermore, though the female rib cages in this example are less pyramidal, and more barrel shaped, they display a sternum that thrusts out from the body, rather than one which is parallel to the spinal column, the flat sternum being seen in the Musée de l'Homme articulated collection. Additionally, in the 3D scan of the thoracic cage (Garcia-Martinez et al. 2016, pp. 471, 472, 474) the vertebral spinous processes show robust angles of 45 degrees or larger.

Contrastingly, Bellemare et al. do not indicate a difference in shape apart from a lengthening of the torso in female skeletons of the same height as their male counterparts. They do note that "the ratios of rib lengths to body length were all significantly greater in females" (Bellemare et al. 2005, p. 235). They do not otherwise consider rib shape as an inherent sexually dimorphic feature, making no mention of the downward or upward facing sternal ends. As there are no images accompanying the article, I am unable to assess whether such images would show a difference in vertebral angle, sternal end direction, or rib shape.

Thus, current studies which address the shape of the rib cage either fail to see or fail to address any sexually dimorphic characteristics of spinous process angle or rib shape. Absent any indication of abnormalities, and keeping in mind that no one raised the issue of dimorphism in any anatomical textbooks that exist on the subject, any quantifiable and consistent differences between the shapes expressed in male and female skeletons from a time period where corseting was the norm able to be attributed to the influence of the corset on developing bone, particularly where other physical factors (metabolic diseases, injury, etc.) have been ruled out. Similarly, this applies to the spinous process angle as well.

In personal correspondence with Rachel Ives (2015), I was able to rule out rickets[5] and other metabolic disorders as a potential cause for deformation of the spinous processes. Thus, the combination of anatomically abnormal rib curvature with spinous process deformation can be positively associated only with corseting, and with no other known phenomenon, so long as it is seen across a collection of female skeletons who one can safely assume to have corseted, and not seen prevalently in the male skeletons of the same collection.

Far from curving downward toward the sternum, many of the female ribs curved directly forward, leaving a gap of a very small size, indicating that the cartilage which connected them to the sternum had been deformed as well, and that the sternal ends of the ribs would have been nudging up against the sternum itself. This abnormal curvature markedly tends to differentiate itself from rickets in two ways—it is uniform between T4 and T9, and the ribs do not exhibit a flattening of their most lateral curvature, but an accentuation of curvature at the most anterior portion of the rib, the sternal rib end (Brickley and Ives 2008; Ives 2015; Ortner and Putschar 1981).

To continue to examples of vertebrae in bioarchaeological discussions, the various anatomical textbook photographs showing the side

---

[5]Rickets, also known as Vitamin D deficiency, causes a systemic inability to process and accumulate calcium in the bones. The result of such deficiency are very flexible bones with low calcium density, which bend under the body's own weight. With the deficiency, the pressure of a person's arms against their rib cage causes a bending inward of the side curvature of the ribs, and a front pointing roundness to the front of the rib cage, commonly referred to as "pigeon breast." Several of my fellow bioanthropologists and I believe that the corseting deformation present in the St. Bride's population, and other populations, has been overlooked for decades because of being misattributed to Rickets.

view of a thoracic vertebra (Bass 1987, p. 101; Byers 2008, p. 42; Evans 2015, p. 97; White et al. 2011, p. 133), each show an approximately 45° angle, but there is no indication that this is either normal or abnormal. Thus, between 40 and 45 degrees was my cutoff point for normal, based on the above illustrations and on the control group of male skeletons. Therefore, when examining the St. Bride's and Musée de l'Homme collections, I coded anything over 45° as robust, and anything below 40° as remodeled due to corseting. The exception to this was T4, which was uniformly non-robust throughout the entire collection, in both male and female skeletons, and so did not factor into my equations.

Results from the St. Bride's Lower Churchyard (FAO90) Collection

For relevant measurements, I focused on finding the place on the skeleton where I might reasonably expect to find deformation away from anatomical normal. To reiterate, in no anatomical text that I have consulted do **either** the shape of the ribs **or** angles of the spinous processes of male and female skeletons show quantifiable sexual dimorphism (Bass 1987; Brickley and Ives 2008; Byers 2008; Evans 2015; Ives 2015; Ortner and Putschar 1981; Ubelaker 1978; White et al. 2011).

Because the corset creates an unnatural waist, rather than the natural one created by the bottom of the rib cage in uncorseted women, I surmised that corseting would create a distinct deformation of the ribs and spinous processes, and anything T6 and below would show deformation in all cases of corseting. All corset shapes, whether underbust or overbust, produce pressure and constriction below breasts, where the sixth rib meets the sternum.

However, in the St. Bride's collection, not all skeletons had one or both of their sixth ribs or T6. Additionally, it was often not possible to create multiple pairings of consecutive ribs in order to see the overall shape of the thoracic cage, though I did so when I could. Therefore, it was necessary to use all available vertebrae/rib pairs, which allowed me to recreate as much of the thoracic cage as possible. For both collections, I either measured the circumference at the sixth rib around the thoracic cage (Musée de l'Homme) or estimated using an online calculator for all extant rib circumferences (St. Bride's). I also measured the total dimension for both the coronal and the sagittal aspects of all rib pairs. I further measured the angle of all available spinous processes in both collections.

Additionally, as this particular deformation of the spinous processes had never been fully described before (although it has now been confirmed by Moore and Buckberry [2016] and was quasi-described by Angel et al. [1985]), there are no discussions of spinous process abnormality, apart from those related to spina bifida, in the abovementioned texts.

In the St. Bride's collection, when I compared ages regardless of sex across the entire sample, there was no difference in the deformation of the spinous processes or in the coronal dimension of the ribs— respectively younger and older women had similarly shaped rib cages, and similar spinous process angles, and older and younger men also had similarly shaped rib cages compared to each other. However, when I compared the two sexes to each other without considering age, there were distinct differences in both aspects of the skeletal structure. The spinous processes of women displayed both mean and individual angles that were significantly smaller than those of men. Furthermore, this was across the sample, with all women (sample size of 70 for these measurements) displaying the same trend.

In regard to the coronal measurements, there was also no difference when I used age as a factor, but there was a noticeable difference in the ratio of coronal to sagittal measurements when I compared the sexes. The difference thus shown was that female skeletons had markedly smaller coronal dimensions relative to the size of the sagittal dimension, giving them a rounder, more barrel-shaped thoracic cavity, whereas most of the measured male skeletons had longer coronal dimensions giving them the ovoid thoracic shape that is characteristic of a "normal" skeleton, as pictured in the above texts.

From initial observations of the St. Bride's skeletons conducted by the Museum of London, Archaeology division (MOLA) upon excavation, only two sets of remains had been previously identified as having corset damage (Walker 2012). Such damage as was specifically observed, the curvature of the ribs and deformation of the spine, was not mentioned in the subsequent MOLA report of pathology of the vertebrae, which concentrated on the accession data of individual bones rather than looking at sets of bones.

One male skeleton did not at all conform to these results, however. FAO90 1312, an adult male between 36 and 45, had the spinous process deformation and rounded rib shape typical of a corset wearing female. His coronal and sagittal dimensions were almost 1:1 for all measured rib pairs (T4–T7) and the angles of his spinous processes were smaller than the mean for males. In examining his recorded pathologies, I found that he had been recorded as having scoliosis and spina bifida. The indicated treatment for those conditions regardless of sex was, during the time period under consideration, the long-term use of a corset, as it is today (Photos 7.10, 7.11, and 7.12).

This type of treatment—the medical use of corsets—and the fact that it can be seen in the skeletal record, is discussed in considerably more detail by Moore and Buckberry (2016), where they detail a male burial from the 1800s which shows evidence of both corseting, and of Pott's Disease, a tuberculotic infection of the spine.

Moving to a discussion of the ribs and vertebrae themselves, we can see that female skeletons demonstrated a marked deformation away from both textbook normal and anatomical normal from the sample. Specifically, that the mean ratio of the coronal dimension to the sagittal dimension at T6 was 1:90, and that the overall trend of female ratios was greater than 1:74, that found in the to be anatomically normal for males in the collections. The ribs in the female skeletons as a whole also demonstrate a shape that deviates from both textbook and sample normal, with a lack of downward curvature and a forward lateral straightening, making the body of the rib sit level or very close to level with the vertebral body. Furthermore, accounting for the space of the intervertebral disks and carefully articulating the superior and inferior articular facets of each vertebra in the St. Bride's collection revealed that the female spinal columns did not conform to the s-shaped curvature of normal spines, and in many cases there was possible vertebral disc atrophy to accommodate the newly straightened spinal shape.

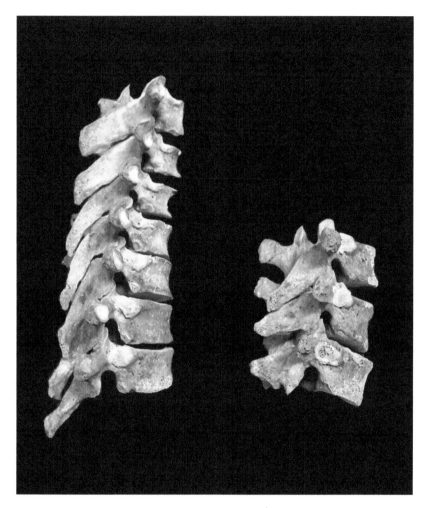

Photo 7.10 Right side view of vertebrae T1-T7 and T9-T11 of FAO90 1312 (photo © Museum of London)

Additionally, the vertebrae of the female skeletons acquired a plastically deformed set of angles from the vertebral body to the tip of the spinous process, as well as a less robust spinous process appearance overall. This lack of robusticity cannot be attributed only to sex, however, because of the evidence of the anomalous male skeleton in the

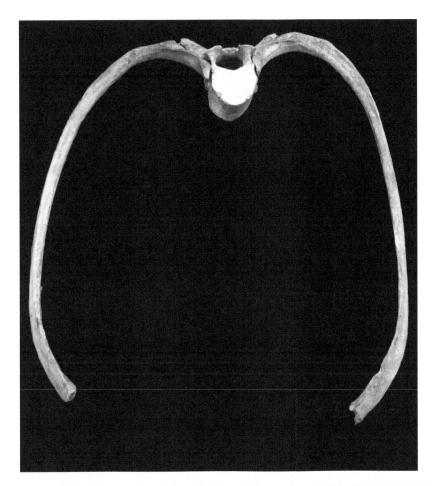

Photo 7.11 Superior view of vertebra T4 and associated ribs of FAO90 1312 (photo © Museum of London)

St. Bride's sample. This male skeleton, presenting to the Museum of London's bioarchaeologists as having scoliosis and spina bifida, shows the same deformations as the female skeletons, with a ratio of coronal to sagittal dimensions of 1:1.02 at T6, and a lack of overall robusticity in his spinous process angles. During the time period in question, and indeed in modern medicine, the accepted practice for "curing" people of scoliosis was a back brace, or a corset. It is an absolute certainty

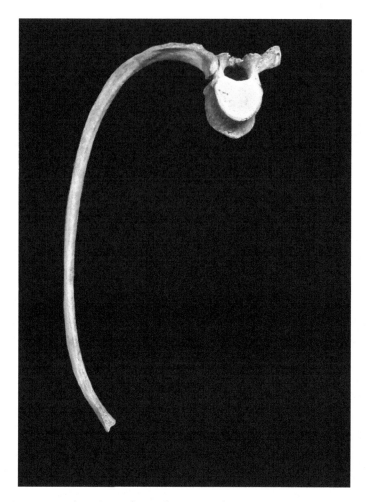

Photo 7.12 Superior view of vertebra T6 and associated ribs of FAO90 1312 (photo © Museum of London)

that to survive to the age at which he died, between 36 and 45 years, he would have had to wear a corset. However, his spinous processes are not nearly as extreme in their non-normality than many of the female skeletons in the sample. The fact that his spinous processes show somewhat less damage can be attributed to the fact that his corset was worn for support rather than fashion, and most likely would not have had to be reimagined as each decade decided on its newest trend.

Finally, as shown by the photos of the articulated vertebral columns, compared to the male vertebrae, the female spinous processes are not only diverted downward, they are also diverted laterally, to one side or the other, where they have met with resistance from the next most inferior vertebra. While the females have greater maximum angle sizes, the males have larger minimum sizes by far across the board, and there is a greater standard deviation in the female sample, leading to the conclusion that outlying female vertebrae with robust angles somewhat skewed the maximum values in the sample. The means of the male sample are also much higher, indicating that they have more larger angles in general.

Use of Comparative Samples

In such a study, comparative samples are useful as they tend to minimize confirmation bias, by demonstrating that the same phenomenon can be seen in different populations, even if the presentation of that phenomenon contains variations on the theme. Some differences in the two collections of the overall study bear discussing. As noted before, the Musée de l'Homme collection contrasts in many ways with the St. Bride's population. It is not representative of female skeletons from France during this time period, as it contains only 4 skeletons from France, and 7 from French-controlled colonial territories. The only thing these skeletons have in common as a group is the fact that at some point they attracted the attention of the curators or naturalist friends of the curators, and through that attention they ended up as the first part of the Musée de l'Homme's comparative anatomy collection. This produces obvious ethical problems as discussed at the beginning of this chapter and in Chapter 1, as the likelihood of someone with the power to refuse such collection ending up in it is low, meaning that a few statements can be concretely made about women who did: they would have been poor, without much in the way of family or personal wealth; certainly many of them were enslaved people or indentured servants; and they were potentially sourced by grave robbing or medical-school based dissection.

However, despite this intense poverty or lack of control over their lives, they must have moved about polite society in one way or another. Most were not from remote or "uncivilized" areas of the world, and as many are listed as living in specific cities, they would have dressed to the times as did the women of London's St. Bride's. Thus, considering what I have shown about cities in previous chapters, we can know that the women who inhabited European or Europeanized cities wore the corset as a standard undergarment. Using the aforementioned information about the St. Bride's population, particularly the anomalous male, we can now discuss how to determine whether or not women in this sample are showing the same deformation, and to what extent. First, a discussion of the variation in evaluation technique and the challenges it posed.

With articulated skeletons, which had been reconstructed by experts in the field, I was no longer concerned with the proper alignment of the ribs and spinal column. However, I no longer had unfettered access to all of the surfaces of the bone, and my photography became somewhat limited. For example, getting a clean photograph of the superior angle of the ribs and vertebrae was not going to happen. Nor, it turned out, was a clear scan of the spinous processes, once I began 3D scanning. There were simply too many things in the way, from other bones to the metal bar of the stand creating both a physical impediment and a surface off which the laser could scatter. And yet the detail of the photographs I was able to take allowed me to do the above side-by-side comparison of the non-Europeanized and Europeanized skeletons. Additionally, the 3D modeling technique gives a better sense of the rounded rib cage than looking at a 2D photograph. This technology was beneficial in creating better data points for analysis.

However, the only female skeletons at or below 1:.74 for their coronal to sagittal ratios were those that were anomalous or non-Europeanized, which is shown when the non-Europeanized skeletons were removed from consideration. Overall, the female thoracic cages demonstrated a barrel shape, with the ribs showing an abnormal curvature as defined in relation to the photograph in White et al. (2011, p. 158) and the discussions in Amores et al. (2014), Bastir et al. (2014), Bellemare et al. (2005), and Garcia-Martinez et al. (2016) and the sternal cartilage presented as deformed. The spinal column for many of the female skeletons lacked its anatomically normal curvature.

As in the St. Bride's collection, the vertebrae of the female skeletons acquired plastic deformation to their spinous process angles, and a less robust spinous process appearance overall. This was especially pronounced in the anomalous female skeleton, that of the girl who died between 13 and 17 years of age mentioned in the opening vignette. Due to the fact that she was still in her bone growth phase at the time of death, we can clearly see that pressure placed on these particular sets of bones creates early and long-lasting plastic deformation in this pattern, first described in relation to the known-corset-wearing London population.

What, then, do these results "mean"? What purpose has been served by collecting these data and assembling them here? The meaning is twofold—firstly, the data serve to demonstrate that corseting **did** have an effect on the skeletal structure of women, but that the effect was not fatal, nor was it necessarily violent, painful, or traumatic. And secondly, using the cross-cultural comparison shows that this is not a phenomenon unique to the St. Bride's cemetery, nor to the "civilized" urban areas of the world, such as London. I will address these two meanings one at a time.

Regardless of our chosen discourse—exotic/erotic, Freudian/hysterical, medical, domestic, etc.—we have been the recipient of several culturally formed ideas and opinions, myths, about corseting. These opinions, as shown in the above chapters, come to us lacking nuance, and rooted in reinforcing the idea of women's powerlessness, their de-subjectification if you will, turning them from self-actualized subjects to mere objects. This results in painting women as merely incidental participants in the structure of the patriarchal hegemony. While there are theorists who believe that we all are powerless over the shape of our lives, that we do what is culturally constructed for us and we cannot move beyond that because our culture is all-pervasive, I am not one of them. I see that argument as particularly facile and flattening. It minimizes individual contributions, leaving no room for agentive action, despite evidence that individual agency builds to collective agency, creating different hegemonies over time.

What the women of St. Bride's illustrate so beautifully **is** that individuality, despite their uniformity of damage from corseting. If we were to look at *only* the skeletons, if we were to see *only* the damage, then we may be forgiven for looking at them as victims of violent patriarchal harm. But we must look at them as more than that. We must look at them as we have in the previous chapters—as mothers, wives, public facing figures, participants in their own discourses, makers of their own fashions, purchasers of their own clothing. We must look at them as complex. They vary in ages. They vary in their cause of death. They vary in socioeconomic class. They vary in profession and marital status. They, it cannot goes without stating, undoubtedly varied in the way they thought of and used the corset. Some may have vainly tight-laced. Some may have been very casual wearers of the corset. Some may have worn it during pregnancy, while others did not. Some may have been able to afford to follow fashion, while others chose not to, and still others could not afford but one corset in their adult lives, carefully mended when the fabric tore or the boning broke. The point is that the changes in their skeleton caused by corseting were most likely seen by them as incidental, or desired, or possibly not even noticed or remarked upon by women living their daily lives, giving their undergarments no more thought than we give ours today.

The second point illustrated by the above data is that women the world over concerned themselves with fashion, acquired fashion through cultural diffusion, and corseted. Based on our discussion of the non-dimorphic qualities of the ribs and vertebrae, and of the fact that the anatomically normal human rib cage is wider than it is deep, when we see the same deformation on skeletons from London and skeletons from Italy (MNHN-NA-771), Madagascar (MNHN-NA-818), New Caledonia in Canada (MNHN-NA-2277), and Mumbai, in India (MNHN-NA-784), we are seeing the interconnectedness of the world at the time under consideration, as well as the results of colonial expansion, ideas about European exceptionalism and white supremacy, and the desire to "civilize" the savage, as Balch put it in his 1904 discussion of clothing. The idea and function of the corset, like the women who wore it, was complex, and it was effective—remaining the prevailing undergarment of "civilization" for centuries. The next chapter will discuss how such ideas have continued into modern times, and examine the newest trends in corseting; today's own "bioarchaeology of binding."

Bibliography

Angel, J., et al. (1985). *Bony Response to 18th Century Stays Versus Later Corsets* (abstract only, unpublished).

Anonymous. (1866, February 17). A Plea for Tight-Lacing. *Flag of Our Union, 21*(7), 110.

Anonymous. (1883, March 16). The New Skirt. *Knowledge, 3,* 162–163.

Amores, A., Botella, M., & Alemán, I. (2014). Sexual Dimorphism in the 7th Cervical and 12th Thoracic Vertebrae from a Mediterranean Population. *Journal of Forensic Sciences, 59*(2), 301–305.

Balch, E. (1904). Savage and Civilized Dress. *Journal of the Franklin Institute of the State of Pennsylvania, for the Promotion of the Mechanic Arts, 57*(5), 321–332.

Bass, W. (1987). *Human Osteology: A Laboratory and Field Manual* (3rd ed.). Colombia, MO: The Missouri Archaeological Society.

Bastir, M., Higuero, A., Ríos, L., & García Martínez, D. (2014). Three-Dimensional Analysis of Sexual Dimorphism in Human Thoracic Vertebrae: Implications for the Respiratory System and Spine Morphology. *American Journal of Physical Anthropology, 155,* 513–521.

Bellemare, F., Higuero, A., Ríos, L., & García Martínez, D. (2005). Sexual Dimorphism of Human Ribs. *Respiratory Physiology and Neurobiology, 150,* 233–239.

Brickley, M., & Ives, R. (2008). *The Bioarchaeology of Metabolic Bone Disease.* Oxford, UK: Academic Press.

Byers, S. (2008). *Introduction to Forensic Anthropology* (3rd ed.). Boston, MA: Pearson Education.

Dickinson, R. (1887). The Corset: Questions of Pressure and Displacement. *New York Medical Journal, 44,* 507–516.

Evans, E. (2015). *Anatomy in Black.* Chichester, UK: Lotus Publishing.

Garcia-Martinez, D., Torres-Tamayo, N., Torres-Sanchez, I., García-Río, F., & Bastir, M. (2016). Morphological and Functional Implications of Sexual Dimorphism in the Human Skeletal Thorax. *American Journal of Physical Anthropology, 161,* 467–477.

Gould, S. (1982). The Hottentot Venus. *Natural History, 91,* 20–27.

Ives, R. (2015). Personal Correspondence Regarding Identification of Rickets vs. Costume Related Plastic Deformation, via email.

Jenkins, T. (2011). *Contesting Human Remains in Museum Collections: The Crisis of Cultural Authority.* New York, NY: Routledge.

Lai, E., Chang, J. Z., Jane Yao, C. C., Tsai, S. J., Liu, J. P., Chen, Y. J., et al. (2008). Relationship Between Age at Menarche and Skeletal Maturation Stages in Taiwanese Female Orthodontic Patients. *Journal of the Formosan Medical Association, 107*(7), 527–532.

Lord, W. B. (1868/1870). *Freaks of Fashion: The Corset and the Crinoline.* London: Ward, Lock, and Tyler.

Matthew, C. (2000). *Short Oxford history of the British Isles, the Nineteenth Century.* Oxford: Oxford University Press.

Moore, J., & Buckberry, J. (2016). The Use of Corsetry to Treat Pott's Disease of the Spine from 19th Century Wolverhampton, England. *The International Journal of Paleopathology, 14,* 74–80.

Müller, A. (2006). *Fashioning Childhood in the Eighteenth Century: Age and Identity.* New York, NY: Routledge.

Ortner, D., & Putschar, W. (1981). *Identification of Pathological Conditions in Human Skeletal Remains.* Washington, DC: Smithsonian Institution Press.

Shrimpton, J. (2016). *Victorian Fashion.* Oxford, UK: Shire Publications.

Ubelaker, D. (1978). *Human Skeletal Remains: Excavation, Analysis, Interpretation* (2nd ed.). Washington, DC: The Smithsonian Institute.

Walker, D. (2012). *Disease in London, 1st–19th Centuries: An Illustrated Guide to Diagnosis.* Monograph Series 56. London, UK: MOLA.

Walkowitz, J. (1992). *City of Dreadful Delight: Narratives of Sexual Danger in Late Victorian London.* Chicago, IL: University of Chicago Press.

Waugh, N. (1954/2018). *Corsets and Crinolines.* New York, NY: Routledge.

White, T., Black, M., & Folkens, A. (2011). *Human Osteology* (3rd ed.). Burlington, MA: Elsevier Press.

8

Modern Corseting and How We Talk About Today's Women

Perhaps the most persistent pseudo-scientific myth about regarding women who corseted is that of rib removal. Certainly, all areas of science have such issues—Egyptology and aliens building the pyramids; geography and Atlantis; astronomy and astrology; etc. For reasons unknown, what has stuck in the minds of corseting enthusiasts and denunciators alike is that women during the time period, and women today, have their ribs removed to make their waists smaller and their corsets fit better.

To remind you of the historical context outlined above, I shall reiterate a few facts about surgery and medicine from the historical time period: There was limited anesthesia, meaning that surgery was performed with the person conscious and with full sensation (Fitzharris 2017). There was a minimal emphasis on hygiene, leading to almost certain occurrence of infection (ibid.). Many surgeries were not considered or expected to be survivable, including caesarian sections, which, one should note, did not include the removal of bone nor any work near or on the vertebral column. Surgeons would have contests as to who could perform amputations or resection skin the quickest (ibid.), and spinal surgery, or anything requiring that they be knowledgeable and skillful with the nervous system, was still decades off at this point.

© The Author(s) 2020
R. Gibson, *The Corseted Skeleton*,
https://doi.org/10.1007/978-3-030-50392-5_8

While women were going to doctors in increasing numbers, and a result of that was the creation of women as a medical subject, many anatomists still based their practices off of what worked for men, unless the surgery happened on the female reproductive system. At that point, the focus was on removal, rather than repair. Furthermore, at all levels of society, women's contribution to the home and family were seen as necessary for that family to function—taking weeks or months off to recover from a surgery in the name of vanity, and for a surgery that could kill the subject, was socially unthinkable (entire section Aptowicz 2014; Fitzharris 2017). And finally, as shown by the skeletal evidence I compiled, there was absolutely no need to do so.

Enter Dr. Barry Eppley, plastic surgeon, based in Indianapolis, and claiming to have done over 25 rib removal surgeries (Eppley 2016). The one he most publicly lauds is that of Pixee Fox, a self-proclaimed surgery obsessive, who states that Eppley and his team removed six of her ribs (three on each side, nonsequentially). Fox has taken plastic surgery to an extreme, listing herself on Instagram as "the living doll." Certainly, much of the augmentation she has had is evident—her breasts are very large, as is her posterior. Her face is changed dramatically from its original features. Her waist is indeed tiny. Yet, in many of the photographs that bare her abdomen, you can see her rib cage, very clearly defined. You can see her abdominal muscles, and you can see the definition of her lower sternal cartilage and you can see the front portions of her ribs. In fact, you can count them; they are all present.

Also, no photographs of the procedure performed on Fox are posted (Fox 2017) and Snopes.com, a website devoted to debunking fake claims, calls Fox's claim to have had this surgery "questionable" (Lacapria 2015). No before and after photos with a noticeable difference in circumference are posted (Fox 2017), and the "post-surgery photo" shown on the Snopes.com site is far from conclusive (Lacapria 2015) showing only bruising in a very small area, and a similarly small bandage, both of which could be done with makeup. No write-up of this allegedly successful procedure by Eppley exists in medical textbooks, plastic surgery conference abstracts, or medical journals. Eppley has not published this procedure or results from it in the American Journal of Medicine, or the journal of the American Academy of

Cosmetic Surgery, or the proceedings of the American Society of Plastic Surgeons and the Plastic Surgery Foundation's annual meetings. No corroboration from Eppley's surgical team has been posted (Eppley 2017). Eppley has no evident published work with the search terms "rib removal" or "rib resectioning." And although Eppley states that he "definitely did [Fox's] surgery" (Eppley 2016), his website only contains photos of the procedure which appear to have been performed on a cadaver—close examination of the photographs show no bleeding at the site of incision and removal, indicating that said removal is taking place on an already dead body (confirmed in consultation with Wendy Birch, head of the Anatomy Laboratory at University College London) (Eppley 2017).

While Eppley and I agree (Eppley 2016) that it would have been nigh on impossible for the procedure to have been done between the years of 1700 and 1900, it is my contention that it is still not performed cosmetically to this day. As the skeletal evidence shows, there was no need to perform such surgeries—the pressure of the corset on developing bone would do the job of forming the woman into the more desirable shape. And in modern revivals of the corseting trend, standard bone remodeling—osteoclast/osteoblast activity at any age—has been shown to perform the same function (Jung 2017).

Why, then, does this myth persist (and persist it does—I hear it often when I give talks, or teach classes on this subject)? Why do we want to believe that women went to such extremes for a fashionably tiny waist, and how does that fit into this overarching narrative we have built around the corset? To see that, we must look at why the corset fell out of popularity, and how and why it came back again.

*   *   *

The Fall and Rise of the Modern Corset

If the corset was seen as hyper-sexualized feminine, unnatural, unmotherly, and yet not wearing the corset with the fashion of the day, in whatever form that fashion existed, was considered unfeminine, slovenly, and improper, what occurred when women cast off the corset entirely was revolutionary and incendiary. With the Rational Dress movement of the 1870s–1890s, women set the world on its ear. Their reasoning for ridding themselves of the corset was their health and comfort, and a return to the beauty and modesty of nature, though that modesty was under cultural dispute as seen above. Where the corset was seen as contravening nature, going without one was seen as giving into it, a thought that in many ways terrified.

If we grant Sherry Ortner's point (Ortner 1974) that women are an intermediary between nature and culture, what occurs when they decide to abandon that role? Nature is seen as uncontrolled, indeed, as uncontrollable, so if no moderating force exists then perhaps it will take over, overrun, kill, civilization, and culture. Removing the corset opens the possibility that the "natural" woman will de-civilize or unacculturate society. That the female body—that women—will be uncontrolled, and thus uncontrollable. That this movement came when women (among others) were pressing for abolition, for temperance, and for the vote, is no coincidence.

The Rational dress or the Bloomer costume consisted of, "…a loose tunic-dress extending to just below the knee, worn over ankle-length, baggy trousers. An advocate of women's rights, Mrs. [Amelia] Bloomer was primarily concerned with the hygienic and comfortable aspects of 'pantaloons,'" (Steele 1985, p. 145). Kunzle states that "the first formally organized dress reform societies appeared in the United States, in the aftermath of the Anti-Slavery movement which did so much to inspire subsequent feminism in that country.…This same year [1873] the first Dress Reform Society was founded in Boston by a group of laywomen and women doctors headed by Abba Gould Woolson" (Kunzle 1982, p. 172). Agreeing with the medical community that fashionable corseting was detrimental to the health of women and the children they bore, the Dress Reform Society produced practical, modest suggestions for a new type of clothing for women.

With complaints about how women could be reasonably expected to fully participate in society if she remained corseted, and the force of modern medicine behind them, the reformers advocated loose clothing and—if not trousers—sensible divided skirts for ease of motion. Kunzle states:

The 'New Dispensation' in dress hoped to protect the vital organs from compression and cold; attain uniformity of body-temperature, divided at present between frigid (shoulder and upper chest), temperate (thorax) and torrid (waist and hip) zones; reduce the total weight and bulk of clothing; and suspend it from the shoulders rather than the hips. Problems of compression, temperature, weight and bulk would all be solved by altering the system of suspension.

Suspension was a critical matter. Recognizing that there was no way of eliminating pressure at the waist as long as the hips were the sole point of support, and that an accumulation of up to sixteen thicknesses of material at the waist invited its compression in order to restore it optically to its natural size, Mrs. Woolson demonstrated that all clothing may be conveniently, decently and pleasingly suspended from the shoulders. (Kunzle 1982, pp. 172–173)

One can rather see their point, as temperature was thought to effect health to an immoderate degree. If parts of the body were to remain cold while others overheated, ill-health would result. Furthermore, the multitude of layers of female dress—underclothing, petticoats, a chemise, the corset, an overdress, and any addition of bustle, hoops, or tapes to shape the garment, would be quite heavy, and the locus of that weight was the hips.

It was the contention of the reformers that this severely overbalanced the woman, making her bottom heavy, unwieldy on top—stiff, like the handle of the bell she resembled—and required a corset to give her any aspect of the curvaceous feminine form. Their answer was to remove curves to a bare hint, intuited by the person viewing the garment, from the form underneath. Kunzle's rather snarky aside that "The poor aesthetic result may be judged from the accompanying illustrations" (Kunzle 1982, p. 173), is not borne out by pictures or illustrations of the day. In fact, I beg to differ with his opinion: while it may have shocked the public of the early twentieth century, certainly it is no longer shocking, nor any more aesthetically displeasing than many of the fashions today.

O'Followell, writing four decades after the beginning of the reform movement, agrees that the classical, also called the Greek, or Roman, style of dress, was more beautiful than the artificial contortions of the corset. Comparing the unadorned female to the classical ideal, he writes:

> We see the Venus de Milo, and find her fair and beautiful, but if she were wearing the current styles, surely you would see her as ugly, for the clothing of today would not fit her size. You admire the Venus de Milo, and you admire the small woman of today, yet if the small woman were without her clothing you would be obliged to conclude that she must be ugly because she would not resemble the Venus. (O'Followell 1908, p. 239)

While his logic is not impeccable on this point, for surely a person can find more than one type of body beautiful, it does make a fair point—that if the unclothed natural body of the Venus de Milo is held up as a societal pinnacle of female perfection, then the corset contravenes that perfection, makes a woman grotesque and unnatural. He is also not alone in this—both one of the anonymous contributors to the journal Knowledge (Anonymous 1883), and D. O. Teasely (1904), make the comparison to the various statues. It is ironic, therefore, that the dress reformers were seen to be mentally disturbed for wishing to return the body to the state of nature.

It was during the time of the dress reform that the psychological trope of female hysteria, which I have discussed earlier in this work, came to prominence. The blanket term hysteria served for a number of problems of the female body and psyche. A woman was thought to be hysterical if she ranted, if she were melancholy, if she wanted sex, if she would not submit to sex, if she tight-laced, if she wore no corset, and if she was at all agitated, in mind, in body, or politically. Steele states:

> According to the American reformer Mary Tillotson, the phrase 'to wear the breeches' carried with it 'the implied idea that pants are allied to power'; and bloomers were widely regarded as both feminist and masculine. Many men responded with anger and ridicule; according to the New York Times (May 27, 1876), the 'thirst for trousers' was a 'curious nervous disorder,' probably 'hysteria, attended by…mental hallucination,' (Steele 1985, p. 146)

It is to this that Foucault refers when he writes, "[the female body] … was placed in organic communication with the social body (whose regulated fecundity it was supposed to ensure,)" (Foucault 1978, p. 104). This equation of the corsetless, natural body with the hysterical woman underscored the idea that a woman without a corset was nature uncontrolled—something no longer regulated—childbearing out of control of the male-headed household. As the women of the period were leaving the strict confines of the late Victorian house and entering the public–social sphere, entering politics, entering the workforce, they were escaping the control of the corset and of society. Society in this case was personified by the male.

However, feminists were not the only proponents of Rational dress. Putting forth the case of healthy pregnancy and motherhood, many women shunned the corset for its bodily constriction and its link to moral degeneracy. Steele states,

> 'True health' and 'true virtue' were allied…. Thus at the religious community at Oneida, New York, women wore, 'trousers and loose, short gowns, like children's, that thus clad they could regain health and equilibrium of forces adequate to the high influence they must wield in the harmonization of society.' Dress reform was but the first step by which women should exert their 'ennobling influence' on society. (Steele 1985, p. 146)

This accepts the idea of the corset as contra nature, but rejects completely the idea that it was needed to regulate the female form as society saw it. This alternate view can be explained by the theories of Jean Comaroff, who states, "the waxing and waning of bodily space and the presence or absence of attractiveness at its centre [sic] are thus realized through the process of reciprocal identity definition that occurs in a social exchange, a process which also tightens or loosens bodily margins" (Comaroff 1985, p. 548). For the nonfeminist reformers, Rational dress brought nature into society, as the mediating force discussed by Ortner. However, the rational dress soon began to signify something else to women—reform movements in general.

One did not have to be a feminist to want reform, as seen by the above. Nonfeminists also pressed for an end to slavery, and for prohibition, wanting not equality, but temperance in all things. It is in this way that dress reform was seen by them: temperance in dress and a repression of the sexuality inherent in the corset would contribute further to the cause of temperance in industry and in alcohol.

The period of the fight for women's rights in England and America overlapped with the First World War. Necessity had removed women from the home with far more urgency and permanence than their own fight for independence from their husbands, fathers, and governments. During the period immediately following the war, fashion reflected this independence, and the rebellion expressed by throwing off the constricting corset. The actions of the flapper, the drop-waisted dresses she wore, and the dance craze of the Charleston, would not allow for the restriction of movement. For a small chested, thin woman, an option was to do without supporting undergarments entirely. However, not all women's forms fit the styles of the day. For them, corsets moved down off the chest and became waist cinchers and girdles, while the top part separated from the bottom and became a brassiere—a garment which could emphasize or conceal, and served both purposes during its tenure as the mainstay of lingerie.

Modern Corseting, and Why It Has Found a Resurgence

The above text has taken us to the age of dress reform—women fought for their right to dress as they pleased, to remove the corset and move more freely into a different style of undergarment, the bra and girdle pairing, and eventually, just the bra. With the removal of the corset, myriad opportunities both physical and social opened to women. As they had replaced men in the wartime factories, so too did they replace the uncomfortable corset and voluminous skirts with flexible, elastic lingerie and shorter, more manageable skirts. Yet it is important to realize that this was very much a choice and that opinions on that choice differed significantly. When government intervened during the

Second World War to regulate their support garments, the women again rebelled. Jill Fields discusses this rebellion in her book on sexuality:

> In February 1947…[Christian] Dior['s] style featured a long and full skirt, rounded shoulders, and a cinched waist. This silhouette was a dramatic departure from the shape of women's clothing in the United States and Great Britain during World War II. In both countries, wartime shortages had prompted government regulation of fabric and materials that kept skirts straight and hems knee length….In the United States, though Women's Bureau director Mary Anderson declared corsets essential to women's war work in factories, the government banned elastic from foundation garments…. Distinctions between New Look and World War II-era styles also provoked arguments against its adoption, and a short but pointed debate ensued. For many the New Look marked a welcome return of peacetime femininity for women, but some viewed it as a step backward in women's comfort, convenience, and beauty in dress. (Fields 2007, p. 256)

With elastics and synthetics replacing steel boning, corsets were becoming easier to don, and cheaper to produce and purchase. Advertisements for girdles and bras, the fashion that replaced corsets, make certain to announce the new materials, sometimes using an amalgamation of them in the name of the product. An advertisement for Perfolastic Girdle allows you to try the garment for ten days, and has such statements as "Reduce Quickly, Easily, and Safely!" and "The inner surface of the Perfolastic Girdle is a delightfully soft, satinized fabric, especially designed to wear next to the body…. A special adjustable back allows for perfect fit as inches disappear" (Photobucket).

Also, one can see an attempt to renaturalize the unnatural figure made by the girdle, in an advertisement for Werner's Tru-Lift: "So divinely comfortable, too—because Tru-Lift supports you *lightly,* in the manner nature intended" (Weirduniverse). This emphasis on innovation, fashion, and a return to nature, was exemplary of the postwar ideal of comfortable yet stylish women, working during the day and being somewhat sexual at night—the products were versatile, and showed that the women who wore them could be as well.

The twentieth century became the era of the brand name designer and the brand name knockoff with Dior spearheading fashion and the lesser designers rushing to copy his lines. The new corsetry became a counter-rebellion, though this time the argument was for comfort and freedom within a newly defined femininity, rather than for the vote and freedom by throwing off tightly defined eroticized femininity. While styles of lingerie would fade in and out of fashion, the corset and its binding restrictive properties would remain ever at the back of the collective mind, and continue to make periodic resurgences in fashion and fetishistic behavior.

If we grant ethnographer and theorist Terance Turner's idea that the natural is socially unintegrated, we could counter-argue that so is that which is seen as very unnatural. The corset, as far as possible from the comfort driven, natural lines of the jean and t-shirt combination found on many of today's women, is then an extreme of social unintegration. This is very similar to many things which are sexually fetishized. For example, in escalating order of the "bizarre-ness" of the fetish named, shoes, latex wear, bondage and domination, scarification, and coprophilia. These all have similarities to the focus of anthropologist Mary Douglas' theories on liminality and the body as a physical boundary (Douglas 1966). That which is in is designed to stay in (without further bulwarking) and that which comes out of the body is designed to stay out (without reintegration). Corseting or tight-lacing, therefore lies pretty securely in the middle range of fetish-types—it shapes and shores up the body (making it unnatural) but does not release things by breaching the skin's liminal barrier (as do scarification and coprophilia). This redefining of the corset as fetish is seen most recently with the revival of tight-lacing, and the dissemination of information about it as an aesthetic practice via the internet.

Among the sites devoted to tight-lacing is that of Cathie Jung, the woman with the smallest waist of anyone currently living. Jung has been tight-lacing for the last several decades, and has a 15-inch waist when she is laced into one of the many corsets she owns. She also occasionally dons an all-silver corset, which seems to be a reproduction of the sixteenth-century metal corsets discussed at the beginning of this paper.

Jung's original adult waist size was 26 inches, and her uncorseted size currently is 19 inches. Although she, and people who have interviewed her, speak to why she began and continues such extreme body modification, there is little talk of symbolism or restriction or repression—except in the literal meanings of the word: the restriction and repression of the waist, the modification of the body itself. Her husband enjoyed the look of the wasp waist, and she did also, and so she embarked on a lifelong pursuit of waist training. For her, it is simply a mode of dress, extreme certainly, but not politically or socially symbolic in her own opinion (Jung 2017). Determining whether or not those who admire her efforts and wish to emulate them also see the practice as lacking political symbolism is as yet undetermined.

This is echoed on other websites devoted to the practice. These websites are not just a tool for those making use of an existing fashion meme, but are perpetuators of that meme through commerce; they often sell corsets for fashion, fetish, or body modification. In this way, a person may build an identity not only as a tight-lacer or waist-trainer, but also as a consumer of a certain style or brand of corset. While there is a proliferation of generic fashion corsets, there are also many specialty sites, where a custom-made corset will cost hundreds of dollars and be fitted to the wearer directly. Here, too, we see the divide in the social monde, where the wealthier denizens can afford the more prestigious fashion, the better-quality work, and the finer materials.

Most sites devoted to corseting give a nod to the historicity of tight-lacing, mentioning (occasionally counter-factually) the beginning of corsetry and cautioning modern individuals to avoid starting out too fast and damaging the ribs. Although they do recommend wearing the corset the entire day, perhaps with one hour without it, they give instructions on proper lacing techniques, with a focus on slowly making your body conform to the size of the corset rather than forcing it into the desired dimensions too soon. Furthermore, while there are a few extremes like Jung, the majority of photographs—as opposed to drawn illustrations—show women who have only deviated a few inches from their full adult waist size (Corsetconnection).

The social and political facts of the current age are therefore reflected in its fashions. There are no longer explicit political restrictions on women, nor are there explicit economic restrictions—either in the workforce or the materials used—which restrict women to wearing one type of garment, or restrict that type of garment to one that includes a corset. Women who tight-lace today do it not out of necessity, whether that necessity was to obtain a husband or to follow a dictatorial fashion. By and large, it appears that they do it because they want to. Women are still creating their own bodyscapes, and yet these desires are still socially motivated as we saw during the pre-twenty-first- century corseting. Playing into that motivation, one can see the power of sex, the strength of modern consumerism, and the work of fashion, or anti-fashion—the desire to be socially unintegrated.

Kim Kardashian West and the Modern Corset

I would be remiss if I did not mention the most widely recognized proponents of the modern corset, the Kardashians, and more specifically, Kim Kardashian West and her implicit and explicit use of corsets as "waist training." At the time of this writing, Kardashian West has 62.9 million Twitter followers, 156 million Instagram followers, and a net worth of 370 million dollars.[1] To say that she is culturally relevant would be an extreme understatement. With her marriage to rapper and Yeezy designer Kanye West, Kardashian West has united two very disparate demographics among fan groups, those who follow fashionistas and beauty icons, and those who follow music and clothing designers. And those subscribers, followers, and fans are all exposed to her use of corsetry.

At the 2019 Met Gala, Kardashian West donned a dress that left her looking like she had just emerged, nude, from seafoam—cascades

---

[1]Your author: 1703 Twitter followers, 278 Instagram followers, and a negative net worth due to massive amounts of student loan debt. Culturally relevant among other scholars, for the most part. Pretty fun at parties, though.

of water-like decorations streamed down her skin-toned garment, and her hair was styled into a wet-look. It was gloriously beautiful, and while some might say that it did not entirely fit the theme of the year ("camp," which is generally more over-the-top enthusiastic-sexy than slinky-sexy), it certainly made the statement that she was aiming for. It was also placed over a corset that gave her already voluptuous figure a much more rigidly slender waistline. Potential problems with the dress on the night of the gala were preempted by the fact that she "had to take 'corset breathing lessons' from Mister Pearl, the famous corset-maker who crafted it for her" (Fakuade 2019), that she decided to just endure the pain of the evening, which left marks on her body (Harding 2019), and by developing a plan to have one of her sister's clean her up if she had to urinate: "'If I have to pee, it's a problem. Honestly, if it's an emergency, I think I pee my pants and then have my sister wipe my leg up,' Kardashian West said. 'I'm not even joking. She can wipe my leg up'" (Frey 2019).

While her advocacy for corseting has spiked sales on Amazon.com (Kinney 2017), such special occasion garments are still seen as entirely sensational. We also see the resurgence of the rib removal myth: "Some speculated that Kim went so far as to have her ribs removed to wear the item (!!), [punctuation emphasis sic] but instead the star donned a hectic corset that was fastened so tight, it took three fully grown men to fasten it up…" (Harding 2019). The perniciousness of this myth fascinates me; we, the viewing public, are willing to both accept and normalize the idea that a woman would secretly go through extensive, painful, unnecessary cosmetic surgery for the fit of just one garment worn just one time. Putting aside for the moment the abovementioned doubtfulness of the procedure ever having been done in a cosmetic surgery practice at all, Kim Kardashian West has several small children, and she is often photographed picking them up and holding them. A compromised rib cage would render such physical actions very, very painful. And to connect this point back to the introductory chapter, Kardashian West and her sisters have been criticized in recent years for both "acting Black" with their photographic emphasis on their enlarged posteriors, and for marrying or having children with Black men. They are, to use the parlance of this narrative, "uncivilized" for doing so.

Renn Faires and Steampunk: Ye Olde Modern Corseting

Two other examples of the modern use of corsetry can be found in the Renaissance and Medieval reenactments found in faires around the country, and in the Steampunk fashion movement. These examples are both ones of false nostalgia, a yearning to recreate something that never was. No matter how much one reads about the Renaissance and Medieval periods, it is impossible to remake them accurately in terms of ambiance, which is why part of what the faires attempt to do is ramp up the mysticism and lore of the time, while being somewhat lax on the details. There is a romanticizing of what must, by all accounts, have been a brutal and hard time to exist, an oversimplification that occasionally involves accurately remaking the corset (there are truly amazing fiber artists who sell at the faires) while removing it from its context. Reenactors can, of course, remove their garb at the end of the faire and return to modern life, and most do. From personal experience, the relief of removing one's corset at the end of the day is unparalleled.

This removal of context is even more evident in the Steampunk movement, as it epitomizes a time that exists only in fantasy; a use of retroactive continuity (retcon, in current parlance) where the Victorian era continued past Queen Victoria's death. It contains steamships of the air, massive dirigibles in which people rode through the sky like pirate frigates, and the fashion reflected this technological diversion containing gears paired with leather, corsetry paired with mechanics, in sepia-toned opulence. Thus the modern corset has been redefined to cast off the idea of restriction and embrace the idea of expression. And again, we see almost a negative image of the beginning of modern corsetry. Where once women's restriction was social and political, and mostly involuntary, modern fashion has allowed women to recreate restriction as a form of free expression of their own sexuality. To corset in modern clothing is to choose to be restricted, to choose when and where your agency will be exercised, and who can see you exercising it. To corset in modern clothing is to be socially without restraint, creating your own bodyscape.

Summation

As shown in the above work, there are several discourses that drive the way we think and speak about corsets: the discourse of the exotic/erotic corset wearer, the discourse of the everyday/ordinary corset wearer, the Freudian/hysterical discourse, and the discourse that privileges the authority of doctors. All of these discourses have been challenged by the bioarchaeological evidence, which showed lifelong corset use creating definite changes to the skeletal anatomy, but not correlating with either a shortened lifespan or demonstrably correlating with other types of incipient morbidity. We can no longer assume that the corset is about sex, nor that the corset is a killer. The textual and physical evidence does not bear this out. In challenging these assumptions, this work may make inroads on the ways in which we talk about women, both from the 1700 to 1900 period, and our contemporary discourse on women's strengths and capabilities.

Our ways of thinking, of talking about women, are all bound up in the language of corsets. Whether we are saying someone is too tight-laced, or that they should loosen up, or that they are acting hysterically, these words come from the time of the corset. When we talk about who can wear the pants in the family, or if women are strong enough to lead, that stems from our view of corseted women. If we doubt a woman's ability to carry their own weight, or view them as fragile, frail, or breakable, that derives directly from this discourse that led us to assume that women were oversexed, underdeveloped, and so tightly corseted that they were occasionally pictured as being snapped in half by their own garments. Through changing the discourse, we change the perception.

We continue to judge women by these standards, set for women during the eighteenth and nineteenth centuries, not just in their actions, but in their capacity to act. In effect, we treat women who are agentive in society as though they were wearing corsets and could faint at any time. The exploration of what the lives of corseted women were like may contribute to changing that perception, and by doing so change how we approach many issues that have implications in the law and in creating and sustaining an environment that recognizes women's equality and, more importantly, equal abilities.

This work challenges such issues as the way women are treated in the political sphere, maternity leave, women in combat, the wage gap, access to birth control and abortion, attitudes toward childbirth and child-rearing, transgender, and intersexual issues, the American "rape culture," and other instances of outdated patriarchal thinking. We have been thinking of women who corseted as fragile, and we understood them as though they were created as varying types of subjects by their society, instead of by our own cultural assumptions and popular interpretations. Today, those creations continue their influence.

We can see these issues in the headlines all around us. In 2008 and 2016, Hillary Clinton was held to "womanly" standards during her presidential campaigns. People raised doubts as to who would be running the country, her, or her former-president husband. Presidential candidate Michelle Bachman and vice-presidential candidate Sarah Palin were both called hysterical and/or crazy during the 2008 election cycle. Palin was mother to a young child and grandmother to a new grandchild during her campaign for vice-president, and doubts were expressed about her ability to care for her extended and expanded family along with the implied "family" of the American public. And yet, all of these women were held to "bad subject" standards, never stepping into the disidentified realm.

We see this in the way women are treated as though they will go on maternity leave and never come back. The book "Lean In" by Sheryl Sandberg deals with strategies to combat this forced subjectivity with action, and brings her strategies to work with her. During her first pregnancy, she was head of certain operations at Google, where she fought for rights and protections for pregnant women. Her book, though well received overall, encountered massive amounts of pushback from people who claimed she was not being womanly enough. She was, in effect, a bad subject, judged by pre-twenty-first-century standards.

Representative Tammy Duckworth, a naturalized American citizen who lost both legs in combat for America, has had her patriotism and ability to represent the American people challenged by her opponents. Her opponent, Joe Walsh, questioned her actual heroism because she talks about it in her campaign speeches, something that could be considered unwomanly (Tribune 2012), but would be praised if she were a man. She was also denied the ability to vote by proxy while pregnant, an ability which would be afforded to any other person unable to fly due to a temporary inability (Hotair 2014).

In 2015, a case hit the California courts—The People of the State of California v. Brock Allen Turner. Eventually convicted for his crimes, but given a very, very light sentence which was then mostly commuted to time served, Turner raped an unconscious woman behind a dumpster. The woman, referred to in the court proceedings as Emily Doe, was vilified in the court and in the press, notably by the judge overseeing the case, who went out of his way to be lenient to Turner. This lenience was "explained" by the desire to preserve Turner's quality of life—to not "ruin" the promising career of the former Stanford swim-team member, over what was considered "youthful indiscretions" by the judge and others. Turner, his previous record clear of verifiable wrongdoing, with wealth, status, and privilege on his side, got to mostly return to his normal life. His subjectivity was unquestioned, due to many factors, but primarily his maleness. Men—if they are young, white, wealthy men, because the intersections of privilege do play a part here—are de facto good subjects, even when they have done bad, so long as it is the first time they have done so. Women, on the other hand, are de facto bad subjects when they have participated (willingly or not) in anything sexual.

The ordinary questions and assumptions that come with reporting a rape were loud and public during this fiasco: it was assumed from the start that she was lying, even with eye-witnesses in the form of the two men who pulled Turner off of her and saved her from more abuse. People asked what she was wearing, how much had she been drinking, why had she been in a frat house? These assumptions and questions all lead back recursively into the notions of subjectivity. The good subject wears the proper clothes and acts in ways that would not invite unwanted sexual acts. The bad subject wears short skirts, drinks, and visits men in places where men are in a position of power. The womanly woman subverts her own agency and meekly accepts responsibility for what happened to her. The unwomanly woman reports a rape, whether it is a lie or the truth. The woman in question, the bad subject who is actually good, has to re-violate herself, over and over again, in pursuit of justice or even to own her own narrative, each retelling of the sequence of events poured over and dissected for faults by the courts and the media. This particular victim, Chanel Miller, will never be whole again, though she did manage to get the final word by publishing a book in 2019, titled, appropriately for our discussion of agentive behavior and subjectivity, "Know My Name" (NPR 2019).

I began this project expecting to create a purely bioarchaeological study. I would measure and report on the unique changes in women's skeletons due to the use of the corset, and that would be that. But along the way, I discovered that to do so, I would have to ignore the countless other aspects of their lives, the other discourses that had set our cultural ideas about corseting and what it means to be a woman. These voices do not speak in concert with each other, but rather enter into a dialogue, a dialogue which creates and forms women's subjectivity, and can either erase or amplify female agency.

In expanding this book to look at more than their skeletons, I was able to bust a few myths about corseting—corseting is not a killer; women did not die young during this time; waist sizes were not uniformly small; women did not have their ribs removed to make their waists smaller, either then or now; the corset was not originally meant to be exotic or erotic; women who tight-laced or who did not wear the corset at all were not hysterical; the corset was not a tool of patriarchal violence. I also was able to give some of the women, the women of St. Bride's parish and some of the women in the Musée de l'Homme, back their stories. Anthropology has a lot to answer for in terms of silencing those who we purport to study. Our history is rife with racism and colonialism, with misogyny and patronizing attitudes, and the acceptance and normalization of slavery, and other unethical practices. We owe it to ourselves and to the future of the discipline to use work such as this to mitigate the effect of past misdeeds, and to strive to create better more ethical scholarship.

The final question of this work comes down to this: do we want to continue to use the previously held model of women's agency which uses erasure of women's voices, negation of their agency, and ignores disidentification to create the good subject, a passive, weak, "womanly" woman, who respects the patriarchy and who does not believe in her own power and equality? Or do we want to acknowledge our roots, but move beyond this model, taking a more nuanced and balanced view of women's contributions to their own cultures? If the latter sounds better to us, if the woman is allowed out of our viewpoint of her as a corset-bound woman with no judgments or restrictions, what would that world look like? It is important to continue reevaluate our assumptions, so that we may project for ourselves a future that involves women creating their own power and merging their belief in themselves with actions toward a fair and equitable society.

Bibliography

Anonymous. (1883, January 12). Stays and Statues. *Knowledge, 3*, 23–24.

Aptowicz, C. (2014). *Dr. Mütter's Marvels*. New York, NY: Penguin.

CBSNews. (2015). http://www.cbsnews.com/news/rolling-stone-retracts-article-on-college-fraternity-rape-at-university-of-virginia/.

Comaroff, J. (1985). Bodily Reform as Historical Practice: The Semantics of Resistance in Modern South Africa. *International Journal of Psychology, 20*, 541–567.

Corsetconnection. (n.d.). corsetconnection.com/tight_lacing.htm; pinupsart-n-style.com/waist-training.html.

Douglas, M. (1966/2001). *Purity and Danger: An Analysis of Concepts of Pollution and Taboo*. New York, NY: Routledge.

Eppley, B. (2016). Pers. Corrs.

Eppley, B. (2017). http://exploreplasticsurgery.com/.

Fakuade, M. (2019, July 8). Just How Painful was Kim Kardashian West's Met Gala Corset? *The Cut*. https://www.thecut.com/2019/07/kim-kardashians-met-gala-corset-pain.html.

Fields, J. (2007). *An Intimate Affair: Women, Lingerie, and Sexuality*. Berkeley, CA: University of California Press.

Fitzharris, L. (2017). *The Butchering Art: Joseph Lister's Quest to Transform the Grisly World of Victorian Medicine*. New York, NY: Macmillan Publishers.

Foucault, M. (1978). *The History of Sexuality* (Vol. 1). New York, NY: Random House Books.

Fox, P. (2017). https://www.thepixeefox.com/.

Frey, K. (2019, October 11). Kim Kardashian's Met Gala Dress Was So Tight, She Considered Peeing Her Pants in 'an Emergency'. *People*. https://people.com/style/kim-kardashian-met-gala-2019-pee-pants-emergency/.

Harding, N. (2019, July 9). Kim Kardashian Reveals What Her Met Gala Corset Really Did to Her Body. *Cosmopolitan*. https://www.cosmopolitan.com/uk/fashion/celebrity/a28331296/kim-kardashian-met-gala-corset-body/.

Hotair. (2014). http://hotair.com/archives/2014/11/14/tammy-duckworth-refused-proxy-vote-in-dem-caucus/.

Jung, C. (2017). cathiejung.com/history.htm. cathiejung.com/corset36.htm.

Kinney, T. (2017). Cinch for Instacurves: The Discursive Assemblage of Waist Trainers in New Media. *Fat Studies*, 6(2), 152–169.

Kunzle, D. (1982). *Fashion and Fetishism*. London, UK: George Prior Associated Publishers Ltd.

Lacapria, K. (2015). https://www.snopes.com/news/2015/12/01/pixee-fox/.

NPR. (2019). https://www.npr.org/2019/09/04/757626939/victim-of-brock-turner-sexual-assault-reveals-her-identity.

O'Followell, L. (1908). *Le Corset: Histoire, Médicine, Hygiène*. Paris: A. Maloine.

Ortner, S. (1974). *Is Female to Male as Nature is to Culture? From Women, Culture and Society* (M. Ronaldo, Ed., pp. 67–87). Stanford: Stanford University Press.

Photobucket. (n.d.). i156.photobucket.com/albums/t21/what-i-found/Screen%20Play%20June%201934/ScreenPlayJune1934-4.jpg.

Steele, V. (1985). *Fashion and Eroticism: The Ideals of Feminine Beauty from the Victorian Era to the Jazz Age*. New York: Oxford University Press.

Teasley, D. (1904). *Private Lectures to Mothers and Daughters on Sexual Purity: Including Love, Courtship, Marriage, Sexual Physiology, and the Evil Effects of Tight Lacing*. Moundsville, WV: Gospel Trumpet Company.

Tribune. (2012). http://articles.chicagotribune.com/2012-07-04/news/chi-rep-joe-walsh-appears-to-question-tammy-duckworths-hero-status-20120703_1_duckworths-congressman-walsh-joe-walsh.

Turner, T. (1993). *The Social Skin in Reading the Social Body* (C. Burroughs & J. Ehrenreich, Eds., pp. 15–39). Iowa City: University of Iowa Press.

Wierduniverse. (n.d.). media.weirduniverse.net/girdle3.jpg.

Appendix A: A Timeline of World and Corset-Related Events

© The Editor(s) (if applicable) and The Author(s),
under exclusive license to Springer Nature Switzerland AG 2020
R. Gibson, *The Corseted Skeleton*,
https://doi.org/10.1007/978-3-030-50392-5

World events	France	The UK	Year	Corset events	Medicine	St. Bride's and Musée de l'Homme
			43			St. Bride's Church is founded in Londinium
			1510		Ambroise Paré is born	
			1514		Andreas Vesalius is born	
			1550	Busks and stays are prevalent in fashion, but not made from whalebone		
			1560	Conical waistline is in fashion		
			1564		Andreas Vesalius dies	
			1570	Low pointed waistline is in fashion		
			1590		Ambroise Paré dies	
			1610	Square tabs at the waist are in fashion		
			1660	Narrow pointed tabs and a long front waistline are in fashion		
			1666		The Great Fire of London destroys St.Bride's Church structure	
			1675		Sir Christopher Wren opens new St. Bride's Church structure	

World events	France	The UK	Year	Corset events	Medicine	St. Bride's and Musée de l'Homme
			1690	Low waistlines flaring into mantuas are in fashion		
		Georgian period begins	1714			
			1720	Soft fabric has replaced hard tabs at the waistline		
Industrial Revolution begins			1760	Low square waistline is in fashion		
		Mention of Queen entitled to receive whale as "Royal Fish"	1765			
	Georges Cuvier born		1769			
			1770			St. Bride's Lower Churchyard opens
American Revolution			1776			
		The Times of London (originally The Daily Universal Register) begins publication on Fleet St. near St. Bride's Church	1785			
	French Revolution		1789			Saartjie Baartman "The Hottentot Venus" is born
			1790	High empire waistlines and neoclassical styles begin to be in fashion		
	Muséum National d'Histoire Naturelle (MNHN) (re)formed under Cuvier		1793			

World events	France	The UK	Year	Corset events	Medicine	St. Bride's and Musée de l'Homme
Mary Wollstonecraft publishes A Vindication of the Rights of Women			1793			
Cotton gin invented in America			1793			
		Regency period begins	1811			
		Destruction of Stocking Frames Act passed	1812			
Analine dyes are popularized giving the fashion world magenta, fuchsia, and Paris and Scheele's greens			1814			
			1815			Saartjie Baartman dies, is skeletonized by Cuvier
		Regency period ends	1820			
			1825	Waistline at mid-body approaching 'natural' waist		
	First silk revolution in Lyon		1831			
	Georges Cuvier dies		1832			
	Second silk revolution in Lyon		1834			
		Georgian period ends	1837			
		Victorian period begins	1837			

World events	France	The UK	Year	Corset events	Medicine	St. Bride's and Musée de l'Homme
Alexis de Tocqueville coins the Separate Spheres ideology			1840	Lower pointed waist-line returns to fashion		
Industrial Revolution ends			1840			
	Third silk revolution in Lyon		1848			
			1849			St. Bride's Lower Churchyard closes
Cold formed steel popularized, becomes an affordable alternative to whalebone			1850			
		Victoria and Albert Museum created	1852			
			1860	Higher waist returns to fashion		
American Civil War begins			1861			
		Lancashire "Cotton Famine" begins	1861			
		Lancashire "Cotton Famine" ends	1865			
American Civil War ends			1865			
		National Museum of Antiquities in Scotland established (became the National Museums Scotland)	1866			

World events	France	The UK	Year	Corset events	Medicine	St. Bride's and Musée de l'Homme
			1868	William Berry Lord publishes "Freaks of Fashion or Corsets and Crinolines"		
			1870	Natural-level waistline returns to fashion		
			1872		Ludovic O'Followell is born	
Dress Reform Society is formed			1873			
			1878			Musée d'Ethnographie du Trocadéro formed under the MNHN
			1880	Pointed basque waistline is in style		
Freud publishes works on hysteria			1893			
			1900	Straight front corset comes into fashion		
		Victorian period ends	1901			
		Edwardian period begins	1901			
			1908		Ludovic O'Followell revises and publishes Le Corset—Medicine Histoire et Hygeine	
		Edwardian period ends	1910			
World War I begins			1914			
World War I ends			1918			

World events	France	The UK	Year	Corset events	Medicine	St. Bride's and Musée de l'Homme
			1937			Musée de l'Homme replaces Musée d'Ethnographie du Trocadéro
World War II begins (Europe)			1939			
			1940			St. Bride's Church is bombed by air raid during WWII
America enters WWII			1941			
World War II ends			1945			
		St. Fagans Museum established in Cardiff	1948			
			1954			Excavation of St. Bride's Lower Churchyard
		Fashion Museum Bath established	1963			
			1965		Ludovic O'Followell dies	
			2002			Saartjie Baartman's skeleton is repatriated to South Africa
			2003			Centre for Human Bioarchaeology established at the Museum of London

Appendix B: Aggregate Data from the Corset Collections

Location	Date	Accession #	Bust	Waist	Hips	B/W/H ratio
V&A	1905	T.90-1928—wedding corset, highly decorated	68.0	46.0	61.0	1:.67:.89
	1660–1680	T.148a-1951—salmon colored corset with sleeves	64.0	51.0	36.0	1:.79:.56
	1885	T.429&A-1990—two piece ball gown, silk, with lace overlay	68.0	62.0	46.0	1:.91:.67
	1895	T.234-1968	53.0	50.0	54.0	.98:.92:1
	1908–1910	T.53-1960—fancy corset with purple ribbons	38.0	57.5	66.5	.57:.86:1
	1880–1899	T.236-1989	70.0	70.0	68.0	1:1:.97
	1905	T.228-1968	55.0	56.0	59.5	.92:.94:1
	1890–1900	T.184-1962	61.0	60.0	65.0	.93:.92:1
	1875–1899	T.938A-1984—white corset with added lace	68.0	52.0	56.0	1:.76:.82
	1825–1835	T.57-1948—plain cotton, no boning, closed with buttons in rear	56.0	52.0	68.0	.82:.76:1
	1900	T.158 to D-1962—full wool riding costume	62.0	46.0		NA
	1905	CIRC.638&A-1964	42.0	71.5		NA
	Fabric 1770s, Dress 1840s	T.854-1974—silk jacquard ball gown	76.0	48.0		NA
	1909	T.33-1960—full dress, purple with green lace overlay	90.0	60.0	84.0	1:.67:.93
	1900–1905	T.91&A-1984	54.0	48.0		NA
	1895–1900	T.95&A-1984	49.0	45.0	41.0	1:.91:.84
		T.92&A-1984—corset with added lace	61.5	56.0	49.0	1:.91:.80

Location	Date	Accession #	Bust	Waist	Hips	B/W/H ratio
	1900	T.94&A-1984	55.0	50.8	48.0	1:.92:.95
	1870s	T.129-1963	47.5	44.5	43.5	1:.94:.92
	1875–1899	T.33-1965	86.0	76.0	78.0	1:.88:.90
	1900	T.232-1968	57.0	57.0	58.0	.98:.98:1
	1900	T.233-1968	82.0	80.0	58.0	1:.97:.71
	1875–1899	T.97&A-1984	70.0	62.0	57.0	1:.88:.81
	1830–1840	T.124-1968—padded corset for stage	62.0	53.0	68.0	.91:.78:1
	1840	T.227-1968	60.0	55.5	53.0	1:.93:.88
	1830	T.38-1968	69.0	65.5	60.0	1:.95:.87
	1885–1889	T.654-1996	57.0	52.0	48.0	1:.91:.84
	1900	T.96&A-1984	84.0	77.0	68.0	1:.92:.81
	1888–1889	T.407-2001—Green velvet dress	80.0	58.0	84.0	.95:.69:1
St Fagans	1760–1790	51.410/30	84.0	76	86	.98:.88:1
	1760–1780	49.469/17	84.0	60	50	1:.71:.60
	1780–1800	38.262—in jill's book	95.0	70	63.5	1:.74:.67
	1770–1780	53.119	87.5	68	66	1:.77:.75
	1760–1790	47.165/69	119.0	100.5	90	1:.84:.76
	1890	F78.277—in jill's book	79.0	50.5	69	1:.64:.87
	1900–1910 c.1905	F78.80.1—in jill's book	54.5	50	56.5	.96:.88:1
	1910–1920	F.75.181/27	70.0	78.5	100.5	.70:.78:1
	1900–1907	48.363	69.0	52	93	.74:.56:1
	1890–1900	F.70/378/23	92.0	60.5	93.5	.98:.65:1
	1900	F.76.180/19	90.5	73	98	.92:.74:1
	1910–1920	F.76.180.20	96.5	72	107	.90:.67:1
	1900–1910	F.75.181/28	94.0	79	114.5	.82:.69:1
	1880–1890	F77.168/8	81.0	72.5	60	1:.90:.74
	1890–1893	60.527/26	89.5	78	62.5	1:.87:.70

Location	Date	Accession #	Bust	Waist	Hips	B/W/H ratio
	1898	F73.209/17	84.5	64.5	61	1:.76:.72
	Late 19th c	F77.170/19	80.0	70	72	1:.88:.90
	1860s	F.74-233/10	87.0	80	69	1:.92:.79
	1850–1860	F.81.37-1	94.0	75	60	1:.80:.64
	1864–1867	60.527/45	90.0	82	63	1:.91:.70
	1860	F.73-209/10	80.0	68	62	1:.85:.78
	1840	38-179/3	88.0	69	64	1:.78:.73
	1880s	61.363/12	70.0	70	88	.80:.80:1
	1880	65-81/30	76.0	62	66	1:.82:.88
	1875	F.73-129/2	72.0	63	71	1:.88:.99
	1860–1888	47-256/4	76.0	65	63	1:.86:.83
	1888–1889	F77-168/7	95.5	61	59.5	1:.64:.62
	1880s	F44-168/5	82.0	53	93.5	.88:.57:1
	1897	47-293/6	88.0	65	72	1:.74:.82
	1880–1895	F.45-405/25	71.0	62	64	1:.87:.90
	1883	F83.173.4	86.0	51.5	93.5	.92:.55:1
	1900–1910	F80.212.4	99.0	67	91.5	1:.68:.92
	nd	F75-405-38	65.0			NA
	19th c., brocade from previous century	46-424/1	80.0	66.5	55.5	1:.83:.69
	1832–1837	42.367.16	82.0	70	63.5	1:.85:.77
	1845–1850	49.469/65	85.0	67	64	1:.79:.75
	1850–1860	49.469/60	84.0	63	130	.65:.48:1
	1868–1869	36-244/1	89.0	69	66	1:.78:.74
	1865–1870	49-469/75	83.0	59.5		NA
	1870s	F77-170.13/4	85.0	78	62.5	1:.92:.74
	1875	58.272-1	83.0	60.5		NA
	1878	F72.250/1	71.5	59		NA

Location	Date	Accession #	Bust	Waist	Hips	B/W/H ratio
	1876	55-227-3	90.0	74	138	.65:.54:1
	1870s	67-347/1	92.0	60	66.5	1:.65:.72
	1870s	F80-278-1	90.5	66.5	91	.99:.73:1
	1870s	46-113/3	91.0	73		NA
	1880	F48.35-26/7	99.0	76		NA
	late 19th c	46-424/5	97.0	63.5		NA
	19th c	F77.261.1	87.5	66.5		NA
	1890–1892	60.527/16A	84.0	58	76	1:.73:.90
	1893–1895	60.208/2-3	86.5	60	67	1:.69:.77
	1898–1900	60.527/20A	91.0	62	63.5	1:.68:.70
	1890s	65-81/24	88.0	73		NA
	1890–1895	F70-356/9	86.0	65		NA
	1882	F72.334/2	84.0	67	93	.90:.72:1
	1890s	53-137/1	92.5	53.5	66	1:.58:.71
	1890s	F75-181/8	94.0	76		NA
	1890s	65.374/1	92.0	62		NA
	1890s	WFM4-3-173/3	107.0	68		NA
	1879	55–199	98.5	74		NA
	1902	SS47	90.0	62		NA
	1895	SS225	90.0	59		NA
	1890s	F78.127/1	82.0	56		NA
	1890s	SS30A	88.5	60		NA
	1890s	66-426/3	95.0	68		NA
	1893–1895	60.527/5	92.0	64.5		NA
	1900s	68.555/12-13	101.0	82.5		NA
	1880s	65.81/21	95.0	68		NA
	1883	58-297/1	96.0	58.5		NA
	1893	65-364/1	81.5	59		NA

Location	Date	Accession #	Bust	Waist	Hips	B/W/H ratio
National Museum of Scotland	1700s	L1965.35/Q.L. 1965.35	82.0	52.5		NA
	1700s	N.P. 05-984/A.1905.984	87/88/81.5	68.5/60/55		NA
	mid-1700s	1935.772/A.1935.772	97.5	58.5		NA
	mid-1700s	1935.721/A.1935.721	82.0	67.0		NA
	1700s	1960.2923/HTVD6/H.TVD 6	83.5	55.0		NA
	1700s	TQ 1/H.TQ 1	83.0	63.0		NA
	1750–1770	K.2015.85	79.8	57.0		NA
	1800s	H.TVD.8/TVD.8	81.0	53.0	82.0	.99:.65:1
	1820–1840	TQ 18/H.TQ 18	85.0	48.0	74.5	1:.56:.88
	1800s	TQ 13/H.TQ 13	84.0	63.5	90.0	.93:.71:1
	1890–1900	A.1989.60 A&B	82.0	57.0	81.0	1:.70:.99
	ND	A.1989.62 A&B	86.5	66.0	98.5	.88:.67:1
	ND	A.1989.61	78.5	94.5	121.5	.65:.78:1
	1820–1830	1982.1212/A.1983.1212	75.0	54.5	71.0	1:.73:.95
	1880–1890	1986.4/A.1986.4	89.0	55.5	86.0	1:.62:.97
	1820–1830	1983.1213/A.1983.1213	69.0	47.0	65.5	1:.68:.95
	late 19th c.	1970.1063/A.1970.1063	79.5	59.0	83.0	.96:.71:1
	1890–1900	NAB.131/H.NAB 131	88.0	49.0	84.0	1:.56:.95
	ND	1957.537.132	77.5	49.0	76.0	1:.63:.98
	late 19th c.	1970.1062/A.1970.1062	75.5	59.5	85.5	.88:.70:1
	1750–1800	I.27.44	85.5	73.5	62.5	1:.86:.73
Bath Fashion Museum	1775–1800 (possibly, as mislabeled)	Number unknown, mislabeled as I.27-85 (Green)	81.0	61.0	59.0	1:.75:.73
	1775–1800	I.27.85	89.5	76.5	71.0	1:.85:.79
	1775–1799	I.27.866	82.5	75.0	69.5	1:.91:.84

Location	Date	Accession #	Bust	Waist	Hips	B/W/H ratio
	1700–1800	I.27.83	95.0	73.0	54.0	1:.77:.57
	1750–1850	I.27.86	57.0	55.0	54.0	1:.96:.95
	1700–1799	I.27.865	75.5	63.5	51.0	1:.84:.68
	1860–1880	2016.301	71.0	56.5	79.0	.90:.72:1
	1840–1850	I.27.88	85.0	76.5	98.0	.87:.78:1
	1820–1830	I.27.1	92.0	92.0	86.0	1:1:.93
	1830–1840	I.27.87	85.0	57.5	91.0	.93:.63:1
	1860–1870	I.27.90	101.5	87.5	108.0	.94:.81:1
	1870–1880	I.27.44	66.0	45.0	77.0	.86:.58:1
	1860–1870	I.27.77	87.0	57.5	86.0	1:.66.99
	1875–1885	I.27.79	104.0	80.0	110.0	.95:.72:1
	1870–1880	I.27.107	110.5	80.5	122.0	.91:.66:1
	1870–1875	I.27.3	80.5	51.5	79.0	1:.64:.98
	1870–1880	I.27.215	82.0	53.0	80.5	1:.65:.98
	1860–1870	I.27.89	96.5	71.0	90.5	1:.74:.94
	1880–1890	I.27.6	80.0	54.0	82.0	.98:.66:1
	1883–1887	I.27.81	84.5	53.5	87.0	.97:.61:1
	1883–1887	I.27.78	80.0	55.0	83.5	.96:.66:1
	1880–1885/1890	I.27.8 and 8A	69.5	50.5	69.0	1:.73:.99
	1880	I.27.82	98.0	74.5	115.0	.85:.65:1
	1880–1890	I.27.9	106.0	72.0	107.5	.99:.67:1
	1890–1900	I.27.10	88.0	47.0	86.0	1:.53:.98
	1890–1900	I.27.60 and 60A	100.0	41.0	87.0	1:.41:.87
	1890–1900	I.27.75	89.0	56.0	91.0	.98:.62:1
	1890–1899	I.27-867	83.0	47.0	76.0	1:.57:.92
		Averages	81.5	59.8	74.4	1:.73:.90
		Min	38.0	41.0	36.0	
		Max	119.0	94.5	122.0	

Appendix C: Musée de l'Homme Skeletal Data

Location	Acces-sion #	Museum's Notes	Circum-ference ribs at T6	Coronal	Sagittal	Ratio c:s	Known age
DJ 5	3786	Acquired 1879, French, potential other information in archive held at Musee de l'Homme–reference number 998, collected by Dumoutier, acquired by M. Barbier	65.20	18.5	19	1:1.03	
DO 6	765	English, died in 1843	84.00	26	19	1:.73	
DK 3	3636	French	68	22	16.6	1:.75	
DK 7	5825	French, acquired 1869, from Alsace	69	20.6	20	1:.97	
DE 6 SA 24	28216	Polonaise, given by the Polish anth. Soc. To the Paris anth. Soc., in 1878	60	19	15	1:.79	
DL 8	7774	"Canaque" from the island of Spiritu Santo in the New Hibrides, donated by Charles Saintyves, from Vanuatu, collected in 1883	65	19	16	1:.84	
DM 9	1604	"Hottentot[e]" aged 28–30 years at death "recueille" with the help of naturalist Delalande the son (fils) during his voyage to the cape of Africa and to the "Cafrerie" during the years 1818–1820, given to Cuvier. From South Africa. Docummented in Hamy, l'Anthropologie, 1907, page 264	68.5	24	15.5	1:.64	28–30
DH 10	10279	"Femme Ona, sud de la Terre de Feu au Chili" Collected by Rousson and Williams, date of accession 1892	66.5	21	17.5	1:.83	
DH 7	3398	Chinese	72	22.5	18	1:.80	

Location	Acces-sion #	Museum's Notes	Circum-ference ribs at T6	Coronal	Sagittal	Ratio c:s	Known age
DH 4	810	Bengali, died at the cape de Bonne Esperance (Cape of Good Hope), "recueilli" with the help of the naturalist Delalande the son during his journey of three years to the Cape and to the "Cafrerie" in 1818–1820, and given to Cuvier. "Bengladesh" Documented in Hamy l'Anthropologie 1907, page 264	63.5	20	15	1:.75	
DH 6	784	Indian from Bombay (Mumbai), a domestic, who died in hospice Beaujon in 1839	60	19.5	17	1:.87	
DJ 8	10283	"Yaghan, sud de la Terre de Feu" South American, collected by Rousson and Willems in 1892	74.5	23.5	18.5	1:.78	
DG 9	781	from the Ile of Bourbon, died in Paris in November 1850 at the age of 38, from La Reunion ***NOTE*** Both tag and ink on skull note this as Negresse du Mozambique, morte a Paris 1850 coll. Serres	71.5	21	16.5	1:.79	38
DG 2	2092	From Brazil, but originated in Mozambique, marked in ink on skull as negresse	67	21	15.5	1:.73	

Location	Acces-sion #	Museum's Notes	Circum-ference ribs at T6	Coronal	Sagittal	Ratio c:s	Known age
DF 4	1763	Aeta, environ de Binangonan cote est de Lucon Phillippines, given by the Anatomie comparee "rapporte" by M. de la Gironiere, Archive number 2	64	21.5	15	1::70	
DF 1	2918	Javanaise "[certainement metisse sinon tout a fait europeenne]" keep horizontal because the pelvis and legs have fallen off. Collected by Dr. Steenstra-Toussaint, of Batavia, collected in 1862	61	19.6	15	1::77	
DI 5	17883	the skeleton of "Lapon de Nosseby, Ostfinmarken, Varangerfiord" acquired by "Nordvi" and is Norwegian, archive number 371, collected in 1885	71.7	22.2	19	1::86	
DJ 2	819	Peruvian, of "Owankai" "versant des Andes orientales" From Peru	68.3	22.5	18.4	1::82	
DG 7	818	From Madagascar, recueilli with the help of naturalist Delalande the son on his voyage of three years to the Cape and "Cafrerie in the years of 1818–1820, given to Cuvier, archived at Hamy l'Anthropologie, 1907, page 264	67.6	19.8	20	1:1.01	

Location	Acces-sion #	Museum's Notes	Circum-ference ribs at T6	Coronal	Sagittal	Ratio c:s	Known age
DA 10	2277	From "Canala" (Canada, I think), "Nouvelle Caledonie", collected by Bourgarel, surgeon of the imperial marines	68.8	21	20.3	1:.96	
DE 8	782	Origin indeterminable, 20 years old	55.6	18	16	1:.89	20. Very, very incorrect
DB 2	3571	Died in Paris, collected by Serres, marked in ink on skull as Negresse	63.8	20.8	20	1:.96	
DE 9	815	Origin unknown	61	21.4	15	1:.70	
DA 10	771	Piemontaise, 30 years old, from Italy	63.3	20.5	16.8	1:.81	30
DK 9	28194	From the Caraibe (caribbean) Suriname, collected in 1897	61	20.4	16	1:.78	
DJ 4	10287	Fuegienne Yaghan, 30 years olve, from de l'ile Hoste, Chili, Collected in 1885	67	21.6	17	1:.79	30
DG 5	17874	Betsimisaraka, Tamatave, Madagascar, collected in 1903	58	19	15	1:.79	
		Mean	66.14	20.96	17.13		
		Median	66.50	21.00	16.80		
		Mode	61.00	21.00	15.00		
		Max	84.00	26.00	20.30		
		Min	55.60	18.00	15.00		

Appendix D: Museum of London FAO90 Data

© The Editor(s) (if applicable) and The Author(s),
under exclusive license to Springer Nature Switzerland AG 2020
R. Gibson, *The Corseted Skeleton*,
https://doi.org/10.1007/978-3-030-50392-5

Context	Sex	Age	T4	T5	T6	T7	T8	T9	T10
1123	F	>46							
1127	F?	>46							
1151	F	>46				11.4(22.8)*16.9	10.4(20.8)*16.4	9.6(19.2)	
1152	F	>46	19*17.5			12.1(24.2)	11.6(23.2)*19.1		15.4(30.8)*15.4
1166	F	26–35							
1199	F	36–45							
1203	F	>46					11.3(22.6)*19		
1207	F	26–35							
1278	F	26–35	22.3*16	20*18.4					
1281	F	26–35							11.6(23.2)*19.2
1291	F	>46	10.7(21.4)*16.7	13.2(26.4)*17	13.9(27.8)*27.4				14.8(29.6)
1326	F	>46							
1336	F	36–45	20.2*17.3	10.8(21.6)	10.8(21.6)				
1343	F	>46	19.5*15.5	25*24	21*21.5				
1352	F	>46	24*18.5						
1373	F?	>46							
1376	F	26–35	23.5*23.9	10.2(20.4)*23.4			21.5*15.3		
1386	F	18–25							
1417	F	>46							
1422	F	36–45	19.6*15.9	20*16	20*17.4				
1428	F?	36–45		10.3(20.6)*13.2		10(20)*19.4	11.5(23)*17	12.9(25.8)*16.5	11.5(23)*16.5
1474	F?	36–45				31.3*17.1	32.6*17.5	33.5*17.6	
1495	F	>46							
1519	F	26–35	13.9(27.8)						
1547	F?	>46							
1611	F	26–35	21.2*17.9	11.1(22.2)*21.4	21.6*19.4	10.5(21)*18.9			
1637	F	>46	21.7*16.9		11.5(23)*18.8				
1641	F	36–45	11(22)		12.3(24.6)		13(26)		
1653	F	26–35						9.6(19.2)*16.2	
1671	F	>46	11.4(22.8)*17	22.5*19					
1691	F	>46	10.5(21)	10(20)	20.2*20.2	10.7(21.4)			
1703	F	36–45							

Context	Sex	Age	T4	T5	T6	T7	T8	T9	T10
1709	F?	>46	11.6(23.2)	23.5	12.8(25.6)	25.5	12.4(24.8)	10(20)*14	
1711	F?	36-45			12.9(25.8)				
1741	F	>46		11.4(22.8)	12.5(25)				
1755	F	26-35	21.8*18.3	23.4*17.4		22.5*18.7	23.2*19.1	21.4*17.1	
1781	F	>46	20.2			21.8			
1793	F	36-45							
1795	F	>46							
1799	F	36-45							
1809	F	36-45	19.7*14.6	21.6*17	10(20)*17.6	22*17.8			
1887	F	>46							
1891	F	>46							
1895	F	>46							
1903	F?	36-45	16.8*13.8	10(20)*16.9	22.4*17.9	22.8*18	23.4*18	15.4(30.8)	
1913	F	>46							
1936	F?	UNCLASSIFIED ADULT				14.7(29.4)*18			
1940	F?	>46				11.9(23.8)*19.8			
1946	F	36-45							
1952	F	36-45							
1995	F	18-25	21.8*16.8	21.4*16.8	20.4*18.7	18.5*20.9	18.7*19.4		
2005	F?	>46				9.9(19.8)	12.4(24.8)		
2049	F	36-45	18*16.8	19.2*17.5	19.8*19	24.2*17.5			
2055	F	>46							
2065	F?	26-35	19.9*15.4	19.9*17.4	22.5*19	24*20	24.6*18.9	23.9*18.6	22*16.9
2071	F?	>46							
2073	F	>46							
2105	F	>46		11.1(22.2)*16.8		12.5(25)	12.9(25.8)*16.9		
2116	F	>46	10.9(21.8)*17.4	12.4(24.8)	11.5(23)				
2134	F	26-35							
2136	F?	>46							
2158	F	>46	9.9(19.8)						
2161	F	26-35	12(24)*15.4	25*20.2	21.4*20.4				22.6*19.2

Context	Sex	Age	T4	T5	T6	T7	T8	T9	T10
2171	F	26–35							
2199	F	26–35	20.2*16.9	11.1(22.2)*18			20.8*18.2	11.7(23.4)*17.4	20.6*15.4
2214	F	>46							
2216	F	36–45	21*17	22.4*17.4	24.3*17.1		12.5(25)*17.3		
2233	F	>46							
2245.1	F	>46							
2255	F	36–45	23.5	11.7(23.4)		13.4(26.8)			
2308	F	36–45							
2332	F	36–45							
2353	F	36–45	10.3(20.6)*16.6	10.8(21.6)	12(24)				

Appendix E: Selections from the St. Bride's Archive Data*

© The Editor(s) (if applicable) and The Author(s),
under exclusive license to Springer Nature Switzerland AG 2020
R. Gibson, *The Corseted Skeleton*,
https://doi.org/10.1007/978-3-030-50392-5

Year	Month	Date	Name	Cause of Death—codes: C=consumption; CV=convulsions; F=fever; D=dropsy (water-swollen body tissue); DC= decline (emaciation, wasting, end-stage syphilis); W=from the workhouse; O=old age; S=small pox; M=mortification (gangrene); P=palsy (paralysis, hemiplegia [Bell's Palsy]); CB=childbed; PR=prison; E=executed; SD=sudden death; PF=Putrid fever (Typhus); CR=cancer; V=visitation of God; DY=decay DYN=decay of nature; R=Rheumatism/ Rheumatic fever/Rheumatic decline; A=Asthma; AP=Apoplexy; I=Inflammation (type added if specified); L=lunatic or lunacy; IN=insanity; TIN=Temporary insanity; MC=Miscarriage; CH=Cholera	Age	Where buried— codes: L = lower churchyard; U = upper churchyard; P = pauper's yard; SWV = south west vault; D (no recorded meaning attached to D)
1801	January	4	Ann Phelps (83 Shoe Lane)	F	22	L
		14	Lydia Johnson	DC	65	P
		14	Sarah Smith (Bride Lane)	F	24	P
		18	Mary Sutton (69 Shoe Lane)	DC	70	L
		18	Elizabeth Vale	DC W	65	P
		19	Mary Edwards	O	79	W Vault
		22	Elizabeth Sanders (10 Gt New St)	F	26	U

Year	Month	Date	Name	Cause of Death—codes: C=consumption; CV=convulsions; F=fever; D=dropsy (water-swollen body tissue); DC= decline (emaciation, wasting, end-stage syphilis); W=from the workhouse; O=old age; S=small pox; M=mortification (gangrene); P=palsy (paralysis, hemiplegia [Bell's Palsy]); CB=childbed; PR=prison; E=executed; SD=sudden death; PF=Putrid fever (Typhus); CR=cancer; V=visitation of God; DY=decay DYN=decay of nature; R=Rheumatism/ Rheumatic fever/Rheumatic decline; A=Asthma; AP=Apoplexy; I=Inflammation (type added if specified); L=lunatic or lunacy; IN=insanity; TIN=Temporary insanity; MC=Miscarriage; CH=Cholera	Age	Where buried— codes: L = lower churchyard; U = upper churchyard; P = pauper's yard; SWV = south west vault; D (no recorded meaning attached to D)
		22	Mary Walker (15 King's Head Ct)	DC	45	L
		28	Susanna Sines (12 Black Horse Alley)	DC	34	L
	February	1	Mary Evans (47 Fleet Market)	DC	47	SWV
		11	Ann Marshall	F W	50	P
		11	Elizabeth Gilpin	DC W	56	P
		11	Ann Price (39 Ludgate Hill)	DC	41	L
		15	Mary Olliver (13 Blackhorse Alley)	DC	46	L

Year	Month	Date	Name	Cause of Death—codes: C=consumption; CV=convulsions; F=fever; D=dropsy (water-swollen body tissue); DC= decline (emaciation, wasting, end-stage syphilis); W=from the workhouse; O=old age; S=small pox; M=mortification (gangrene); P=palsy (paralysis, hemiplegia [Bell's Palsy]); CB=childbed; PR=prison; E=executed; SD=sudden death; PF=Putrid fever (Typhus); CR=cancer; V=visitation of God; DY=decay DYN=decay of nature; R=Rheumatism/Rheumatic fever/Rheumatic decline; A=Asthma; AP=Apoplexy; I=Inflammation (type added if specified); L=lunatic or lunacy; IN=insanity; TIN=Temporary insanity; MC=Miscarriage; CH=Cholera	Age	Where buried—codes: L = lower churchyard; U = upper churchyard; P = pauper's yard; SWV = south west vault; D (no recorded meaning attached to D)
		18	Margaret Honor	DC W	68	P
		18	Elizabeth Hulet	DC W	65	P
		18	Mary Biggs	DC W	62	P
		20	Ann Burk (Charlotte Street, St. George)	A	64	Mid
		20	Rachael King (7 Brides Lane)	D	41	U
		21	Lucinda Grace (Salisbury Ct)	CB	22	U
		24	Beatrice Murry	DC PR	45	U
		25	Mable Cheal	W	68	P
		25	Ann Murford (Shoe Lane)	F	21	P

Year	Month	Date	Name	Cause of Death—codes: C=consumption; CV=convulsions; F=fever; D=dropsy (water-swollen body tissue); DC= decline (emaciation, wasting, end-stage syphilis); W=from the workhouse; O=old age; S=small pox; M=mortification (gangrene); P=palsy (paralysis, hemiplegia [Bell's Palsy]); CB=childbed; PR=prison; E=executed; SD=sudden death; PF=Putrid fever (Typhus); CR=cancer; V=visitation of God; DY=decay DYN=decay of nature; R=Rheumatism/ Rheumatic fever/Rheumatic decline; A=Asthma; AP=Apoplexy; I=Inflammation (type added if specified); L=lunatic or lunacy; IN=insanity; TIN=Temporary insanity; MC=Miscarriage; CH=Cholera	Age	Where buried—codes: L = lower churchyard; U = upper churchyard; P = pauper's yard; SWV = south west vault; D (no recorded meaning attached to D)
	March	1	Mary Morley (126 Fleet St)	DC	46	Mid
		1	Ann Short	A W	70	L
		8	Mary Ayros (Temple Lane)	A W	43	U
		11	Susanna Sinkwell	A W	61	P
		25	Mary Lane	A W	55	P
	April	1	Elizabeth Paryar (13 Stone Cutter)	DC	33	L
		6	Ann Pridden (100 Fleet St)	D	65	Chancel
		10	Rebecca Pratt	F W	57	P

Year	Month	Date	Name	Cause of Death—codes: C=consumption; CV=convulsions; F=fever; D=dropsy (water-swollen body tissue); DC= decline (emaciation, wasting, end-stage syphilis); W=from the workhouse; O=old age; S=small pox; M=mortification (gangrene); P=palsy (paralysis, hemiplegia [Bell's Palsy]); CB=childbed; PR=prison; E=executed; SD=sudden death; PF=Putrid fever (Typhus); CR=cancer; V=visitation of God; DY=decay DYN=decay of nature; R=Rheumatism/ Rheumatic fever/Rheumatic decline; A=Asthma; AP=Apoplexy; I=Inflammation (type added if specified); L=lunacy or lunacy; IN=insanity; TIN=Temporary insanity; MC=Miscarriage; CH=Cholera	Age	Where buried— codes: L = lower churchyard; U = upper churchyard; P = pauper's yard; SWV = south west vault; D (no recorded meaning attached to D)
		19	Elizabeth Challener (4 Parsons Ct)	F	32	L
		21	Ann Gale	Evil W	61	L
		21	Elizabeth Stroud (5 Bride Lane)	D	64	U
		26	Esther Scoffield (3 Crown Ct)	CV	19	L
	May	3	Jane Till (54 Dorset St)	D	32	
		15	Ann Curtis (108 Shoe Lane)	Fits	38	L
		20	Mary Bagshaw	DC	70	P

Year	Month	Date	Name	Cause of Death—codes: C=consumption; CV=convulsions; F=fever; D=dropsy (water-swollen body tissue); DC= decline (emaciation, wasting, end-stage syphilis); W=from the workhouse; O=old age; S=small pox; M=mortification (gangrene); P=palsy (paralysis, hemiplegia [Bell's Palsy]); CB=childbed; PR=prison; E=executed; SD=sudden death; PF=Putrid fever (Typhus); CR=cancer; V=visitation of God; DY=decay DYN=decay of nature; R=Rheumatism/ Rheumatic fever/Rheumatic decline; A=Asthma; AP=Apoplexy; I=Inflammation (type added if specified); L=lunatic or lunacy; IN=insanity; TIN=Temporary insanity; MC=Miscarriage; CH=Cholera	Age	Where buried— codes: L = lower churchyard; U = upper churchyard; P = pauper's yard; SWV = south west vault; D (no recorded meaning attached to D)
	June	29	Ann Hurt (26 Great New St)	DC	23	U
		20	Susan Bennet	D W	78	P
		7	Mary Gurrier	F	50	P
		3	Sarah Tabernacle	F W	32	F
		4	Elizabeth Tallends (11 George Alley)	CB	28	L
		8	Elizabeth Finch (2 Bride Lane)	Complications	60	Vault
		24	Elizabeth Mc Donough	F W	50	P
		26	Mary Mathews	DC W	60	P

Year	Month	Date	Name	Cause of Death—codes: C=consumption; CV=convulsions; F=fever; D=dropsy (water-swollen body tissue); DC= decline (emaciation, wasting, end-stage syphilis); W=from the workhouse; O=old age; S=small pox; M=mortification (gangrene); P=palsy (paralysis, hemiplegia [Bell's Palsy]); CB=childbed; PR=prison; E=executed; SD=sudden death; PF=Putrid fever (Typhus); CR=cancer; V=visitation of God; DY=decay DYN=decay of nature; R=Rheumatism/ Rheumatic fever/Rheumatic decline; A=Asthma; AP=Apoplexy; I=Inflammation (type added if specified); L=lunatic or lunacy; IN=insanity; TIN=Temporary insanity; MC=Miscarriage; CH=Cholera	Age	Where buried—codes: L = lower churchyard; U = upper churchyard; P = pauper's yard; SWV = south west vault; D (no recorded meaning attached to D)
			Note: much of June and July are blank with dates and locations but no names or ages			
July		8	Ann Phelps	O	77	P
August		4	Ann Hedlington	DC W	65	L
		13	Ellener Allin (Black Horse Alley)	F	45	L
		16	Ester Savoy (13 Crown Ct. Fleet St)	DC	42	L

Year	Month	Date	Name	Cause of Death—codes: C=consumption; CV=convulsions; F=fever; D=dropsy (water-swollen body tissue); DC= decline (emaciation, wasting, end-stage syphilis); W=from the workhouse; O=old age; S=small pox; M=mortification (gangrene); P=palsy (paralysis, hemiplegia [Bell's Palsy]); CB=childbed; PR=prison; E=executed; SD=sudden death; PF=Putrid fever (Typhus); CR=cancer; V=visitation of God; DY=decay DYN=decay of nature; R=Rheumatism/ Rheumatic fever/Rheumatic decline; A=Asthma; AP=Apoplexy; I=Inflammation (type added if specified); L=lunatic or lunacy; IN=insanity; TIN=Temporary insanity; MC=Miscarriage; CH=Cholera	Age	Where buried—codes: L = lower churchyard; U = upper churchyard; P = pauper's yard; SWV = south west vault; D (no recorded meaning attached to D)
	September	28	Mary Hodges	F W	62	L
		9	Mary Bryers (11 Great New St)	DC	61	L
		23	Elizabeth Williams	C	37	L
		29	Ann Eddridge	A W	75	L
	October	3	Jane Cox	DC W	55	L
		8	Sarah Low (45 New St Sq)	DC	18	U
		14	Catharine Sullivan	DC W	22	L
		25	Ann Rowe	DC	18	L
		28	Ann Jewill (Goldsmith St)	D	63	U

Year	Month	Date	Name	Cause of Death—codes: C=consumption; CV=convulsions; F=fever; D=dropsy (water-swollen body tissue); DC= decline (emaciation, wasting, end-stage syphilis); W=from the workhouse; O=old age; S=small pox; M=mortification (gangrene); P=palsy (paralysis, hemiplegia [Bell's Palsy]); CB=childbed; PR=prison; E=executed; SD=sudden death; PF=Putrid fever (Typhus); CR=cancer; V=visitation of God; DY=decay DYN=decay of nature; R=Rheumatism/ Rheumatic fever/Rheumatic decline; A=Asthma; AP=Apoplexy; I=Inflammation (type added if specified); L=lunatic or lunacy; IN=insanity; TIN=Temporary insanity; MC=Miscarriage; CH=Cholera	Age	Where buried— codes: L = lower churchyard; U = upper churchyard; P = pauper's yard; SWV = south west vault; D (no recorded meaning attached to D)
November	2		Elizabeth James (3 King's Head Ct)	F	25	
	5		Ann Parker (17 Shoe Lane)	I	20	L
	8		Elizabeth Wicker (3 King's Head Court)	F	48	L
December	16		Elizabeth Fledged	CB	35	U
	2		Elizabeth Hicks	DC W	72	L
	6		Elizabeth Smith (Water Lane)	DC	61	L
	6		Catherine Brewer (Falcon Lane, Shoe Lane)	A	62	L

Year	Month	Date	Name	Cause of Death—codes: C=consumption; CV=convulsions; F=fever; D=dropsy (water-swollen body tissue); DC= decline (emaciation, wasting, end-stage syphilis); W=from the workhouse; O=old age; S=small pox; M=mortification (gangrene); P=palsy (paralysis, hemiplegia [Bell's Palsy]); CB=childbed; PR=prison; E=executed; SD=sudden death; PF=Putrid fever (Typhus); CR=cancer; V=visitation of God; DY=decay DYN=decay of nature; R=Rheumatism/ Rheumatic fever/Rheumatic decline; A=Asthma; AP=Apoplexy; I=Inflammation (type added if specified); L=lunatic or lunacy; IN=insanity; TIN=Temporary insanity; MC=Miscarriage; CH=Cholera	Age	Where buried— codes: L = lower churchyard; U = upper churchyard; P = pauper's yard; SWV = south west vault; D (no recorded meaning attached to D)
		11	Elizabeth Wiliams	DC W	63	L
		11	Mary Hazard	DC W	50	L
		13	Elizabeth Hazard	DC	64	L
		17	Ann Grislock (9 falcon, 6 shoe lane)	DC	16	L
		20	Ann Burk (Charlotte Street, St. George)	DC W	90	L
		23	Sarah Jones (Poppins Ct)	DC	78	L
		23	Elizabeth Brimston	DC	70	U
		30	Ann Hughes	DC	43	L

Year	Month	Date	Name	Cause of Death—codes	Age	Where buried—codes

Cause of Death—codes: C=consumption; CV=convulsions; F=fever; D=dropsy (water-swollen body tissue); DC= decline (emaciation, wasting, end-stage syphilis); W=from the workhouse; O=old age; S=small pox; M=mortification (gangrene); P=palsy (paralysis, hemiplegia [Bell's Palsy]); CB=childbed; PR=prison; E=executed; SD=sudden death; PF=Putrid fever (Typhus); CR=cancer; V=visitation of God; DY=decay DYN=decay of nature; R=Rheumatism/Rheumatic fever/Rheumatic decline; A=Asthma; AP=Apoplexy; I=Inflammation (type added if specified); L=lunatic or lunacy; IN=insanity; TIN=Temporary insanity; MC=Miscarriage; CH=Cholera

Where buried—codes: L = lower churchyard; U = upper churchyard; P = pauper's yard; SWV = south west vault; D (no recorded meaning attached to D)

Year	Month	Date	Name	Cause of Death	Age	Where buried
1802	January	8	Mary Tim	DC W	56	L
		20	Elizabeth Prosser	DC W	24	L
		20	Frances Keatholm	DC W	46	L
		23	Mary Simpson (Falcon Court)	CB	40	L
		31	Sarah Bath (5 Salisbury Ct)	D	51	New Vault
	February	3	Catharine Delzoph (St. Clement's)	D	72	U
		6	Esther Varley	D	53	New Vault
		12	Mary Adkins (2 Fleet Market)	D	62	U

Year	Month	Date	Name	Cause of Death—codes: C=consumption; CV=convulsions; F=fever; D=dropsy (water-swollen body tissue); DC= decline (emaciation, wasting, end-stage syphilis); W=from the workhouse; O=old age; S=small pox; M=mortification (gangrene); P=palsy (paralysis, hemiplegia [Bell's Palsy]); CB=childbed; PR=prison; E=executed; SD=sudden death; PF=Putrid fever (Typhus); CR=cancer; V=visitation of God; DY=decay DYN=decay of nature; R=Rheumatism/ Rheumatic fever/Rheumatic decline; A=Asthma; AP=Apoplexy; I=Inflammation (type added if specified); L=lunatic or lunacy; IN=insanity; TIN=Temporary insanity; MC=Miscarriage; CH=Cholera	Age	Where buried— codes: L = lower churchyard; U = upper churchyard; P = pauper's yard; SWV = south west vault; D (no recorded meaning attached to D)
		24	Penelope Nichols (Fleet Street)	DC	78	L
		26	Elizabeth Smith	DC W	52	L
		26	Elizabeth Deacon (Fleet Market)	DC	79	L
	March	4	Lady Esther Hope (St George)	DC	35	New Vault
		6	Mary Wright (7 Belle…)	DC	40	U
		10	Mary Kint (92 Dorset Ct)	DC	75	L
		13	Amelia Hare (27 Poppins Ct)	DC	27	U
		14	Elizabeth Speller	DC W	75	L

Cause of Death—codes: C=consumption; CV=convulsions; F=fever; D=dropsy (water-swollen body tissue); DC= decline (emaciation, wasting, end-stage syphilis); W=from the workhouse; O=old age; S=small pox; M=mortification (gangrene); P=palsy (paralysis, hemiplegia [Bell's Palsy]); CB=childbed; PR=prison; E=executed; SD=sudden death; PF=Putrid fever (Typhus); CR=cancer; V=visitation of God; DY=decay DYN=decay of nature; R=Rheumatism/Rheumatic fever/Rheumatic decline; A=Asthma; AP=Apoplexy; I=Inflammation (type added if specified); L=lunatic or lunacy; IN=insanity; TIN=Temporary insanity; MC=Miscarriage; CH=Cholera

Where buried—codes: L = lower churchyard; U = upper churchyard; P = pauper's yard; SWV = south west vault; D (no recorded meaning attached to D)

Year	Month	Date	Name	Cause of Death	Age	Where buried
	April	14	Hannah Stevens	DC W	44	L
	May	10	Elizabeth Forster (91 22 Fleet Lane)	DC	56	L
		26	Ann Goodwin	DC W	59	L
		30	Catherine Mitchell (18 Poppins Ct)	D	57	L
		30	Jane Giffin (87 Shoe Lane)	F	69	L
	June	22	Ann Wilkinson (Bell savage ludgate)	DC	73	L
	July	2	Ann Bronn (St. Sepulchre)	CV	21	L

Year	Month	Date	Name	Cause of Death—codes: C=consumption; CV=convulsions; F=fever; D=dropsy (water-swollen body tissue); DC= decline (emaciation, wasting, end-stage syphilis); W=from the workhouse; O=old age; S=small pox; M=mortification (gangrene); P=palsy (paralysis, hemiplegia [Bell's Palsy]); CB=childbed; PR=prison; E=executed; SD=sudden death; PF=Putrid fever (Typhus); CR=cancer; V=visitation of God; DY=decay DYN=decay of nature; R=Rheumatism/ Rheumatic fever/Rheumatic decline; A=Asthma; AP=Apoplexy; I=Inflammation (type added if specified); L=lunatic or lunacy; IN=insanity; TIN=Temporary insanity; MC=Miscarriage; CH=Cholera	Age	Where buried— codes: L = lower churchyard; U = upper churchyard; P = pauper's yard; SWV = south west vault; D (no recorded meaning attached to D)
		25	Catherine Seaton (14 Stone Cutter St)	CR	44	L
	August	3	Ann Ansley (14 Bride Lane)	SD	22	L
		4	Deborah Read (135 Salisbury Ct)	DC	27	New Vault
		5	Frances Taylor (11 New Great...)	D	66	L
		8	Ann Hall (Great New St)	Rupture (could be Rapture)	60	L
		14	Sarah Lovell (St. Giles in the Fields)	DC	65	U

Year	Month	Date	Name	Cause of Death—codes: C=consumption; CV=convulsions; F=fever; D=dropsy (water-swollen body tissue); DC= decline (emaciation, wasting, end-stage syphilis); W=from the workhouse; O=old age; S=small pox; M=mortification (gangrene); P=palsy (paralysis, hemiplegia [Bell's Palsy]); CB=childbed; PR=prison; E=executed; SD=sudden death; PF=Putrid fever (Typhus); CR=cancer; V=visitation of God; DY=decay DYN=decay of nature; R=Rheumatism/ Rheumatic fever/Rheumatic decline; A=Asthma; AP=Apoplexy; I=Inflammation (type added if specified); L=lunatic or lunacy; IN=insanity; TIN=Temporary insanity; MC=Miscarriage; CH=Cholera	Age	Where buried—codes: L = lower churchyard; U = upper churchyard; P = pauper's yard; SWV = south west vault; D (no recorded meaning attached to D)
		15	Martha Holland (30 Poppins Ct)	Scarlet Fever	28	L
	September	18	Rose Vesey (1 Little New St)	AP	59	L
		23	Maria Gray (8 Bell Savage…)	Bowel Complaint	16	U
		24	Mary Chippendall	DC	38	New Vault
	October	6	Jane Smith	DC W	36	L
		22	Esther Bath	DC PR	23	L
		24	Sarah Rider (White Friars)	F	40	U
	November	4	Elizabeth Harber (Cutter Stone St)	DC	33	L

Year	Month	Date	Name	Cause of Death—codes: C=consumption; CV=convulsions; F=fever; D=dropsy (water-swollen body tissue); DC= decline (emaciation, wasting, end-stage syphilis); W=from the workhouse; O=old age; S=small pox; M=mortification (gangrene); P=palsy (paralysis, hemiplegia [Bell's Palsy]); CB=childbed; PR=prison; E=executed; SD=sudden death; PF=Putrid fever (Typhus); CR=cancer; V=visitation of God; DY=decay DYN=decay of nature; R=Rheumatism/ Rheumatic fever/Rheumatic decline; A=Asthma; AP=Apoplexy; I=Inflammation (type added if specified); L=lunatic or lunacy; IN=insanity; TIN=Temporary insanity; MC=Miscarriage; CH=Cholera	Age	Where buried— codes: L = lower churchyard; U = upper churchyard; P = pauper's yard; SWV = south west vault; D (no recorded meaning attached to D)
		6	Sarah Price (94 Shoe Lane)	SD	44	U
		8	Jane Fletcher (Dove Court New St)	DC	43	L
		13	Mary Patmore (St Bartholomew's St)	DC	29	L
		17	Jane Goff (Pattern Maker Shoe Lane)	F	45	L
		24	Mary Ann Cahppel (108 Dorset st)	Fitts	20	U
		24	Mary Valentine	DC W	70	L

Cause of Death—codes: C=consumption; CV=convulsions; F=fever; D=dropsy (water-swollen body tissue); DC= decline (emaciation, wasting, end-stage syphilis); W=from the workhouse; O=old age; S=small pox; M=mortification (gangrene); P=palsy (paralysis, hemiplegia [Bell's Palsy]); CB=childbed; PR=prison; E=executed; SD=sudden death; PF=Putrid fever (Typhus); CR=cancer; V=visitation of God; DY=decay DYN=decay of nature; R=Rheumatism/ Rheumatic fever/Rheumatic decline; A=Asthma; AP=Apoplexy; I=Inflammation (type added if specified); L=lunatic or lunacy; IN=insanity; TIN=Temporary insanity; MC=Miscarriage; CH=Cholera

Where buried— codes: L = lower churchyard; U = upper churchyard; P = pauper's yard; SWV = south west vault; D (no recorded meaning attached to D)

Year	Month	Date	Name	Cause of Death	Age	Where buried
		24	Mary Shelton (15 Poppins Ct)	DC	74	L
		24	Sarah Hunter (8 George Alley)	DC	67	L
		24	Esther Deane (8 Bridge St)	DC	42	U
	December	2	Henrietta Barrat	F W	45	L
		5	Mary Bronn (6 Brides Lane)	DC	77	L
		6	Elizabeth Godden	F PR	23	L
		10	Elizabeth Bevet (St Ann Black)	DC	83	U
		19	Eleanor Woodroffe (99 Sugar Loaf Court)	DC	51	U
		31	Sarah Bembridge	DC W	58	L

Year	Month	Date	Name	Cause of Death—codes: C=consumption; CV=convulsions; F=fever; D=dropsy (water-swollen body tissue); DC= decline (emaciation, wasting, end-stage syphilis); W=from the workhouse; O=old age; S=small pox; M=mortification (gangrene); P=palsy (paralysis, hemiplegia [Bell's Palsy]); CB=childbed; PR=prison; E=executed; SD=sudden death; PF=Putrid fever (Typhus); CR=cancer; V=visitation of God; DY=decay DYN=decay of nature; R=Rheumatism/ Rheumatic fever/Rheumatic decline; A=Asthma; AP=Apoplexy; I=Inflammation (type added if specified); L=lunatic or lunacy; IN=insanity; TIN=Temporary insanity; MC=Miscarriage; CH=Cholera	Age	Where buried—codes: L = lower churchyard; U = upper churchyard; P = pauper's yard; SWV = south west vault; D (no recorded meaning attached to D)
1803	January	8	Ann Williams (77 Fleet Market)	DC	74	L
		14	Elizabeth Turner (George Alley)	DC	30	L
		17	Hanna Bamber	DC	32	L
		23	Mary Macqures	DC W	47	L
		30	Esther Freeman (Hanging Sword Alley)	DC	36	L
	February	2	Elizabeth Jackson (George Alley)	DC	48	L

Year	Month	Date	Name	Cause of Death—codes: C=consumption; CV=convulsions; F=fever; D=dropsy (water-swollen body tissue); DC= decline (emaciation, wasting, end-stage syphilis); W=from the workhouse; O=old age; S=small pox; M=mortification (gangrene); P=palsy (paralysis, hemiplegia [Bell's Palsy]); CB=childbed; PR=prison; E=executed; SD=sudden death; PF=Putrid fever (Typhus); CR=cancer; V=visitation of God; DY=decay DYN=decay of nature; R=Rheumatism/ Rheumatic fever/Rheumatic decline; A=Asthma; AP=Apoplexy; I=Inflammation (type added if specified); L=lunatic or lunacy; IN=insanity; TIN=Temporary insanity; MC=Miscarriage; CH=Cholera	Age	Where buried—codes: L = lower churchyard; U = upper churchyard; P = pauper's yard; SWV = south west vault; D (no recorded meaning attached to D)
		4	Mary Warner (St. Mary Islington)	C	26	U
		6	Caroline Tisdale (St. Giles in the Fields)	D	40	U
		6	Ann Carter (18 Harp Alley)	DC	60	U
		9	Rebecca Ralph (20 Poppins Ct)	DC	61	L
		16	Sarah Pritchard (Salisbury Ct)	DC	70	D
		22	Elizabeth Tagget	DC W	74	L
	March	6	Eleanor Hartill	A	65	L

Year	Month	Date	Name	Cause of Death—codes: C=consumption; CV=convulsions; F=fever; D=dropsy (water-swollen body tissue); DC= decline (emaciation, wasting, end-stage syphilis); W=from the workhouse; O=old age; S=small pox; M=mortification (gangrene); P=palsy (paralysis, hemiplegia [Bell's Palsy]); CB=childbed; PR=prison; E=executed; SD=sudden death; PF=Putrid fever (Typhus); CR=cancer; V=visitation of God; DY=decay DYN=decay of nature; R=Rheumatism/Rheumatic fever/Rheumatic decline; A=Asthma; AP=Apoplexy; I=Inflammation (type added if specified); L=lunatic or lunacy; IN=insanity; TIN=Temporary insanity; MC=Miscarriage; CH=Cholera	Age	Where buried—codes: L = lower churchyard; U = upper churchyard; P = pauper's yard; SWV = south west vault; D (no recorded meaning attached to D)
		16	Elizabeth Bodmore (85 Fleet market)	A	61	L
		16	Elizabeth Nobbs (St. Andrews)	C	68	L
		20	Elizabeth Vaughan	CB	24	U
		21	Catherine Beens (Crown Ct)	Fell out of window	40	L
		23	Ann Margaret Locker (33 Water Lane)	DC	29	L
		25	Sarah Palmer	DC W	26	L
	April	1	Catherine Clark (George Alley)	DC	32	L

Year	Month	Date	Name	Cause of Death—codes: C=consumption; CV=convulsions; F=fever; D=dropsy (water-swollen body tissue); DC= decline (emaciation, wasting, end-stage syphilis); W=from the workhouse; O=old age; S=small pox; M=mortification (gangrene); P=palsy (paralysis, hemiplegia [Bell's Palsy]); CB=childbed; PR=prison; E=executed; SD=sudden death; PF=Putrid fever (Typhus); CR=cancer; V=visitation of God; DY=decay DYN=decay of nature; R=Rheumatism/ Rheumatic fever/Rheumatic decline; A=Asthma; AP=Apoplexy; I=Inflammation (type added if specified); L=lunatic or lunacy; IN=insanity; TIN=Temporary insanity; MC=Miscarriage; CH=Cholera	Age	Where buried— codes: L = lower churchyard; U = upper churchyard; P = pauper's yard; SWV = south west vault; D (no recorded meaning attached to D)
		1	Mary Davis (Great New St)	Suicide	70	L
		13	Elizabeth Bickington	F W	16	L
		14	Susanna Jones (St Ann Black Friars)	DC	42	U
		20	Marth Whitehead (16 Poppins Ct)	DC	20	L
			NOTE: 20: William Clement Stroud DC St Ann Blackfriars at 29, relevent to Hannah Fulford, buried U			

Cause of Death—codes:
C=consumption; CV=convulsions; F=fever; D=dropsy (water-swollen body tissue); DC= decline (emaciation, wasting, end-stage syphilis); W=from the workhouse; O=old age; S=small pox; M=mortification (gangrene); P=palsy (paralysis, hemiplegia [Bell's Palsy]); CB=childbed; PR=prison; E=executed; SD=sudden death; PF=Putrid fever (Typhus); CR=cancer; V=visitation of God; DY=decay DYN=decay of nature; R=Rheumatism/ Rheumatic fever/Rheumatic decline; A=Asthma; AP=Apoplexy; I=Inflammation (type added if specified); L=lunatic or lunacy; IN=insanity; TIN=Temporary insanity; MC=Miscarriage; CH=Cholera

Where buried—codes: L = lower churchyard; U = upper churchyard; P = pauper's yard; SWV = south west vault; D (no recorded meaning attached to D)

Year	Month	Date	Name	Cause of Death—codes:	Age	Where buried—codes:
	May	27	Mary Holyland (POOR house not Workhouse) ***Note: workhouse becomes poorhouse, designated by W (P)***	DC W (P)	60	L
		4	Sarah Blackman	DC	62	U
		12	Mary Robertson (18 Poppins Ct)	DC	58	L
		13	Grace Gleadhall	CB W	32	L
		18	Elizabeth Skildon	W A	53	L

Year	Month	Date	Name	Cause of Death—codes: C=consumption; CV=convulsions; F=fever; D=dropsy (water-swollen body tissue); DC= decline (emaciation, wasting, end-stage syphilis); W=from the workhouse; O=old age; S=small pox; M=mortification (gangrene); P=palsy (paralysis, hemiplegia [Bell's Palsy]); CB=childbed; PR=prison; E=executed; SD=sudden death; PF=Putrid fever (Typhus); CR=cancer; V=visitation of God; DY=decay DYN=decay of nature; R=Rheumatism/ Rheumatic fever/Rheumatic decline; A=Asthma; AP=Apoplexy; I=Inflammation (type added if specified); L=lunatic or lunacy; IN=insanity; TIN=Temporary insanity; MC=Miscarriage; CH=Cholera	Age	Where buried— codes: L = lower churchyard; U = upper churchyard; P = pauper's yard; SWV = south west vault; D (no recorded meaning attached to D)
		22	Elizabeth Pennelow (Fleet Market)	DC	39	U
	June	27	Mary Spencer	DC W	74	L
		8	Martha Simpson (1 Dove Ct)	DC	78	L
		19	Mary Bolton	DC W	26	L
		20	Mary Willmott (Islington)	DC	80	Mid
		24	Margaret Dawson (140 Salisbury Ct)	DC	50	U
		26	Elizabeth Newman (St Andrews Ct)	D	50	L

Cause of Death—codes: C=consumption; CV=convulsions; F=fever; D=dropsy (water-swollen body tissue); DC= decline (emaciation, wasting, end-stage syphilis); W=from the workhouse; O=old age; S=small pox; M=mortification (gangrene); P=palsy (paralysis, hemiplegia [Bell's Palsy]); CB=childbed; PR=prison; E=executed; SD=sudden death; PF=Putrid fever (Typhus); CR=cancer; V=visitation of God; DY=decay DYN=decay of nature; R=Rheumatism/ Rheumatic fever/Rheumatic decline; A=Asthma; AP=Apoplexy; I=Inflammation (type added if specified); L=lunatic or lunacy; IN=insanity; TIN=Temporary insanity; MC=Miscarriage; CH=Cholera

Where buried—codes: L = lower churchyard; U = upper churchyard; P = pauper's yard; SWV = south west vault; D (no recorded meaning attached to D)

Year	Month	Date	Name	Cause of Death	Age	Where buried
	July	1	Mary Andrew (3 New St. Sq)	DC	66	L
		6	Mary Price	DC W	70	L
		17	Eleanor Brown (Crown Ct. Fleet St)	F	27	P
	August	20	Ann March (28 Poppins Ct)	DC	47	L
		12	Elizabeth Dismont	DC W	27	L
		17	Jane Thorn	DC W	72	L
		17	Ann Clark	DC W	73	L
	September	8	Ann Wright (1 New Ct. Great New St)	DC	35	L

Year	Month	Date	Name	Cause of Death—codes: C=consumption; CV=convulsions; F=fever; D=dropsy (water-swollen body tissue); DC= decline (emaciation, wasting, end-stage syphilis); W=from the workhouse; O=old age; S=small pox; M=mortification (gangrene); P=palsy (paralysis, hemiplegia [Bell's Palsy]); CB=childbed; PR=prison; E=executed; SD=sudden death; PF=Putrid fever (Typhus); CR=cancer; V=visitation of God; DY=decay DYN=decay of nature; R=Rheumatism/ Rheumatic fever/Rheumatic decline; A=Asthma; AP=Apoplexy; I=Inflammation (type added if specified); L=lunatic or lunacy; IN=insanity; TIN=Temporary insanity; MC=Miscarriage; CH=Cholera	Age	Where buried—codes: L = lower churchyard; U = upper churchyard; P = pauper's yard; SWV = south west vault; D (no recorded meaning attached to D)
		11	Ann Stroud (Poppins Ct)	DC	27	U
		13	Ann Cooper (Bridewell)	DC	43	U
		19	Harriet Bell (11 Bell Building)	SD	29	SWV
		29	Diana Simpson	DC PR	16	L
	October	1	Ann Pineger (37 Ludgate Hill)	F	49	U
		2	Mary Reeves (2 Brides Passage)	DC	76	U
		6	Sarah Bigg (All Hallows London Wall)	DC	49	U

Cause of Death—codes:
C=consumption; CV=convulsions; F=fever; D=dropsy (water-swollen body tissue); DC= decline (emaciation, wasting, end-stage syphilis); W=from the workhouse; O=old age; S=small pox; M=mortification (gangrene); P=palsy (paralysis, hemiplegia [Bell's Palsy]); CB=childbed; PR=prison; E=executed; SD=sudden death; PF=Putrid fever (Typhus); CR=cancer; V=visitation of God; DY=decay DYN=decay of nature; R=Rheumatism/ Rheumatic fever/Rheumatic decline; A=Asthma; AP=Apoplexy; I=Inflammation (type added if specified); L=lunatic or lunacy; IN=insanity; TIN=Temporary insanity; MC=Miscarriage; CH=Cholera

Where buried— codes: L = lower churchyard; U = upper churchyard; P = pauper's yard; SWV = south west vault; D (no recorded meaning attached to D)

Year	Month	Date	Name	Cause of Death—codes	Age	Where buried—codes
		15	Martha Copland (7 Salisbury Ct)	Paraletic Stroke	59	U
	November	19	Ann Graham (Little New St)	DC	35	L
		21	Elizabeth Branham	DC W (P)	74	L
		28	Elizabeth Vickrey	D W (P)	53	L
		2	Sarah Veerey	D W (P)	53	L
		10	Mary Smith (107 Fleet St)	DC	50	U
		11	Ann Combes	DC W (P)	62	L
		16	Ann Stone	DC W (P)	82	L

Year	Month	Date	Name	Cause of Death—codes: C=consumption; CV=convulsions; F=fever; D=dropsy (water-swollen body tissue); DC= decline (emaciation, wasting, end-stage syphilis); W=from the workhouse; O=old age; S=small pox; M=mortification (gangrene); P=palsy (paralysis, hemiplegia [Bell's Palsy]); CB=childbed; PR=prison; E=executed; SD=sudden death; PF=Putrid fever (Typhus); CR=cancer; V=visitation of God; DY=decay DYN=decay of nature; R=Rheumatism/ Rheumatic fever/Rheumatic decline; A=Asthma; AP=Apoplexy; I=Inflammation (type added if specified); L=lunatic or lunacy; IN=insanity; TIN=Temporary insanity; MC=Miscarriage; CH=Cholera	Age	Where buried— codes: L = lower churchyard; U = upper churchyard; P = pauper's yard; SWV = south west vault; D (no recorded meaning attached to D)
		20	Eleanor Buckley (St Giles in the Fields)	F	50	L
		25	Elizabeth Davis	DC W (P)	60	L
		25	Elizabeth Vickery	DC W (P)	70	L
		27	Mary Taylor (114 Fleet St)	DC	75	U
		30	Mary Langton (white friars)	DC	60	L
	December	5	Martha Tale (New St. Hill)	DC	71	L
		16	Jane Thyne (53 Dorset St)	F	39	U
1804	January	1	Mary Mumford (St Paris Covent Garden)	DC	73	U

Year	Month	Date	Name	Cause of Death—codes: C=consumption; CV=convulsions; F=fever; D=dropsy (water-swollen body tissue); DC= decline (emaciation, wasting, end-stage syphilis); W=from the workhouse; O=old age; S=small pox; M=mortification (gangrene); P=palsy (paralysis, hemiplegia [Bell's Palsy]); CB=childbed; PR=prison; E=executed; SD=sudden death; PF=Putrid fever (Typhus); CR=cancer; V=visitation of God; DY=decay DYN=decay of nature; R=Rheumatism/ Rheumatic fever/Rheumatic decline; A=Asthma; AP=Apoplexy; I=Inflammation (type added if specified); L=lunatic or lunacy; IN=insanity; TIN=Temporary insanity; MC=Miscarriage; CH=Cholera	Age	Where buried—codes: L = lower churchyard; U = upper churchyard; P = pauper's yard; SWV = south west vault; D (no recorded meaning attached to D)
		11	Elizabeth Karr (1 Bride Lane)	P	84	U
		13	Elizabeth Gilbert (86 Shoe Lane)	F	84	L
		23	Elizabeth Douglas (38 New St Square)	DC	50	L
		27	Mary Tawneray (2 Dorset Ct)	DC	62	L
		30	Mary Suck (St George's Place)	F	52	U
	February	2	Mary Tucker (77 Fleet Market)	DC	61	L
		19	Elizabeth Hamling (4 Shoe Lane)	DC	39	U

Year	Month	Date	Name	Cause of Death—codes: C=consumption; CV=convulsions; F=fever; D=dropsy (water-swollen body tissue); DC= decline (emaciation, wasting, end-stage syphilis); W=from the workhouse; O=old age; S=small pox; M=mortification (gangrene); P=palsy (paralysis, hemiplegia [Bell's Palsy]); CB=childbed; PR=prison; E=executed; SD=sudden death; PF=Putrid fever (Typhus); CR=cancer; V=visitation of God; DY=decay DYN=decay of nature; R=Rheumatism/Rheumatic fever/Rheumatic decline; A=Asthma; AP=Apoplexy; I=Inflammation (type added if specified); L=lunatic or lunacy; IN=insanity; TIN=Temporary insanity; MC=Miscarriage; CH=Cholera	Age	Where buried—codes: L = lower churchyard; U = upper churchyard; P = pauper's yard; SWV = south west vault; D (no recorded meaning attached to D)
	March	26	Mary Ford (Covent Garden)	DC	31	L
		1	Catharine Smith (St Martins Ludgate)	I of the Lungs	37	L
		4	Jane Broughton (5 King's Head Court Shoe Lane)	DC	61	U
		6	Sarah Allen (23 Poppins Ct)	DC	75	U
		29	Sarah Mepowder (Black Horse Ct)	DC	61	U
	April	5	Mary Pincott (34 Potter Lane)	DC	46	U

Year	Month	Date	Name	Cause of Death—codes: C=consumption; CV=convulsions; F=fever; D=dropsy (water-swollen body tissue); DC= decline (emaciation, wasting, end-stage syphilis); W=from the workhouse; O=old age; S=small pox; M=mortification (gangrene); P=palsy (paralysis, hemiplegia [Bell's Palsy]); CB=childbed; PR=prison; E=executed; SD=sudden death; PF=Putrid fever (Typhus); CR=cancer; V=visitation of God; DY=decay DYN=decay of nature; R=Rheumatism/ Rheumatic fever/Rheumatic decline; A=Asthma; AP=Apoplexy; I=Inflammation (type added if specified); L=lunatic or lunacy; IN=insanity; TIN=Temporary insanity; MC=Miscarriage; CH=Cholera	Age	Where buried— codes: L = lower churchyard; U = upper churchyard; P = pauper's yard; SWV = south west vault; D (no recorded meaning attached to D)
		22	Mary Wright (12 West Harding St)	DC	63	U
	May	29	Ann Sheens (37 Water Lane)	DC	47	U
		20	Elizabeth Benoiment (19 Brides Lane)	I in the Bowels	74	U
		20	Sophia Wheeler (Black Horse Ct)	D	53	U
	June	6	Mary Felleet	DC W	69	L
		13	Harriet Richards (24 Harp Alley)	DC	30	L

Cause of Death—codes: C=consumption; CV=convulsions; F=fever; D=dropsy (water-swollen body tissue); DC= decline (emaciation, wasting, end-stage syphilis); W=from the workhouse; O=old age; S=small pox; M=mortification (gangrene); P=palsy (paralysis, hemiplegia [Bell's Palsy]); CB=childbed; PR=prison; E=executed; SD=sudden death; PF=Putrid fever (Typhus); CR=cancer; V=visitation of God; DY=decay DYN=decay of nature; R=Rheumatism/Rheumatic fever/Rheumatic decline; A=Asthma; AP=Apoplexy; I=Inflammation (type added if specified); L=lunatic or lunacy; IN=insanity; TIN=Temporary insanity; MC=Miscarriage; CH=Cholera

Where buried—codes: L = lower churchyard; U = upper churchyard; P = pauper's yard; SWV = south west vault; D (no recorded meaning attached to D)

Year	Month	Date	Name	Cause of Death	Age	Where buried
	July	25	Ann Bennett (White Fryars)	SD	46	L
		5	Margaret James (Islington)	DC	79	U
		31	Mary Roswell (Black Horse Ct)	D	65	L
	August	8	Mary Raymus	DC W	60	L
		8	Mary Hutton	Paraletic stroke W	58	L
		8	Elizabeth Ford	DC W	56	L
	September	8	Ann Fawthrop (69 Dorset St)	DC	74	L
		16	Rebecca Berg (12 Bell's Buildings)	L	46	U
		25	Mary Hempel (White Friars)	A	32	L

Year	Month	Date	Name	Cause of Death—codes: C=consumption; CV=convulsions; F=fever; D=dropsy (water-swollen body tissue); DC= decline (emaciation, wasting, end-stage syphilis); W=from the workhouse; O=old age; S=small pox; M=mortification (gangrene); P=palsy (paralysis, hemiplegia [Bell's Palsy]); CB=childbed; PR=prison; E=executed; SD=sudden death; PF=Putrid fever (Typhus); CR=cancer; V=visitation of God; DY=decay DYN=decay of nature; R=Rheumatism/Rheumatic fever/Rheumatic decline; A=Asthma; AP=Apoplexy; I=Inflammation (type added if specified); L=lunatic or lunacy; IN=insanity; TIN=Temporary insanity; MC=Miscarriage; CH=Cholera	Age	Where buried— codes: L = lower churchyard; U = upper churchyard; P = pauper's yard; SWV = south west vault; D (no recorded meaning attached to D)
	October	28	Mary Dingley	DC W	48	L
		5	Ann Wood	DC W	68	L
		12	Mary Henery	DC W	50	L
		21	Susanna Paulson (Great New ST)	DC	75	L
	November	24	Margaret Dallanger	DC W	64	L
		18	Mary Belton (noted as Mary Boston by mistake) (23 Harp Alley)	DC	90	L

Year	Month	Date	Name	Cause of Death—codes: C=consumption; CV=convulsions; F=fever; D=dropsy (water-swollen body tissue); DC= decline (emaciation, wasting, end-stage syphilis); W=from the workhouse; O=old age; S=small pox; M=mortification (gangrene); P=palsy (paralysis, hemiplegia [Bell's Palsy]); CB=childbed; PR=prison; E=executed; SD=sudden death; PF=Putrid fever (Typhus); CR=cancer; V=visitation of God; DY=decay DYN=decay of nature; R=Rheumatism/Rheumatic fever/Rheumatic decline; A=Asthma; AP=Apoplexy; I=Inflammation (type added if specified); L=lunatic or lunacy; IN=insanity; TIN=Temporary insanity; MC=Miscarriage; CH=Cholera	Age	Where buried—codes: L = lower churchyard; U = upper churchyard; P = pauper's yard; SWV = south west vault; D (no recorded meaning attached to D)
		19	Mary Phillips (St. Bartholomew's Hospital)	F	44	L
		25	Mary-Ann Fleming (57 Crown Ct)	P	52	SWV
	December	12	Sarah Jones (St. Catherine Coleman)	DC	83	U
		20	Mary Alewood (White Friars)	DC	39	L
		24	Hanna Welstead (70 Fleet Market)	F	38	L

Year	Month	Date	Name	Cause of Death—codes: C=consumption; CV=convulsions; F=fever; D=dropsy (water-swollen body tissue); DC= decline (emaciation, wasting, end-stage syphilis); W=from the workhouse; O=old age; S=small pox; M=mortification (gangrene); P=palsy (paralysis, hemiplegia [Bell's Palsy]); CB=childbed; PR=prison; E=executed; SD=sudden death; PF=Putrid fever (Typhus); CR=cancer; V=visitation of God; DY=decay DYN=decay of nature; R=Rheumatism/ Rheumatic fever/Rheumatic decline; A=Asthma; AP=Apoplexy; I=Inflammation (type added if specified); L=lunatic or lunacy; IN=insanity; TIN=Temporary insanity; MC=Miscarriage; CH=Cholera	Age	Where buried— codes: L = lower churchyard; U = upper churchyard; P = pauper's yard; SWV = south west vault; D (no recorded meaning attached to D)
1805	January	2	Mary Pryce (St. Mary Newington)	A	71	U
		6	Ann Powell (90 Crown Ct. Dorset St)	DC	32	L
		10	Mary Baldock (12 New St)	D	51	U
		16	Elizabeth Clarke (St. Sepulchre's)	DC	81	L
		16	Mary Boucher	IN W	32	L
		16	Ann Head (Stone Cutter St)	DC	66	U
		29	Ann Legger (Stone Cutter St)	DC	22	L

Year	Month	Date	Name	Cause of Death—codes: C=consumption; CV=convulsions; F=fever; D=dropsy (water-swollen body tissue); DC= decline (emaciation, wasting, end-stage syphilis); W=from the workhouse; O=old age; S=small pox; M=mortification (gangrene); P=palsy (paralysis, hemiplegia [Bell's Palsy]); CB=childbed; PR=prison; E=executed; SD=sudden death; PF=Putrid fever (Typhus); CR=cancer; V=visitation of God; DY=decay DYN=decay of nature; R=Rheumatism/Rheumatic fever/Rheumatic decline; A=Asthma; AP=Apoplexy; I=Inflammation (type added if specified); L=lunatic or lunacy; IN=insanity; TIN=Temporary insanity; MC=Miscarriage; CH=Cholera	Age	Where buried—codes: L = lower churchyard; U = upper churchyard; P = pauper's yard; SWV = south west vault; D (no recorded meaning attached to D)
February		3	Ann Flindell	DC W	65	L
		5	Elizabeth Wright (105 Fleet St)	DC	58	Chancel
		7	Mary Dodd (Stone Cutter St)	DC	38	L
		10	Elizabeth Talour (West Harding St)	DC	27	L
March		1	Catherine Osborne (Love's Grove)	D	40	L
		1	Hannah Crane	D W	33	L

Year	Month	Date	Name	Cause of Death—codes: C=consumption; CV=convulsions; F=fever; D=dropsy (water-swollen body tissue); DC= decline (emaciation, wasting, end-stage syphilis); W=from the workhouse; O=old age; S=small pox; M=mortification (gangrene); P=palsy (paralysis, hemiplegia [Bell's Palsy]); CB=childbed; PR=prison; E=executed; SD=sudden death; PF=Putrid fever (Typhus); CR=cancer; V=visitation of God; DY=decay DYN=decay of nature; R=Rheumatism/ Rheumatic fever/Rheumatic decline; A=Asthma; AP=Apoplexy; I=Inflammation (type added if specified); L=lunatic or lunacy; IN=insanity; TIN=Temporary insanity; MC=Miscarriage; CH=Cholera	Age	Where buried— codes: L = lower churchyard; U = upper churchyard; P = pauper's yard; SWV = south west vault; D (no recorded meaning attached to D)
		3	Elizabeth Small (38 Wilderness Lane)	DC	38	U
		20	Elizabeth McLean	DC W	75	L
		20	Elizabeth Search (85 Dorset St)	DC	44	U
		27	Elizabeth Maddox	A W	30	L
		31	Ann Marshall (46 Water Lane)	D	30	L
		31	Mary Wood (Wilderness Lane)	DC	62	L
	April	4	Jane Boucher (Fleet Market)	DC	54	L
		10	Esther Turner	DC W	78	L

Year	Month	Date	Name	Cause of Death—codes: C=consumption; CV=convulsions; F=fever; D=dropsy (water-swollen body tissue); DC= decline (emaciation, wasting, end-stage syphilis); W=from the workhouse; O=old age; S=small pox; M=mortification (gangrene); P=palsy (paralysis, hemiplegia [Bell's Palsy]); CB=childbed; PR=prison; E=executed; SD=sudden death; PF=Putrid fever (Typhus); CR=cancer; V=visitation of God; DY=decay DYN=decay of nature; R=Rheumatism/ Rheumatic fever/Rheumatic decline; A=Asthma; AP=Apoplexy; I=Inflammation (type added if specified); L=lunatic or lunacy; IN=insanity; TIN=Temporary insanity; MC=Miscarriage; CH=Cholera	Age	Where buried— codes: L = lower churchyard; U = upper churchyard; P = pauper's yard; SWV = south west vault; D (no recorded meaning attached to D)
	May	17	Elizabeth Shaw	SD W	21	L
		2	Martha Roofe	C W	62	U
		5	Ann Perry (Wilderness lane)	AP	39	U
		17	Elizabeth Church	D W	56	L
		22	Elizabeth Churchman	D W	74	L
		23	Ann Brewell (Middle New St)	DC	33	L
		27	Sarah Ann Rogers (Crown Court)	DC	45	U
		29	Jane Waters (Umberton Row)	CB	32	U
	June	7	Mary Richardson	DC W	59	L

Year	Month	Date	Name	Cause of Death—codes: C=consumption; CV=convulsions; F=fever; D=dropsy (water-swollen body tissue); DC= decline (emaciation, wasting, end-stage syphilis); W=from the workhouse; O=old age; S=small pox; M=mortification (gangrene); P=palsy (paralysis, hemiplegia [Bell's Palsy]); CB=childbed; PR=prison; E=executed; SD=sudden death; PF=Putrid fever (Typhus); CR=cancer; V=visitation of God; DY=decay DYN=decay of nature; R=Rheumatism/ Rheumatic fever/Rheumatic decline; A=Asthma; AP=Apoplexy; I=Inflammation (type added if specified); L=lunatic or lunacy; IN=insanity; TIN=Temporary insanity; MC=Miscarriage; CH=Cholera	Age	Where buried— codes: L = lower churchyard; U = upper churchyard; P = pauper's yard; SWV = south west vault; D (no recorded meaning attached to D)
		11	Eliza-Frances Robertson	DC PR	32	U
		19	Elizabeth Young (Love's Grove)	DC	56	L
		19	Elizabeth Charles	DC W	76	U
		25	Mary Wells (Camberwell)	DC	77	
		7	Catherine Catesby (Red Lion Passage)	DC	27	L
	July	17	Sarah Miles (George Alley)	Venereal Disease	24	L
		24	Sophia Cook (9 Great New St)	DC	33	L

Cause of Death—codes: C=consumption; CV=convulsions; F=fever; D=dropsy (water-swollen body tissue); DC= decline (emaciation, wasting, end-stage syphilis); W=from the workhouse; O=old age; S=small pox; M=mortification (gangrene); P=palsy (paralysis, hemiplegia [Bell's Palsy]); CB=childbed; PR=prison; E=executed; SD=sudden death; PF=Putrid fever (Typhus); CR=cancer; V=visitation of God; DY=decay DYN=decay of nature; R=Rheumatism/Rheumatic fever/Rheumatic decline; A=Asthma; AP=Apoplexy; I=Inflammation (type added if specified); L=lunatic or lunacy; IN=insanity; TIN=Temporary insanity; MC=Miscarriage; CH=Cholera

Where buried—codes: L = lower churchyard; U = upper churchyard; P = pauper's yard; SWV = south west vault; D (no recorded meaning attached to D)

Year	Month	Date	Name	Cause of Death	Age	Where buried
	August	11	Harriet Bollard (2 Fleet Market)	S	47	L
		11	Ellinor Gilfiling (Little New St)	F	55	L
		14	Elizabeth Simmons	DC W	65	L
		26	Ann Hortham (Temple Lane)	Pleurisy	40	U
		27	Elizabeth Lambart (Bride's Wharf)	F	57	L
		28	Elizabeth Ellis	DC W	60	L
	September	4	Sarah Damon	DC W	19	L

Year	Month	Date	Name	Cause of Death—codes: C=consumption; CV=convulsions; F=fever; D=dropsy (water-swollen body tissue); DC= decline (emaci-ation, wasting, end-stage syphilis); W=from the workhouse; O=old age; S=small pox; M=mortification (gangrene); P=palsy (paralysis, hemiplegia [Bell's Palsy]); CB=child-bed; PR=prison; E=executed; SD=sudden death; PF=Putrid fever (Typhus); CR=cancer; V=visitation of God; DY=decay DYN=decay of nature; R=Rheumatism/ Rheumatic fever/Rheumatic decline; A=Asthma; AP=Apoplexy; I=Inflammation (type added if specified); L=lunatic or lunacy; IN=insanity; TIN=Temporary insan-ity; MC=Miscarriage; CH=Cholera	Age	Where buried— codes: L = lower churchyard; U = upper churchyard; P = pauper's yard; SWV = south west vault; D (no recorded meaning attached to D)
	October	12	Elizabeth Swinton Daffy Flower	DC	22	U
		18	Catherine Lucritia Adams	DC PR	27	U
		23	Sarah Boote (Theobald Road)	CB	24	U
	November	10	Elizabeth Hipley (Sugar-loaf Ct)	DC	26	L
		21	Ann Smith (Fleet St)	DC	31	U
		22	Mary Hurvin (Peterborough Ct)	DC	55	U
		24	Mary Kirkman		55	U

Year	Month	Date	Name	Cause of Death—codes	Age	Where buried—codes
				C=consumption; CV=convulsions; F=fever; D=dropsy (water-swollen body tissue); DC= decline (emaciation, wasting, end-stage syphilis); W=from the workhouse; O=old age; S=small pox; M=mortification (gangrene); P=palsy (paralysis, hemiplegia [Bell's Palsy]); CB=child-bed; PR=prison; E=executed; SD=sudden death; PF=Putrid fever (Typhus); CR=cancer; V=visitation of God; DY=decay DYN=decay of nature; R=Rheumatism/ Rheumatic fever/Rheumatic decline; A=Asthma; AP=Apoplexy; I=Inflammation (type added if specified); L=lunatic or lunacy; IN=insanity; TIN=Temporary insanity; MC=Miscarriage; CH=Cholera		L = lower churchyard; U = upper churchyard; P = pauper's yard; SWV = south west vault; D (no recorded meaning attached to D)
December		5	Ann Dumford (2 Love's Grove)	CB	33	L
		21	Elizabeth Leorgan	DC W	48	L
		22	Mary Garner (2 New St Hill)	DC	52	L
		24	Rebecca Batty	O	78	Mid

*For full dataset, see online reference material.

Index